Children, Care and Crime

I0888312

The historical context of colonisation situates the analysis in *Children, Care and Crime* of the involvement of children with care experience in the criminal justice system in an Australian jurisdiction (New South Wales), focusing on residential care, policing, the provision of legal services and interactions in the Children's Court.

While the majority of children in care do not have contact with the criminal justice system, this book explores why those with care experience, and Indigenous children, are over-represented in this system. Drawing on findings from an innovative, mixed-method study – court observations, file reviews and qualitative interviews – the book investigates historical and contemporary processes of colonisation and criminalisation. The book outlines the impact of trauma and responses to trauma, including intergenerational trauma caused by policies of colonisation and criminalisation. It then follows a child's journey through the continuum of care to the criminal justice system, examining data at each stage including the residential care environment, interactions with police, the provision of legal services and experiences at the Children's Court. Drawing together an analysis of the gendered and racialised treatment of women and girls with care experience in the criminal justice system, the book particularly focuses on legacies of forced removal and apprenticeship which targeted Aboriginal and Torres Strait Islander women and girls. Through analysing what practices from England and Wales might offer the NSW context, our findings are enriched by further reflection on how decriminalisation pathways might be imagined. While there have been many policy initiatives developed to address criminalisation, in all parts of the study little evidence was found of implementation and impact. To conclude, the book examines the way that 'hope tropes' are regularly deployed in child protection and criminal justice to dangle the prospect of reform, and even to produce pockets of success, only to be whittled away by well-worn pathways to routine criminalisation. The conclusion also considers what a transformative agenda would look like and how monitoring and accountability mechanisms are key to new ways of operating. Finally, the book explores strengths-based approaches and how they might take shape in the child protection and criminal justice systems.

Children, Care and Crime is aimed at researchers, lawyers and criminal justice practitioners, police, Judges and Magistrates, policy-makers and those working in child protection, the criminal justice system or delivering services to children or adults with care experience. The research is multidisciplinary and therefore will be of broad appeal to the criminology, law, psychology, sociology and social work disciplines. The book is most suitable for undergraduate courses focusing on youth justice and policing, and postgraduates researching in this field.

Alison Gerard is the Head of the Canberra Law School, University of Canberra, Ngunnawal Country. Her research program focuses on social justice and has been published in leading international and Australian journals. She is currently a CI on an ARC Discovery Project examining 'Crimmigration' in Australia. Alison has co-published on the incorporation of Indigenous perspectives in university curriculum.

Andrew McGrath is an Associate Professor of Psychology at Charles Sturt University. His PhD research, in which he interviewed 200 young people after they appeared before the NSW Children's Court, was published as a journal article that won the Allen Austin Bartholomew Award for best article published in the Australian and New Zealand Journal of Criminology in 2009. Since then, he has published a number of articles in both Australian and International journals on topics ranging from the impact of custodial penalties on re-offending, the sentencing of young Indigenous offenders, serious and violent offending careers and juvenile risk assessment.

Emma Colvin is a Senior Lecturer in law and criminology at Charles Sturt University in NSW Australia, Wiradyuri/Wiradjuri Country. Her research explores the criminalisation of groups of people, such as children with experience of the out-of-home care system. Her research also examines bail and the impact of risk determinations on people perceived as risky because of their vulnerability or disadvantage, such as homelessness or substance use. Emma's work has been published by high-quality publishers and high-impact journals, and she has attracted government and charitable funding to support her research interests.

Annette Gainsford is a Wiradyuri woman from Bathurst NSW and is the Associate Dean Indigenous Teaching and Learning in the Office of the Pro Vice-Chancellor Indigenous Leadership and Engagement at the University of Technology, Sydney. Annette has extensive experience in Indigenous curriculum development that embeds Indigenous graduate attributes across higher education curriculum. Her experience specifically covers the disciplines of law, criminal justice, business and education. She is a recognised leader and expert in the field of Indigenous pedagogy, andragogy and Indigenous research methodologies.

Routledge Studies in Crime and Society

Oppressed by Debt
Government and the Justice System as a Creditor of the Poor
Edited by Saul Schwartz

A Criminological Biography of an Arms Dealer
Yarin Eski

The Rise of Politically Motivated Cyber Attacks
Actors, Attacks and Cybersecurity
Tine Munk

Violence
Situation, Speciality, Politics and Storytelling
David Wästerfors

Motherhood, Respectability & Baby-Farming in Victorian & Edwardian London
Joshua G. Stuart-Bennett

The Intersections of Family Violence and Sexual Offending
Gemma Hamilton and Patrick Tidmarsh

Children, Care and Crime
Trauma and Transformation
Alison Gerard, Andrew McGrath, Emma Colvin and Annette Gainsford

For more information about this series, please visit www.routledge.com/Routledge-Studies-in-Crime-and-Society/book-series/RSCS

Children, Care and Crime

Trauma and Transformation

Alison Gerard, Andrew McGrath, Emma Colvin and Annette Gainsford

Routledge
Taylor & Francis Group
LONDON AND NEW YORK

First published 2023
by Routledge
4 Park Square, Milton Park, Abingdon, Oxon OX14 4RN

and by Routledge
605 Third Avenue, New York, NY 10158

Routledge is an imprint of the Taylor & Francis Group, an informa business

British Library Cataloguing-in-Publication Data
A catalogue record for this book is available from the British Library

Library of Congress Cataloging-in-Publication Data
Names: Gerard, Alison, author. | McGrath, Andrew, author. | Colvin, Emma, author. | Gainsford, Annette, author.
Title: Children, care and crime : trauma and transformation / Alison Gerard, Andrew McGrath, Emma Colvin and Annette Gainsford.
Description: Milton Park, Abingdon, Oxon ; New York, NY : Routledge, 2021. |
Series: Routledge studies in crime and society | Includes bibliographical references and index.
Identifiers: LCCN 2022020378 (print) | LCCN 2022020379 (ebook) | ISBN 9780367554033 (hardback) | ISBN 9780367554057 (paperback) | ISBN 9781003093367 (ebook)
Subjects: LCSH: Child welfare—New South Wales. | Children—Institutional care—New South Wales. | Juvenile courts—New South Wales.
Classification: LCC HV802.Z8 N4944 2021 (print) | LCC HV802.Z8 (ebook) | DDC 362.709944—dc23/eng/20220512
LC record available at https://lccn.loc.gov/2022020378
LC ebook record available at https://lccn.loc.gov/2022020379

ISBN: 978-0-367-55403-3 (hbk)
ISBN: 978-0-367-55405-7 (pbk)
ISBN: 978-1-003-09336-7 (ebk)

DOI: 10.4324/9781003093367

Typeset in Times New Roman
by codeMantra

Contents

Acknowledgements

We would like to thank the respondents and agencies with whom we worked to collect and analyse data that appears in this manuscript. We were guided in our research design and analysis by our Advisory Board who, through their thoughtful and engaged advice, greatly enriched our work. We were also supported in the early stages of this project by the research assistance provided by Dr Natasha Sugden and Maureen Bates-McKay. We also thank our universities, Charles Sturt University, the University of Canberra and the University of Technology Sydney, for providing various practical elements necessary to support and realise quality research. Having an environment of sharp colleagues to bounce ideas off has sharpened the writing that appears on these pages. We particularly thank Professor Leanne Weber. We are also grateful to our copy editor Julia Farrell.

Our pilot study was funded by Charles Sturt University, and the subsequent data collection was funded through a Criminology Research Grant by the Australian Institute of Criminology. We are thankful as this funding enabled the research to take place.

Ultimately, this research was founded upon a commitment to meet research needs identified by community stakeholders. We hope it contributes to a fundamental shift in policy, practices and processes.

We have thoroughly enjoyed working together as an interdisciplinary research team – law, criminology, psychology and Indigenous education. Our diversity in areas other than our academic qualifications has been a significant component in the strength of our teamwork, analysis and contribution to research. Each of the team has this to say to their support crews:

Alison – I'd like to thank Sophie, Sebastien and Zadie for making room for this research and for making family life loving, fun and flexible. I've learned an immense amount from these thoughtful co-authors on this journey and those around us for various parts of it. I have a stronger connection to Country and am stronger as a result.

Andrew – Many thanks to my co-authors. It has been a rewarding experience working in this multi-disciplinary team. Thanks also to the people who agreed to participate in our research, I hope we have done justice to everything you told us. And finally, thanks to my family, Juanita, Maya and Maxine who are always supportive of my work.

Emma – I'd like to thank my family and friends for their support during the course of writing this book. A particular shout out to my co-authors, a great team to work with and thanks for everything. It's been a joy to work with you and I am a better scholar for it.

Annette – I would like to acknowledge my co-authors Alison, Andrew and Emma; it has been a pleasure to work with you and to learn from you throughout this writing journey, thank you for being allies in this work and representing Indigenous voice in such an authentic and integrated way. I would also like to acknowledge Brett, Jessica and Joel and my extended family, you are always at the centre of what I do, thank you for your unwavering love and support across my many research projects, you make me strive to create a better future for our current and future generations.

Acknowledgement of artwork

We would like to acknowledge the Boys to the Bush program; the mission of the program is centred on providing an environment for boys to be surrounded by positive influences and provide opportunities for success through encouraging mateship, resilience and a sense of belonging. The program recognises that there are 50,000 Australian children that are currently living in out-of-home-care arrangements and that four out of five young people in the juvenile system are males. To highlight and support the program, the authors approached Kurt Hancock, the Bathurst Program Manager for Boys to the Bush, to see if the boys from the program would like to create an artwork about their experience for inclusion in the book. Through assistance from Kurt Hancock, Kate Welsh and Brendan Boney, two Wiradjuri boys Joshua Dargin-Carr and Clayton Tarrant created the inspirational artwork Yawarra Dhulubang 'Take Care of Spirit' that appears on the first page of this book. The artwork symbolises the boys' experience through the following story. The emu footprint in the middle is a symbol of a young person moving forward not going back; the circles are support circles with a lot of support from different people on the outside. The dots symbolise a layer of protection. The lines pushing out symbolise a healing place, with four man symbols, to show strong men. The meeting place up top and bottom are two people having one-on-one mentoring. We the authors recognise the significance of this program and the guidance it provides to build strength-based approaches for boys.

Acronyms

ACCP	Aboriginal and Torres Strait Islander Child Placement Principles
ACE	Adverse Childhood Experience
ACWA	Association of Child Welfare Agencies
ADHD	Attention Deficit Hyperactivity Disorder
ADVO	Apprehended Domestic Violence Order
AIATSIS	Australian Institute of Aboriginal and Torres Strait Islander Studies
AIHW	Australian Institute of Health and Welfare
ALRC	Australian Law Reform Commission
APPG	All Party Parliamentary Group
ARC	Attachment, Regulation, Competency (model)
ASD	Aboriginal Strategic Direction
AVL	Audio Visual Link
AVO	Apprehended Violence Order
BAME	Black, Asian and Minority Ethnic
CAN	Court Attendance Notice
DCJ	Department of Communities and Justice
DOCS	Department of Community Services
DSM	Diagnostic and Statistical Manual of Mental Disorders
DOE	Department of Education (UK)
FACS	Family and Community Services
FASD	Foetal Alcohol Spectrum Disorder
HREOC	Human Rights and Equal Opportunity Commission
ISP	Intensive Supervision Program
JJ	Juvenile Justice
LAC	Local Area Command
MOJ	Ministry of Justice (UK)
ODD	Oppositional defiant disorder
OOHC	Out-of-Home Care
PINOP	Person in need of protection
PRT	Prison Reform Trust

PTSD	Post traumatic stress disorder
QAF	Quality Assurance Framework
MASH	Multi-Agency Safeguarding Hubs
NAO	National Audit Office (UK)
NSW	New South Wales
SNAICC	Secretariat of National Aboriginal and Islander Child Care
TAFE	Technical and Further Education
TCF	Therapeutic Care Framework
UK	United Kingdom
YJB	Youth Justice Board (UK)
YP	Young person

Yawarra Dhulubang

'Take Care of Spirit'

Joshua Dargin-Carr (Wiradjuri) and Clayton Tarrant (Wiradjuri)

The emu footprint in the middle is a symbol of a young person moving forward not going back, the circles are support circles with a lot of support from different people on the outside. The dots symbolise a layer of protection. The lines pushing out symbolise a healing place, with four man symbols, to show strong men. The meeting place up top and bottom are two people having one on one mentoring.

Introduction

Introduction

Australia's child protection and criminal justice systems reflect legacies of colonisation, imperialism and globalisation. Contemporary social realities in Australia that see disproportionately large numbers of Aboriginal and Torres Strait Islander people and those with care experience involved with the criminal justice system are indicative of this legacy. We recognise and reflect upon our privilege as part of the academy and as members of key disciplines – criminology, law, psychology and education – that have historically and contemporaneously inhibited engagement with Indigeneity and contributed to these realities (see Porter, 2019).

This book examines the involvement of those with care experience in the criminal justice system in an Australian jurisdiction. The majority of children in care do not come into contact with the youth justice system (Cashmore, 2011). However, among children involved in the youth justice system, those with care experience are over-represented (see Gerard et al., 2019). We focus on the processes of colonisation and criminalisation, rather than crime (see Aliverti et al., 2021). Our research took place in New South Wales (NSW), the most populous state located on Australia's East Coast. Child welfare is the responsibility of individual states and territories, but there are many similarities across jurisdictions. NSW was the site of the first encounters, both peaceful and violent, between Aboriginal and non-Aboriginal people. It was the site of the first colonial 'settlement', although the settlement could be more accurately described as an invasion. The Frontier Wars occurred in Sydney and its surrounds and marked the beginning of a brutal period for Aboriginal and Torres Strait Islander people. The landmark report into the forced removal of Aboriginal and Torres Strait Islander peoples from their families and communities, the Human Rights and Equal Opportunity Commission's *Bringing Them Home* Report found that Indigenous children have been removed from their families since the first few days of European occupation (HREOC, 1997, p. 22). Moreover, Indigenous people's sophisticated practices and social rules around child rearing and family relationships have been, up until the present, poorly understood by

DOI: 10.4324/9781003093367-1

the community, and in particular by case workers, judges and decision-makers in child protection (Behrendt, 2019; Davis, 2019).

The historical context of child protection and colonisation is used to situate the contemporary practices that we observed in our mixed-methods study of care experience and involvement in the criminal justice system in NSW. As a research team, we have backgrounds in law, psychology, criminology and Indigenous education. We draw on theoretical frameworks from critical criminology, psychology and Indigenous standpoint theory to conduct this interdisciplinary study and better understand legacies of colonisation and pathways to transformation. In what follows, we introduce our theoretical approach to the research. We outline our terminology and definitions used and our research design, and we preview the content of each chapter.

Out-of-home care (OOHC)

Across Australia, there are 46,000 children in OOHC (Australian Institute of Health and Welfare [AIHW], 2021). A nationally consistent definition of OOHC was arrived at in 2018–2019, which includes legal and voluntary placements for children who are unable to live with their families due to child safety concerns (AIHW, 2021, pp. 47–48). A legal placement in NSW involves the Department of Communities and Justice successfully applying for a care and protection order to remove a child into the care of the department or a nominated carer. It is meant to be an option of last resort. There are four different types of OOHC: relative/kinship care, foster care, residential care and other forms of home-based care. Just over half of the children in OOHC are in relative or kinship care, with 37% in foster care, 7% in residential care and the remaining 1% in other forms of home-based care. Our research focuses primarily on residential care, which is understood as one of the main sites for the criminalisation of children with care experience and an environment that is potentially unsafe for children and staff, and in particular, culturally unsafe for Aboriginal and Torres Strait Islander children (Cunneen & Libesman, 2000; Davis, 2019; Gerard et al., 2019). Our research was undertaken before and after the commencement of the 2016 NSW Government's *Joint Protocol to Reduce the Contact of Young People in Residential Care with the Criminal Justice System* (the Joint Protocol), prepared by the NSW Ombudsman in conjunction with stakeholders.

Aboriginal and Torres Strait Islander children are over-represented in the Australian child welfare system at a rate of about 11 times that for non-Indigenous children (AIHW, 2021). The over-representation of Aboriginal and Torres Strait Islander children in OOHC is a result of multiple factors explored in this book, including continuing practices of colonisation, intergenerational and transgenerational trauma, bias and systemic racism. Distinguished Professor Larissa Behrendt AO (Behrendt, 2019, p. 192), a Euahlayi/Kamillaroi woman who runs a legal practice in this area, has observed an 'exponential growth in the number of cases of wrongful removal, or of cases where grandparents were deemed unsuitable as carers for children, coming through our doors'. The primary causes of over-representation also include the inaction of successive governments in addressing systemic faults in the child protection and criminal justice systems.

Advocacy by a group of Aboriginal grandmothers in NSW, known as Grandmothers Against Removal, led to a far-reaching inquiry into Aboriginal and Torres Strait Islander children and young people in OOHC. In 2016, the NSW Government commissioned senior law academic and Cobble Cobble woman of the Barrungam nation, Professor Megan Davis, to identify the reasons behind the high and increasing rates of Aboriginal children in OOHC in NSW and strategies to reduce this trend. The review made 125 recommendations, ultimately concluding that 'it is time for the NSW Government to formally acknowledge to Aboriginal communities, as well as the broader Australian community that, as an ostensible "parent", it can and does cause harm to children for whom it has parental responsibility' (Davis, 2020, p. XXXV). None of the recommendations have been responded to by the NSW Government.

Deficiencies in data collection further complicate the picture of child protection and the criminal justice system in NSW, particularly in relation to children in OOHC who cross over into the criminal justice system. Many of the key recommendations by Professor Davis were a commitment to data collection and research so that the picture of child protection can be properly understood and an Aboriginal quality assurance initiative introduced to ensure an appropriate standard of care and protection. Davis also recommended a roundtable with the Aboriginal community and stakeholders to determine how data sovereignty can be realised in the process of designing and collecting data for analysis.

Criminalisation of care experience: gender, trauma, colonisation and individual/structural drivers

Characterisations of the main drivers of the criminalisation of those with care experience have typically fallen into explanations that centre either adverse childhood experiences (ACEs) or the residential care environment. We avoid this unhelpful framing and instead focus on the interaction of multiple and complex factors that contribute to criminalisation, including the ongoing impact of colonisation. Our approach is informed by Scraton's (2007) concept of 'speaking truth to power' and 'pursuing alternative accounts' in critical social research. In our study, we focus on 'how' certain acts are labelled and who has the power to label them (Scraton & Chadwick, 1991, p. 172). Key to this approach is considering the role power plays in creating an official discourse and privileging institutional knowledge (Burton & Carlen, 1979). In our research, we critically analyse what behaviours are valorised and what responses are prioritised – in other words, where agencies place their emphasis and resources in the complex interplay between individuals and stakeholder organisations. In doing so, this book contributes our perspective on the relationship between colonisation and punishment. We agree with Aliverti et al.'s (2021) contention that for too long criminological inquiry has neglected these dimensions.

Structural approaches in critical social research

Scraton and Chadwick (1991) provide a critical analysis framework for understanding the process of criminalisation, particularly through critiquing the role of power in the decision-making of professionals working within the system. They argue that:

> undoubtably professionals, be they employed in the caring agencies, the military, the criminal justice system or private industry, operate on the basis of professional training and work experience enjoying discretionary powers in accordance with their rank and status. Yet whatever the quality and implications of decisions formulated and administered at the interpersonal level of 'agency', their recognition and legitimacy are rooted in the determining contexts of 'structure'. and in their manifestation in the professional ideologies of control and political management. (p. 167)

Further, sometimes criminalisation can occur through repetitious, minor decision-making that at first glance may not appear controversial – as Giddens (1987, p. 9) argues, 'power is at its most intense and durable when running through the repetition of institutionalised practices'. Additionally, Scraton and Chadwick (1991) argue that the focus should be on the action and reaction contexts, not the causation elements as this is reductionist.

Scraton's (2007) work expands on criminalisation through the analysis of routine processes. He draws on C. Wright Mills's critique that policy and practice interventions are prioritised over care and advocacy and that classification and regulation are the driving principles in the training of professionals (p. 6). Gatekeeping information is used to protect official discourse. Key to Scraton's framework is being mindful of the consequences of interviewing 'up' the power structure. He asserts that:

> interviews with senior officials and established professionals, particularly in circumstances where institutions are under scrutiny, usually are prepared and rehearsed by participants. Their purpose is to deflect criticism, negotiate or even reconstruct events. While the 'conditions' of the interview should always be honoured – anonymity, confidentiality, 'off the record' comments and so on – officials undertake interviews to represent and protect the interests of corporate bodies or state institutions. (p. 16)

We are mindful that in our research we interviewed up. Our qualitative interviews in this project thus represent an institutional view. This is a limitation of our research design, as explored in the next section.

The challenge for those in dominant law disciplines, often plagued by assumptions of value neutrality (Foucault, 1980, p. 131), is the ability to access in-depth knowledge in context and seek out the 'view from below'. 'Knowing', presented by Scraton (2007) as an antidote to 'the suppression of truth and the denial of responsibility', comes about in three ways: personal exploration, context and interpretation and understanding. These three factors are underpinned by witnessing and recording by the researcher. Scraton and Chadwick (1991) and Scraton (2007) provide a useful framework for critical analysis of the underlying structural factors that result in criminalisation, in particular, through the critical analysis of official discourse and of the propensity for routine institutional decisions to criminalise the less powerful in the system.

Historically, academic research has reproduced structural inequality, and in many cases, it has reinforced mechanisms of surveillance, control and marginalisation (Scraton, 2007, p. 6). This is particularly true of criminological research in Australia, which 'continues to operate without an acknowledgement of colonialism and its effects' (Porter, 2019; see also Cunneen & Tauri, 2016). Porter argues that:

> criminologists must ask some unsettling questions: has criminology as a discipline failed Indigenous Peoples? And, if so, how can we do things differently? To what degree has criminology been complicit in the rising rates of Indigenous incarceration internationally? And what, if anything, does criminology have to offer these crises in criminal justice experienced by Indigenous Peoples around the globe?
>
> (p. 123)

Cunneen and Tauri (2016, 2017) call for an Indigenous criminology that privileges Indigenous voices and experiences, speaks truth to power and meaningfully engages with Indigenous peoples and communities.

Keeping both individual and structural factors in focus

While this analytical emphasis on structure contributed to the analytical framework used in this book, we also felt that it was important to look at individual differences. We believe that structural approaches often leave out the individual. Cook et al. (2005, p. 390) assert that 'children exposed to complex trauma often experience lifelong problems that place them at risk of additional trauma exposure and cumulative impairment'. In line with this, we felt that a focus on the impact of trauma on behaviour was vital in unpacking lived experiences of criminalisation and victimisation.

Cook et al. (2005) describe the impact of exposure to complex trauma and identify seven domains of impairment. They point out that traditional diagnoses such as post-traumatic stress disorder (PTSD) do not capture the full impact of exposure to complex trauma. Disrupted attachment, particularly disorganised attachment, is likely to result from exposure to trauma. This attachment style results in certain 'themes' of behaviour – specifically, helplessness and coercive control. Disrupted attachment can cause a lifetime of disease and psychosocial dysfunction through increased susceptibility to stress, problems in regulating emotion and altered help-seeking behaviour. Complex trauma has profound neurological impacts, particularly around self-regulation and other executive functions in adolescence. Further, Cook et al. note profound difficulties in identifying, expressing and controlling emotions, disassociation as a coping mechanism, difficulty regulating behaviour, cognitive developmental problems and poor self-concepts. Given that trauma is a common element in the lives of children with care experience, understanding the nature of trauma-informed behaviour is vital to both understanding criminalisation and developing effective responses to such behaviour. Critically, Cook et al. (2005, p. 392) state that 'when the primary caregiver is too preoccupied, distant, unpredictable, punitive, or distressed to be reliably responsive, children become distressed easily and do not learn to collaborate with others when their own internal resources are inadequate'. We are interested in how this manifests when the primary caregiver is a shift worker in a residential care setting.

Harris and Fallot (2001, p. 3) highlight the impact a systemic lack of trauma-informed services has on survivors: 'systems serve survivors of childhood trauma without treating them for the consequences of that trauma' or even without an awareness that clients have experienced childhood trauma. These authors provide guidelines on trauma-informed care practice based on understanding the impact of trauma and incorporating this into every aspect of service delivery. This approach seeks to understand the history of the person being cared for and not just their behaviour. We use this approach to analyse and unpack responses to children's behaviour and how criminalisation can occur through inappropriate responses by OOHC service providers, law enforcement, lawyers and Magistrates. Notably, Harris and Fallot (2001) also discuss how important it is to be aware of power dynamics when implementing a trauma-informed approach within an organisation. This links to our previous discussion on power dynamics, colonisation and official discourse, enabling a more complex, in-depth analysis of trauma-informed responses that we draw on as we unpack our data in the following chapters.

While understanding trauma is an important aspect of our theoretical framework, we felt that there was an absence of cultural understandings of trauma that we saw as pivotal to analysing our data. Comas-Diaz, Hall and Neville (2019) unpack racial trauma, which is imperative to apply to the Australian context in respect of intergenerational trauma among Aboriginal and Torres Strait Islander peoples and the ongoing legacy of colonial and neo-colonial child welfare policies. Racial trauma:

> refers to the events of danger related to real or perceived experiences of racial discrimination. These include threats of harm and injury, humiliating and shaming events, and witnessing harm to other POCI (People of Colour and Indigenous People) due to real or perceived racism.
>
> (Comas-Diaz et al., 2019, p. 1)

Comas-Diaz et al. talk of 'soul wounds' as an illustrative means of understanding the transfer of pain across generations. They also talk of resilience crossing generations alongside trauma. We wanted to unpack this further in our findings as it contrasts with a deficit model of understanding racial trauma and provides a means to adopt a strengths-based approach to addressing issues of criminalisation and victimisation. While Comas-Diaz et al. call for culturally appropriate interventions and recognition of intergenerational trauma is important, we also felt the need to incorporate culturally competent analysis through the lens of Australian Indigenous epistemologies.

We first consider seminal work that explores and unpacks the nature of trauma through an Indigenous/First Nations lens. Much of the literature that theorises in this space have been generated from Canada and Aotearoa New Zealand. We examine these theoretical frameworks generally and then explore how they can be applied to the Australian context. Blackstock et al. (2020) investigate how international law, particularly the *United Nations Declaration on the Rights of Indigenous Peoples* (UNDRIP), has the potential to provide a path forward to promote Indigenous voices, and children's agency, in future initiatives aimed at decolonisation. Our discussion also considers international treaties and agreements. Australia is a signatory to some of these (such as the *UN Convention on the Rights of the Child*), but there is a growing body of international jurisprudence around First Nations rights and this is something we tie into our analysis. However, Blackstock et al. argue that human rights paradigms tend to valorise individual rights over collective rights. They also posit that there are key ontological differences between Indigenous and non-Indigenous conceptualisations of 'care'. Blackstock et al. argue that although there are many different languages, cultural practices and contexts among different Indigenous peoples globally, they all share a common understanding of concepts such as time, land and relationships, and this Indigenous ontological perspective can provide a valuable approach to understanding trauma and how to respond to it. Critically, these authors note that 'Western thinking is deterministic, segmented, privileges new knowledge, and gives primacy to individual rights and current reality' (p. 2). In Blackstock et al.'s characterisation of Western thinking, the value of property is given primacy, and children are seen as chattels. Further, Blackstock et al. argue that understandings of child neglect tend to focus on the individual faults of parents and family rather than on underlying structural elements that lead to poverty and neglect. And, this approach has a disproportionately negative impact upon First Nations families. Blackstock et al.'s argument that problem solving in this space needs to account for Indigenous ontologies and incorporate principles of self-determination has had a significant influence on our analysis and findings. These authors affirm that:

> unless our respective child welfare systems fully embrace self-determination and self-management and embed human rights within child welfare legislation the position of First Nations and Aboriginal and Torres Strait Islander children in child welfare will remain one of over representation and disconnection from family and Nation.
>
> (p. 9)

Blackstock et al.'s research includes a comparison between Canada and Australia, which was useful for providing context to our analysis and offering a basis for international comparison.

Pihama et al.'s (2017) Aotearoa New Zealand–based research on Māori Trauma Informed Care Principles develops a specific set of principles derived from Kaupapa Māori, which is a collective set of ontological principles held by Māori people. These authors highlight the need for therapy to occur within cultural contexts. Dominant framings of trauma and trauma-informed care are grounded in Western definitions and understandings (see, for example, Emmerson & Hopper, 2011), which means that the diverse experiences of trauma among different groups are not fully understood or addressed in current practice (see also Wirihana & Smith, 2014). By applying the Māori Trauma Informed Care Principles, culturally safe and effective practices can be developed for Māori communities. In this regard, it is also noteworthy that current practices do not acknowledge that 'massive group trauma experiences impact on collectives of people and manifest in conditions and behaviour that are often reconstructed within dominant pathologising view[s] as common traits belonging to Indigenous Peoples' (Pihama et al., 2017, p. 23). We were particularly interested in using these principles to inform our analysis. Pihama et al.'s framework is endeavouring to move beyond Western psychological notions of trauma as a one-off event and instead conceptualise trauma as something cumulative. We think critically about this in our analysis of whether and how such a program might be implemented in an Australian context.

Key to our analysis is a thorough understanding of intergenerational and transgenerational trauma. As noted above with reference to Pihama et al. (2017), group trauma, intergenerational trauma and transgenerational trauma are not routinely recognised within or incorporated into Western framings of trauma, nor developed into practice. Atkinson et al.'s (2010) work unpacks transgenerational trauma and group experiences of trauma in the Australian First Nations context, noting in particular that the definition of trauma is not settled. Definitions vary, from those that argue that trauma arises from a single event or events or from an environment to the characterisation of trauma according to an 'extreme/not extreme dichotomy', which, Atkinson et al. (2010) claim, shapes how people process and experience traumatic events as the same event. Yet, scholars have criticised the 'effectiveness of mainstream psychology for Indigenous People' (Atkinson et al., 2010, p. 136). The extent to which concepts like PTSD are able to accurately describe the impact of chronic stressors that pervade the lives of Aboriginal and Torres Strait Islander people has been widely criticised (Atkinson, 2008, 1990, 2002; Cameron, 1998; Milroy, 2005; O'Shane, 1993). Atkinson et al. (2010) characterise these stressors as 'multiple, repeated, and of great severity', and as reinforced by three elements: 'the inability to identify and overcome a single source of stress', 'cumulative stressors' and the fact that those perpetrating the harms are 'well known to the victims'. More specifically, there is a distinction between situational trauma, which occurs as a result of a discrete event such as a car accident, a murder or being taken away, and cumulative trauma, which is more subtle and characterised by feelings that build over time, as occurs in response to racism, for example.

A disproportionately high number of children in OOHC are Indigenous. Therefore, the above observations about the nature of trauma experienced by Aboriginal and Torres Strait Islander peoples and the inadequacy of psychological diagnosis and treatment apply. This may also extend to non-Indigenous children in OOHC, whom we know from the characteristics of those with care experience are likely to experience similar stressors compounded by the three elements referred to above, albeit without the additional layer of the unique trauma facing Indigenous peoples. Atkinson et al.'s examination of how trauma can influence future behaviours, particularly offending behaviours, is useful for our analysis. They critique the DSM-IV-TR definition of trauma, the prevailing diagnostic framework at the time, noting, as do Pihama et al. (2017), that Western definitions and practice are not culturally informed. Their review of the literature on intergenerational trauma provided us with a framework to apply to our analysis of intergenerational trauma. A common theme in the articles referenced in this section was the need for community-led change and culturally safe service provision.

Intersectionality in analysing legacies of colonisation and criminalisation processes

We recognise the need for an intersectional approach to analyse the historical and contemporary realities of colonisation and the specific criminalisation processes examined in this study. Criminology as a discipline has taken a long time to acknowledge and apply concepts of intersectionality (Porter, 2019). The term intersectionality was first coined by law scholar Kimberlé Crenshaw (1989, 1991). Crenshaw's conceptualisation, primarily focused on 'women of colour', takes in 'structural intersectionality', reflecting the structural factors that locate women of colour on the lower rungs of social strata, which, in turn, makes them more vulnerable to violence; 'political intersectionality', relating to discourses in family violence frameworks that silence or erase the experience and voice of women of colour; and 'representational intersectionality', in reference to cultural discourses that marginalise women of colour.

Intersectional theorists argue that by analysing these structural realities in terms of either race or gender, much is lost or erased, in particular the experiences of women of colour (Crenshaw, 1991). In an Australian context, this view is also reflected in Marchetti's (2008, 2013) analysis of the 1991 Royal Commission into Aboriginal Deaths in Custody (RCIADIC), which, by focusing on deaths in police and prison custody, ignored the experiences of Aboriginal women who had been the victims of family violence. Marchetti argues that when politics of race were privileged, and gender was set aside during the Royal Commission, 'a guiding assumption emerged from the investigations into the deaths and from the sociological, anthropological and criminological research: that young Indigenous males were more disadvantaged than Indigenous females' (p. 163). Marchetti's article highlights some confronting and difficult questions with which scholars need to grapple.

An 'additive' approach to intersectionality is not transformative (Porter, 2019). Paik (2016) draws attention to the theoretical tensions between intersectionality and criminology, particularly insofar as quantitative analysis has a tendency to rely on fixed categories. Yuval Davis (2006) stresses that researchers cannot assume that all individuals belonging to a race or gender are the same and that race, gender and class are not the only divisions. Yuval Davis critiques 'additive' approaches to using intersectionality, arguing that they can become essentialist and construct a 'right way' to be a member of a particular group, thereby making certain experiences 'invisible'. Tauri (2017, p.15, in Porter, 2019, p.127) has criticised Australian criminology for seeking to 'add a bit of colour' by incorporating selective Indigenous elements instead of committing to the 'significant overhaul' required to rid the discipline of its 'bias and obstructive prejudice that currently pervades Australian criminology'. British criminology has diluted the focus on race by using the term 'ethnicity' in its place (Parmar, 2017). Parmar suggests that this has been co-constitutive in that 'British criminology's unwillingness to engage with race has resulted in the reticence towards an intersectional approach and vice versa' (p. 35). Parmar argues that a more sophisticated intersectional analysis is required. Yuval Davis (2006) recommends assuming a social divisions approach to intersectionality. In doing so, Parmar argues, 'the point is to analyse the differential ways in which different social divisions are concretely enmeshed and constructed by each other and how they relate to political and subjective constructions of identities' (2017, p. 205).

An intersectional lens allowed us to identify the siloed approach that is prevalent across the board in treatment and support services. When people with multiple intersecting vulnerabilities, such as many of the care-experienced children in our study, come before the courts or are responded to in institutional settings, this siloed approach often results in inadequate responses. Delgado and Stefancic (2012) see intersectionality as a means to engage in 'legal storytelling' and thus to voice and make visible lived experiences of people ordinarily excluded or marginalised. This is particularly important for Indigenous women in the criminal justice system (Marchetti, 2008, p. 156). We thus draw on intersectionality to unpack the deep colonising practices and their impact which we observed in the courts during our research.

In conjunction with an Indigenous ontological approach, intersectionality also offers a framework with which to examine the role of resistance to colonisation and criminalisation processes. Looking at the role of resistance provides a pathway to a strengths-based approach, a relatively novel approach in criminology: 'Criminological studies that illuminate forms of resistance among racialized communities are scarce as are perspectives that interpret ethnic identity as a resource' (Parmar, 2017, p. 36). As Marchetti (2008) discusses, the non-reporting of family violence as a means of protecting children from removal is a good example of resistance from within the community. Our data also revealed instances of resistance by children and we explore this in the context of the systemic view of children as 'misbehaving' or 'troublesome'. The aim of our intersectional approach is not just to understand intersectional dynamics but to transform them (Parmar, 2017).

This chapter has outlined the four theoretical approaches that inform our analytical framework. We draw on structural determinants from Scraton's work, psychological theories of trauma, Indigenous ontologies and intersectionality to enrich our analysis. Our approach combines an individual and a structural lens. The challenge for our book is to meet the requirements set out here – 'intersectionality allows us to avoid overly deterministic structural analyses while also not assuming individuals operate independently of that structural context' (Paik, 2017, p. 9). Psychological models of stress and trauma, while useful in the case of adverse childhood events, do not capture the impact of intergenerational and historical trauma. There is a growing realisation of this, particularly as our understanding of epigenetics increases, and any trauma-informed care program that does not encapsulate this understanding will likely fail, especially in the case of First Nations people. Further, intersectionality offers a way to recognise and explore the diversity of experiences of care. This knowledge is applicable to quantitative research also, as more researchers examine interactions and mediating factors, recognising the complexity of human behaviour.

To explore these issues in the NSW context, we undertook a mixed-methods study consisting of qualitative interviews with key agencies involved in OOHC service provision and the criminal justice system. We also conducted court observation of Children's Court matters and carried out individual file reviews. We now provide an overview of our research design.

Research design

This project was initiated in response to a need identified by a community partner who felt that the involvement of children in residential care in the criminal justice system is both unnecessary and disproportionate. They also expressed concern that it is non-government agencies, charged with looking after children in care, who are calling the police and reporting the behaviour. We, therefore, set out to design a research project to investigate the criminalisation of children in care.

Ethical approval for this study was obtained from the Charles Sturt University Human Research Ethics Committee, protocol H17141. We also obtained approval from the Children's Court of NSW to conduct our court observations. This research is informed by the Australian Institute of Aboriginal and Torres Strait Islander Studies (AIATSIS) Guidelines for Ethical Research in Australian Indigenous Studies. It was also informed by the experiences of one of the authors (Annette Gainsford), who is a Wiradyuri woman with care experience and experience as a carer.

Our research aimed to identify:

- the perceptions of frontline criminal justice professionals of the criminalisation processes that impact children in residential OOHC placements;
- the systems or processes that contribute to the criminalisation of children in OOHC;
- the differential impacts of demographic characteristics such as age, gender, ethnicity and Aboriginality;
- the disparities in representation rates of children in OOHC across regional/metropolitan areas; and
- international decriminalisation practice.

In this book, we explore the processes through which children with care experience come into contact with the criminal justice system, starting with histories of trauma and concluding with contact with the court system. Data supporting this were drawn from three sources: qualitative interviews with key stakeholders, court observations and file reviews. Given this, we do not describe results from each part of the study in turn; rather, we interweave these data into the overall findings presented in the book as they relate to each step in the process. The method pertaining to each part of the study is now described.

Qualitative interviews

Our book draws on qualitative research undertaken with criminal justice and social welfare professionals working on the frontline of the care–criminalisation nexus. These stakeholders are OOHC service providers (*n* = 17), NSW Police Force representatives (*n* = 10), Juvenile Justice officers (Department of Justice employees supervising children on community-based sanctions) (*n* = 19), Department of Family and Community Services employees (*n* = 5), defence lawyers, community legal centre lawyers and lawyers working in the care jurisdiction of the NSW Children's Court (*n* = 14) and Children's Court magistrates (*n* = 10). In the UK case study, interviews were conducted with 10 key stakeholders. Interviews were semi-structured, involving a core set of questions that were followed up by open-ended prompts where necessary. We started by asking about the participant's general experience in the criminal justice system before moving to specific questions relating to care-experienced children.

Our analyses followed the six phases described by Braun and Clarke (2006) but were also informed by these authors' later conceptualisation of 'reflexive' thematic analysis, which sees themes as 'creative and interpretive stories about the data, produced at the intersection of the researcher's theoretical assumptions, their analytic resources and skill, and the data themselves' (Braun & Clarke, 2019, p. 594). We took a semantic approach, identifying themes based on the explicit, rather than latent, meaning of the data. All of the researchers read the interview transcripts, thereby becoming familiar with the data and developing initial ideas to guide subsequent analyses. These were then discussed collaboratively, and codes were developed based on these discussions. The interview data were then entered into NVivo by individual researchers based on separate coding of each interview transcript undertaken independently by each researcher. Where obvious disagreements were observed, these were discussed and resolved by the research team to ensure consistency in coding across the dataset. A further meeting was then held at which the codes were collated into themes using a thematic map. We understood a theme to represent a repeated pattern of meaning across the dataset, substantiated by relevant extracts. Rather than report these themes individually, we contextualise them in reference to certain aspects of the interface between the care and criminal justice systems.

We were not able to interview people directly impacted by the criminalisation of those with care experience in NSW and this is a limitation of our research. Indigenous stories provide a challenge to stereotypes and promote healing and counter-narratives of strength (Anthony et al., 2021; Behrendt, 2019). Behrendt (2019) and Anthony et al.'s articles illustrate the richness created by enabling the conditions for First Nations women to speak directly about experiences of child removal and interactions with the criminal justice system. This scholarship makes us pause, reflect upon and acknowledge the limitations of our own research design. We chose not to interview people in custody or the care system. We decided that we could not effectively surmount the institutional barriers to gaining access to people in custody or under other forms of community supervision. Instead, we spoke to professionals in these organisations charged with responsibility for children in care or with care experience. Our pilot study and our subsequent study started and finished with frontline professionals as interview respondents. We involved those with care experience and Indigenous people in the analysis of the material in an advisory capacity. Our UK case study did interview one person with care experience. Three of the stakeholders we interviewed were Aboriginal and Torres Strait Islander (n = 3). We sought to address these limitations in our sample by establishing an Advisory Board that included Aboriginal representation and people with lived experience of the care system. We also informally consulted Aboriginal lawyers and carers as well as local Elders. In this regard, of immense benefit to our research has been the lived experience of Wiradyuri woman Annette Gainsford (co-author of this book), who was a member of our initial Advisory Board and has experience of the care system as both a care leaver and a carer.

Court files

We reviewed a number of Children's Court files as part of our analysis. We accessed these files through the court registry and later entered relevant details into a database. We reviewed 107 files relating to 92 individuals – 65 males (70%) and 27 females (30%). For 22 (23%) of the files, there was evidence of Indigenous status – 16 males (73%) and 6 females (27%). We also found evidence on file of a care background for 22 (23%) of the children whose matters we reviewed. Other variables coded were whether there were reports on file, such as a Juvenile Justice pre-sentence report (28%), evidence of a mental health condition (30%), homelessness (26%), abuse and neglect (20%), educational problems (33%) and a criminal history (32%). It is likely that these figures are underestimates as only minimal information was provided in a number of files. Figure 1 shows these findings in more detail, highlighting the differences between the children with and without care experience. It is clear from these findings that the care-experienced children whose court files we reviewed were more likely to have a mental health condition, have had educational problems, have been in custody previously, have evidence of abuse and neglect on file and have a history of homelessness.

In addition to these quantitative analyses, we chose a number of files to analyse in greater detail. Specifically, given our interest in intersectionality, we selected four files relating to Indigenous males, four relating to Indigenous females, four relating to non-Indigenous males and four relating to non-Indigenous females. Two of the research team (AM and EC) read each file carefully and made notes. These two researchers then discussed each file in detail and created a file note describing each and highlighting pertinent themes. We refer to these file analyses throughout the book where appropriate.

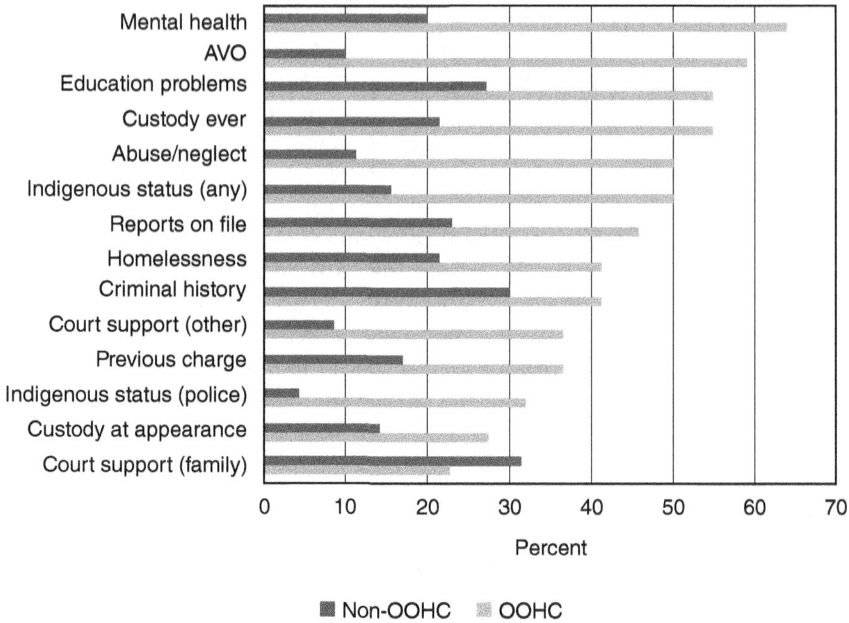

Figure 1 Differences between children with and without care experience (court files).

Court observations

We observed a total of 150 hours of court proceedings spread across three major outer metropolitan Children's Courts. These related to 134 separate matters, involving 83 males (62%), 41 females (31%) and 10 (7%) where the gender could not be determined, as there was no personal appearance by the young person. For 22 (16.4%) of these matters, there was clear evidence of Aboriginal status, determined either by the defendant's Aboriginal status being made known in court or representation by the Aboriginal Legal Service. Our approach was guided by previous court observation studies (Booth, 2012; Hannah-Moffat & Maurutto, 2012; Tait, 2001). Court observation not only allows researchers to collect data on how processes and procedures play out in the court setting but also provides a deeper view of the power structures at play (Garapon, 1997) and the subtle influences on decision-making, such as the physical appearance of children and the presence of family member support in the courtroom (Booth, 2012; Danziger et al., 2011; Tait, 2001).

At least two researchers were present in court for each observation. Each took notes, concentrating on the type of matter being observed but also on other relevant factors such as the demeanour of the child and magistrate, and the presence or absence of support people in court. These notes were collated into a single document, developed by all the researchers. From this document, we developed a series of vignettes that were mapped on to the broader themes relating to the cycle of care and criminalisation. Some quantitative information was also extracted and entered into a database. In particular, we coded for whether the child was supported in court. There was evidence in court of a care background for only six (4.5%) of the young people whose cases we observed. A total of 23 (17%) matters were for sentence, 70 (52%) were bail determinations or extensions and the remaining 41 were Apprehended Violence Order (AVO) matters. As there were only six cases where we could find evidence of care experience, we were unable to make comparisons based on this variable as we did with the file review data.

Table 1 presents the descriptive statistics from the court observations. Approximately 60% of the matters we observed were at one major outer metropolitan court in Sydney; 13% were at a second court and 28% were at a third. There was evidence of Indigenous status in 16.4% ($n = 22$) of the cases. Of these, nine (41%) were female and 12 (59%) were male. Nearly, a quarter of the children (23.9%) coming before court were in custody at the time, with a number of these appearing by video link. Just under 30% of the children were accompanied by family members, and 12% were accompanied by a carer or some other non-family support person. There were significant gender differences in this regard, with males more likely to be supported by family members (38.6% compared to 19.5%, $p = 0.033$) and females more likely to have some other form of support (22% compared to 8.4%, $p = 0.035$).

As with the file reviews, we developed more detailed accounts of the matters we found to be of particular interest or significance and, similarly, make no claim as to how generalisable these are.

Terminology

Care-experienced: We use the term 'care-experienced' to encompass children who have at some stage been in the care system. We understand that children cycle in and out of care and our research includes children who have been in care but may not have been in care at the time of their court appearance.

Cultural competency: For the purposes of this research, 'cultural competency' refers to knowledge of Indigenous peoples and cultures, the ability to communicate effectively and work proficiently with Indigenous peoples and communities and the acknowledgement of cultural difference and associated differing worldviews in the process (Universities Australia, 2011).

Cultural safety: For the purposes of this research, 'cultural safety' relates to creating and providing an environment where Indigenous peoples feel culturally, socially and emotionally safe, and where there is no challenge to a person's Indigenous identity (Williams, 1999).

Indigenous: For the purposes of this research, the terms 'Indigenous', 'Aboriginal and Torres Strait Islander' and 'First Nations' are used

Table 1 Descriptive statistics from court observations broken down by gender

	All[a]	*Male*[b]	*Female*	*p*
Court				
Court 1	58.9	69.9	30.1	$p = 0.301$
Court 2	12.9	50	50	$p = 0.301$
Court 3	28.2	68.6	31.4	$p = 0.301$
Gender	61.9			
Indigenous status	16.4	14.5	22	p = 0.295
Court support (family)	**29.9**	**38.6**	**19.5**	$\boldsymbol{p = 0.033}$
Court support (carer)	**11.9**	**8.4**	**22**	$\boldsymbol{p = 0.035}$
OOHC	4.5	3.6	7.3	$p = 0.366$
Custody at appearance	23.9	19.3	29.3	$p = 0.211$
Sentencing matter	17.2	19.3	17.1	$p = 0.766$
Bail determination/extension	52.2	51.8	56.1	$p = 0.652$
AVO	29.9	30.1	24.4	$p = 0.505$
S28	8.2	7.2	9.8	$p = 0.627$
S32	4.5	3.6	7.3	$p = 0.366$
FTA	9.7	7.2	12.2	$p = 0.360$

Note: a – N = 134, 7.5% (N = 10) gender unknown; b – N = 124, 10 cases where gender was unknown removed from analyses; c – Court 3 had significantly more Indigenous young people than Court 1 ($p < .05$); d – Court 3 had significantly fewer s.28 applications than the other two courts ($p < .05$).

interchangeably throughout, depending on context. The use of Indigenous refers to peoples who are the first inhabitants across Australia, Canada, Aotearoa New Zealand and other colonised countries, depending on context.

Kinship: 'Kinship' refers to Aboriginal social organisation that relates to family relationships and responsibilities.

Self-determination: For the purposes of this research, Indigenous 'self-determination' is defined as Indigenous peoples having autonomy over the cultural, social, economic and political agendas that govern their lives.

FACS/DOCS/Department of Communities and Justice: During the course of the research, the names of relevant NSW government departments changed. When referring to the government department responsible for child protection and child welfare, we generally use the term FACS (Family and Community Services) as this was the department's name at the time of data collection. Previously, this department was known as DOCS (Department of Community Services), so some research participants still referred to this older terminology and some quotes therefore use DOCS. FACS is now a division of the Department of Communities and Justice (DCJ).

Youth Justice/Juvenile Justice: At the time the research was conducted, the relevant department for children in the youth justice system was called Juvenile Justice. We use this term as it is the one used by our research participants. The department is now known as Youth Justice, a division of DCJ.

Understanding the criminalisation of those with care experience

This book begins with an overview of the historical and contemporary context of OOHC in Australia. Chapter 1 outlines the available statistical profile on the characteristics of children in OOHC in Australia and how the current system operates according to official accounts. It then establishes the historical context of the criminalisation of care-experienced children in Australia by examining two key developments. The first is the practices of forced removal that targeted cultural difference and brought about the Stolen Generations, but we focus on more than the Stolen Generations. We illustrate how the frontier wars arrived at our hometown of Bathurst and led to the declaration of martial law and the deaths of many hundreds of Aboriginal people and some 13 Europeans. We chart the various overlapping periods of protection, segregation and assimilation that led to the Stolen Generations and analyse the resistance to, and the impact of, these destructive policies historically and today. Second, we analyse the reception of English approaches to penal welfare that significantly impacted Aboriginal and Torres Strait Islander people and communities, and also ensnared particular non-Indigenous communities. This approach enshrined the focus on 'delinquent' children identified for 'saving' and led to the additive approach of affixing welfare to 'the administration of juvenile justice' (Carrington & Pereira, 2009, p. 26). The final part of Chapter 1 evaluates the research on the impact of 'care experience' on children and adults, and the overlap of children with care experience also engaging with the criminal justice system. It pays particular attention to the research from other colonial countries such as Aotearoa New Zealand and Canada.

Chapter 2 examines the impact of trauma. This chapter overviews the impact of ACEs on physical and mental health, and its relationship with the criminal justice system. We focus particularly on the impact of intergenerational trauma caused by policies of colonisation such as criminalisation and forced removal from families and communities. This chapter then explores the evidence linking trauma to offending and highlights trauma-informed care approaches that decentre immediate behaviour to refocus on the traumatic histories of children in care.

The setting for conflict between behaviour and support services for those with care experience is often the residential care environment, a form of group-based care that is explored in Chapter 3. Residential care in NSW is outsourced to the private sector. Previous research has identified that inadequate responses to challenging behaviour are driving unnecessary criminalisation of children in residential care (Shaw, 2016; Staines, 2016). Based on our data, Chapter 3 examines how OOHC service providers engage with children and other agencies associated with residential care such as law enforcement, Juvenile Justice and the Children's Court. It also reviews the regulatory environment of residential care in NSW. The importance of ensuring cultural safety for Aboriginal and Torres Strait Islander children, effectively a legislative requirement in NSW, is discussed.

The policing of children with care experience forms the focus of Chapter 4. The chapter analyses the relationships between care experience, OOHC service providers, police and involvement in the criminal justice system. In the Australian context, the relationship between police and those with care experience, particularly Aboriginal and Torres Strait Islander people, has a long history (HREOC, 1997). Since European occupation of Australia, police have regularly been on the frontline of the administration of policies of colonisation such as forced removal and forced relocation (Cunneen, 2001).

Chapter 5 analyses the significant role that lawyers play in advising and representing children with care experience who come into contact with the criminal justice system. This chapter explores the interview, file review and court observation data to understand how lawyers interact with children in care. It highlights new research on trauma-informed lawyering that would readily benefit children in care. Chapter 5 concludes with an examination of cultural competence and legal services for children in care.

Chapter 6 examines the relationship between care-experienced young people and the NSW Children's Court, one of the oldest specialist Children's Courts in the world. This chapter reviews Australian and international research on the extent of care-experienced children's contact with the criminal justice system and explores our data against these findings. The court experience itself is examined, before turning to focus on two specific aspects of appearing in court that have serious ramifications for care-experienced children – bail and mental health.

Chapter 7 engages 'legal storytelling' (Bedford, 2019) to draw together a gendered analysis of our data focusing on the differential experience of girls and women with the care system. We unpack gendered understandings of historical approaches to care that included specific institutions for girls and women and use an intersectional framing to centre Aboriginal and Torres Strait Islander children and adults. The global literature on the over-representation of women and girls in care is examined before moving to an analysis of the three key themes that emerged in our research. The first is the narrative that girls are more 'difficult', which pushes girls' propensity for increased trauma to the periphery and instead centres their problematic behaviour. The second relates to how self-harm and responses to it accelerate criminalisation. The third concerns how resistance may result in further criminalisation.

Chapter 8 explores international approaches to care experience by reviewing the results of our case study from England and Wales. In our NSW pilot study, several of our respondents discussed innovations in England and Wales that were leading to a decrease in criminalisation. As a result, we built into our study qualitative interviews with key informants from relevant criminal justice and social welfare agencies in the United Kingdom, including care leavers. The chapter provides an overview of the considerable momentum in the United Kingdom around addressing the criminalisation of children with care experience. This chapter details the changes in policing and the administration of OOHC and the resultant impact on the involvement of those in care in the criminal justice system. While not uniform, these changes reflect what is possible. Chapter 8 draws together what the UK case study can offer the NSW context and, in doing so, the chapter enriches the NSW research by promoting further reflection on how decriminalisation pathways might be imagined.

In our conclusion, we examine the way that 'hope tropes' are regularly deployed in child protection and criminal justice to dangle the prospect of reform, and even to produce pockets of success, only to be whittled away by well-worn pathways to routine criminalisation. We highlight how this serves as a mechanism for the system to breathe: enabling it to attain some level of legitimacy and demonstrate a capacity for reform, only to retract and contract in maintaining the normalisation of criminalisation, in particular of those with care experience and Aboriginal and Torres Strait Islander people. We examine what a transformative agenda would look like and how monitoring and accountability mechanisms are key to new ways of operating. Finally, we explore strengths-based approaches and how they might take shape in the child protection and criminal justice systems.

References

Aliverti, A., Carvalho, H., Chamberlen, A., & Sozzo, M. (2021). Decolonizing the criminal question. *Punishment & Society, 23*(3), 297–316.

Anthony, T., Sentence, G., & Behrendt, L. (2021). 'We're not being treated like mothers': Listening to the stories of First Nations mothers in prison. *Laws, 10*(3), 74.

Australian Institute of Health and Welfare. (2021). *Child protection Australia 2019–20* (Vol. 78).

Atkinson, J. (1990). Violence in Aboriginal Australia: Colonisation and gender. *Aboriginal and Islander Health Worker Journal, 14*(1) (part 1) and (3) (part 2), 5–21.

Atkinson, J. (2002). *Trauma trails, recreating song lines: The transgenerational effects of trauma in Indigenous Australia*. Spinifex Press.

Atkinson, C. (2008). *The violence continuum: Australian Aboriginal male violence and generational post-traumatic stress* [Unpublished doctoral dissertation]. Charles Darwin University.

Atkinson, J., Nelson, J., & Atkinson, C. (2010). Trauma, transgenerational transfer and effects on community wellbeing. *Working Together: Aboriginal and Torres Strait Islander Mental Health and Wellbeing Principles and Practice*, 135–144.

Bedford, N. (2019). Storytelling in our legal system: Healing for the stolen generations. *Australian Feminist Law Journal, 45*(2), 321–331.

Behrendt, Larissa. (2019). Stories and words, advocacy and social justice: Finding voice for Aboriginal women in Australia. *Australian Feminist Law Journal, 45*(2), 191–205.

Blackstock, C., Bamblett, M., & Black, C. (2020). Indigenous ontology, international law and the application of the Convention to the over-representation of Indigenous children in out of home care in Canada and Australia. *Child Abuse and Neglect*, *110*(1). https://doi.org/10.1016/j.chiabu.2020.104587

Booth, T. (2012). 'Cooling out' victims of crime: Managing victim participation in the sentencing process in a superior sentencing court. *Australian and New Zealand Journal of Criminology*, *45*(2), 214–230.

Braun, V., & Clarke, V. (2006). Using thematic analysis in psychology. *Qualitative Research in Psychology*, *3*(2), 77–101.

Braun, V., & Clarke, V. (2019). Reflecting on reflexive thematic analysis. *Qualitative Research in Sport, Exercise and Health*, *11*(4), 589–597. doi: 10.1080/2159676X.2019.1628806

Burton, F., & Carlen, P. (1979). *Official discourse: On discourse analysis, government publications, ideology and the state*. Routledge.

Cameron, S. (1998). *Aboriginal experiences of psychological trauma: Personal, intergenerational and transgenerational* [Unpublished master's thesis]. Victoria University.

Carrington, K. (1993). *Offending girls: Sex, youth and justice*. Allen and Unwin.

Carrington, K., & Pereira, M. (2009). *Offending youth: Sex, crime and justice*. Federation Press.

Comas-Dìaz, Hall G., & Neville, H. (2019). Racial trauma: Theory, research, and healing: Introduction to the special issue. *American Psychologist*, *74*(1), 1–5.

Cook, A., Spinazzola, J., Ford, J., Lanktree, C., Blaustein, M., Cloitre, M., & Van der Kolk, B. (2005). Complex trauma. *Psychiatric Annals*, *35*(5), 390–398.

Crenshaw, K. (1989). Demarginalizing the intersection of race and sex: A Black feminist critique of antidiscrimination doctrine, feminist theory and antiracist politics. *University of Chicago Legal Forum*, *1*(8), 139–167.

Crenshaw, K. (1991). Mapping the margins: Intersectionality, identity politics, and violence against women of color. *Stanford Law Review*, *43*(6), 1241–1299.

Cunneen, C. (2001). *Conflict, politics and crime: Aboriginal communities and the police*. Routledge.

Cunneen, C., & Libesman, T. (2000). Postcolonial trauma: The contemporary removal of Indigenous children and young people from their families in Australia. *Australian Journal of Social Issues*, *35*(2), 99–115. https://doi.org/10.1002/j.1839–4655.2000.tb01088.x

Cunneen, C., & Tauri, J. (2016). *Indigenous criminology*. Policy Press.

Danziger, S., Levav, J., & Avniam-Pesso, L. (2011). Extraneous factors in judicial decisions. *Proceedings of the National Academy of Sciences of the United States of America (PNAS)*, *108*(17), 6889–6892.

Davis, M. (2019). *Family is Culture: Review report*. Independent Review of Aboriginal Children in OOHC.

Delgado, R., & Stefancic, J. (2017). *Critical race theory*. New York University Press.

Emerson, D., & Hopper, E. (2011). *Overcoming trauma through yoga*. North Atlantic Books.

Figley, C. (1985). *Trauma and its wake: The study and treatment of post-traumatic stress disorder*. Brunner/Mazel.

Foucault, M. (1980). *Power/knowledge: Selected interviews and other writings 1972–1977* (C. Gordon Ed.). Harvester Wheatsheaf.

Garapon, A. (1997). *Bien Juger: Essai sur le Rituel Judiciare*. Editions Odile Jacob.

Giddens, A. (1987) *The nation state and violence*. Polity Press.

Hannah-Moffat, K., & Maurutto, P. (2012). Shifting and targeting forms of penal governance: Bail, punishment and specialised courts. *Theoretical Criminology, 16*(2), 201–219.

Harris, M., & Fallot, R. (2001). Envisioning a trauma-informed service system: A vital paradigm shift. *New Direction for Mental Health Services, 89*, 3–22.

Human Rights and Equal Opportunity Commission. (1997). *Bringing Them Home: Report of the national inquiry into the separation of Aboriginal and Torres Strait Islander children from their families*. Commonwealth of Australia.

Marchetti, E. (2008). Intersectional race and gender analyses: Why legal processes just don't get it. *Social and Legal Studies, 17*(2), 155–174.

McFarlane, K. (2010). From care to custody: Young women in out-of-home care in the criminal justice system. *Current Issues in Criminal Justice, 22*, 345–353.

Milroy, H. (2005). Preface. In S. R. Zubrick, S. R. Silburn, D. M. Lawrence et al., *The Western Australian Aboriginal Child Health Survey: The social and emotional wellbeing of Aboriginal children and young people* (pp. xiii–xxvii). Curtin University of Technology and Telethon Institute for Child Health Research.

O'Shane, P. (1993). Assimilation or acculturation problems of Aboriginal families. *Australian and New Zealand Journal of Family Therapy, 14*(4), 196–198.

Paik, L. (2009). Maybe he's depressed: Mental illness as a mitigating factor for drug offender accountability. *Law and Social Inquiry, 34*(3), 569–602.

Paik, L. (2017). Critical perspectives on intersectionality and criminology: Introduction. *Theoretical Criminology, 21*(1), 4–10.

Parmar, A. (2017). Intersectionality, British criminology and race: Are we there yet? *Theoretical Criminology, 21*(1), 35–45. https://doi.org/10.1177/1362480616677496

Pihama, L., Smith, L. T., Evans-Campbell, T., Kohu-Morgan, H., Cameron, N., Mataki, T., Te Nana, R., Skipper, H., & Southey, K. (2017). Investigating Māori approaches to trauma informed care. *Journal of Indigenous Wellbeing, 2*(3), 18–31.

Porter, A. (2019). Aboriginal sovereignty, 'crime' and criminology. *Current Issues in Criminal Justice, 31*(1), 122–142.

Ryan, J. P., & Testa, M. F. (2005). Child maltreatment and juvenile delinquency: Investigating the role of placement and placement instability. *Children and Youth Services Review, 27*(3), 227–249. http://dx.doi.org/10.1016/j.childyouth.2004.05.007

Scraton, P. (2007). Chapter 1: Challenging academic orthodoxy, recognising and proclaiming 'values' in critical social research. In *Power, conflict and criminalisation* (pp. 1–18). Routledge.

Scraton, P., & Chadwick, K. (1991). The theoretical and political priorities of critical criminology. In K. Stenson, & D. Cowell (Eds.) *The politics of crime control* (pp. 161–185). SAGE.

Shaw, J. (2016). Policy, practice and perceptions: Exploring the criminalisation of children's home residents in England. *Youth Justice, 16*(2), 147–161. https://doi.org/10.1177/1473225415617858

Staines, J. (2016). *Risk, adverse influence and criminalisation: Understanding the over-representation of looked after children in the youth justice system*. Prison Reform Trust.

Stanley, E. (2017). From care to custody: Trajectories of children in post-war New Zealand. *Youth Justice, 17*(1), 57–72. https://doi.org/10.1177/1473225416669145

Tait, D. (2001). Popular sovereignty and the justice process: Towards a comparative methodology for observing courtroom rituals. *Contemporary Justice Review*, *4*(2), 201–218.

Taylor, C. (2006). *Young people in care and criminal behaviour.* Jessica Kingsley Publishers.

Wirihana, R., & Smith, C. (2014). Historical trauma, healing and well-being in Māori communities. *MAI Journal*, *3*(3), 198–210.

Yuval Davis, N. (2006). Intersectionality and feminist politics. *European Journal of Women's Studies*, *13*(3), 193–209.

1 Historical and contemporary contexts of out-of-home care

Introduction: the contemporary out-of-home care system

Providing care for children who cannot be raised by their parents is a key task of the modern welfare state. In Australia, with its federated system of government, child welfare is the responsibility of state and territory governments. These child protection systems claim to protect children from abuse and neglect in families. Although there are seven states and two territories in Australia, their approaches to child protection are similar. On the one hand, government departments are generally responsible for the investigation, processing and management of child protection cases; on the other hand, family support services are usually outsourced to a range of non-government organisations.

There are four broad aspects to the formal child protection system in Australia which we set out here but note are more haphazardly applied in practice (AIHW, 2021). The first is the process of notification, investigation and substantiation. Where a child is reported to be at risk of harm, the first step is investigation, which can take the form of interviews with the child and their parents, visits to the family home and the use of other sources of information (such as interviews with teachers). Sometimes, the child is found to be safe; but in other cases, the investigation concludes that the child has been, is currently being or could be harmed. In cases such as these, the relevant department has a duty to ensure the safety of the child, which can take the form of a care and protection order. Under the legislative and policy framework, this is meant to be an option of last resort, only to be triggered where there is a serious risk of harm to the child and other options such as a safety plan negotiated with the family have been exhausted or where a primary carer is in gaol. The Court can give legal responsibility to the parents, to the relevant department or to a nominated carer. In the last two cases, the child is placed in OOHC. The nationally consistent definition of OOHC adopted in 2018–2019 is as follows:

> Out-of-home care is overnight care for children aged under 18 who are unable to live with their families due to child safety concerns. This includes placements approved by the department responsible for child

DOI: 10.4324/9781003093367-2

> protection for which there is ongoing case management and financial payment (including where a financial payment has been offered but has been declined by the carer).
>
> Out-of-home care includes legal (court-ordered) and voluntary placements, as well as placements made for the purpose of providing respite for parents and/or carers.
>
> (AIHW, 2021, pp. 47–48)

In Australia, OOHC can take four forms: relative or kinship care, foster care, residential care and some other form of home-based care. Nationally, approximately 46,000 children were in OOHC at 30 June 2020, which equates to approximately 8 children per 1,000 (AIHW, 2021). Across states and territories, these figures vary from a low of 6.3/1,000 children in Victoria to a high of 16.8/1,000 in the Northern Territory. Most children are admitted to OOHC prior to the age of one, and the majority are discharged between 15 and 17 years of age. A total of 54% of these children are admitted to relative or kinship care, 37% to foster care, 7% to residential care and 1% to other forms of home-based care.

Aboriginal and Torres Strait Islander children are over-represented in the Australian child welfare system. On 30 June 2020, approximately 18,900 Indigenous children were in some form of care (56/1,000, or about 11 times the rate for non-Indigenous children). The reasons for this pattern of over-representation have been canvassed in various reviews and reports over the past 30 years, and while these reasons are contested, most agree that Aboriginal people's contact with the child welfare system has its genesis in the experience of colonisation and subsequent intergenerational traumas, biases against Indigenous modes of parenting and the attrition of community and family capability to care for children (see, for instance, Davis, 2019; Human Rights and Equal Opportunity Commission [HREOC], 1997). Further, incarceration of the parent or primary carer is responsible for driving many children into OOHC (see Davis, 2019, p. 241). The *Family is Culture* report, an independent review into OOHC in NSW by Professor Megan Davis, drawing on the case files of all Aboriginal and Torres Strait Islander children and young people in care for the period 2015–2016 argued that placing an Aboriginal child in OOHC significantly increases the risk of coming into contact with the criminal justice system:

> This 'drift' of children from OOHC into the juvenile justice system is of paramount concern to the Aboriginal community, as Aboriginal children are more likely to be affected by this phenomenon due to their gross over-representation in the OOHC system. Involvement in the juvenile justice system perpetuates a cycle of disadvantage and child removals that must be halted in order to reduce the entry of Aboriginal children into the OOHC system in the longer term.
>
> (Davis, 2019, p. xxxv)

The review provided several recommendations to improve outcomes for Aboriginal children and young people in care in NSW, including:

> Greater data collection and research into the cross-over of children in OOHC and the juvenile justice system, as well as the development of further resources to ensure foster carers and residential home staff are trained about appropriate responses to children exhibiting behavioural difficulties in OOHC.
>
> (Davis, 2019, p. xxxv)

Tracing the historical context of the Australian child protection and criminal justice systems involves analysis of the legacies of colonisation, imperialism and globalisation. In the remainder of this chapter, we will establish the historical context for the criminalisation of care-experienced children that is relied upon in subsequent chapters. We start with an examination of the practices of forced removal that brought about the criminalisation of cultural difference and resulted in the Stolen Generations and continuing practices of removal of Aboriginal and Torres Strait Islander children from their families and communities. The Stolen Generations refers to the forced removal of thousands of children by government and non-government agencies, to live in institutions, foster homes or with families under adoption schemes (AIATSIS, 2022). As Davis (2019, p. xxx) writes, it is not just knowledge about the Stolen Generations that is fundamental to an understanding of contemporary child protection in Australia. A contextual understanding must extend to knowledge of the 'sustained history of oppression, paternalism and cruelty, which included a lengthy period of "protection" or compulsory racial segregation'. We now examine this history.

Frontier violence

> Indigenous children have been forcibly separated from their families and communities since the very first days of the European occupation of Australia.
>
> (HREOC, 1997, p. 22)

Colonisation disrupted traditional and well-established practices for Aboriginal and Torres Strait Islander children, families and communities. Indigenous peoples of the land now known as Australia had sophisticated practices and social rules for child rearing and family relationships (Lonne et al., 2021). Under these traditional practices, kinship, connection to Country and connection to culture are seen as critical to child well-being (Lonne et al., 2021; Priest et al., 2012). Aboriginal children are seen as the greatest asset of an Aboriginal family, and community plays a vital role in their development (Geia et al., 2011). Many policymakers, legislators and practitioners continue to have little understanding of the traditional child-rearing practices of Indigenous Australians, and consequently they have been neither recognised nor valued by authorities. This is important when considering the destructive impact of the Stolen Generations on Indigenous families, which contributed to today's over-representation of Indigenous children in care.

The landmark report *Bringing Them Home* (1997) was the culmination of extensive testimony and evidence collected and collated by the National Inquiry into the Separation of Aboriginal and Torres Strait Islander Children from their Families. The report was 'faithful to the language used by the witnesses quoted' (HREOC, 1997, p. 20) and used respectful 'legal storytelling' in honour of the more than 500 individuals who gave oral and written testimony (Bedford, 2019, p. 325). According to Bedford (2019, p. 322), legal storytelling refers to 'individual accounts of experiences and knowledge' being accepted as part of the legal narrative and treated as evidence. 'Legal storytelling' is a narrative methodology designed to enhance the visibility of marginalised voices, otherwise, excluded from analysis or obscured by quantitative data sets (Bedford, 2019; Smith, 1999). The main themes of the *Bringing Them Home* Report were grief and loss, tenacity and survival. The report documents the historical context of removal and the continuing impact and contemporary resonance of these policies of colonisation. While it will never be known exactly how many people were removed, as official records are incomplete and some fail to record the Aboriginality of children removed, the *Bringing Them Home* Report concludes that 'between one in three and one in ten Indigenous children were forcibly removed from their families and communities in the period from approximately 1910 until 1970' (HREOC, 1997, pp. 3–31).

The forced removal of Aboriginal and Torres Strait Islander children from their families began as frontier violence and went on to become a cornerstone policy of colonisation, similar to the policies used in Canada, Aotearoa New Zealand and the United States (Buti, 2004; Jacobs, 2009; Pihama et al., 2017). In the Australian context, conflict quickly followed the arrival of the First Fleet in Sydney in 1788. The first school for Aboriginal children, the Native Institution at Parramatta, was established by Governor Macquarie in 1814. It soon emerged that its purpose was to 'distance the children from their families and communities', and Aboriginal families subsequently refused to send their children to the school (HREOC, 1997, pp. 2, 33).

We will describe the experience of the Wiradyuri peoples living on the Bathurst plains – the geographic location where the authors are based – as an illustration of resistance to colonial brutality, while noting that these experiences were repeated all over Australia. In 1824, the Wiradyuri people living on the Bathurst plains were thought to number around 600–700 (Salisbury & Gresser, 1971, p. 9). The first meeting between the arriving British and Aboriginal people took place in 1813 and subsequent years were marked by peaceful relations. Bathurst was seen by the British colonisers as having attractive pastures and a road was built from Sydney, which led to Bathurst being proclaimed a town on 7 May 1815; but the increase in settler numbers was slow. Population figures of 1820 show that there were 114 Europeans in the area (Salisbury & Gresser, 1971, p. 15). Salisbury and Gresser argue that this period of colonialisation was also characterised by conflict between 'exclusionist' farmers and 'emancipist' ex-convicts. There was animosity between the two sides, and the exclusionists sought to destabilise Macquarie's leadership. They persuaded the British Government to adopt a policy of land sales and grants, which led to a dramatic increase in the number of settlers in the Bathurst area. By 1821, the year of Macquarie's departure, the population had more than doubled to 287. A growing number of Europeans arrived in the area, seizing land and dispossessing Aboriginal people of vital sources of food, water, accommodation and cultural/spiritual significance. Competition over vital resources ensued and violent conflict took place. Aboriginal people were poisoned with arsenic, and settlers and Aboriginal people alike were massacred although one grazier family, the Suttons, formed a good relationship with the Wiradyuri people and learnt the local language.

The 'potato massacre' was a prominent event in this conflict. In a market garden near the Wambool (Macquarie River), a farmer offered some Aboriginal people potatoes. When these Aboriginal people returned the next day for more, they have driven away and several were killed, including relatives of the Wiradyuri warrior Windradyne, who is understood to have led the resistance after this massacre. Particularly incensed by the killing of cattle, stockholders petitioned for military force (Gapps, 2021; Roberts, 1995, p. 621), and martial law was proclaimed in Bathurst on 14 August 1824. Martial law is defined in the *Australian law dictionary* as 'a state of military control of the general population. Authority may be granted to a state's military forces during war or other emergency situations, or seized, unconstitutionally' (Mann, 2017). Moore (2017, p. 130) has described martial law as a 'strange legal creature' used across the British Empire, and its elasticity may well be its appeal (Evans & Fluence, 2013; Kostal, 2005).

Governor Brisbane's proclamation of martial law was indicative of the level of hostilities at the time, as it was supposedly declared to end the 'mutual bloodshed' (Roberts, 1995, p. 622). Martial law officially ended on 11 December 1824 but arguably continued for much longer. This period has been referred to as the 'First Wiradyuri War of Resistance', the 'Battle of Bathurst' and the 'exterminating war' (Gapps, 2021; Grassby & Hill, 1988; Salisbury & Gresser, 1971). During the conflict, many hundreds of people were killed, with the losses of the Wiradyuri people far outweighing the deaths of non-Aboriginal people. Estimates suggest that 13 Europeans were killed, while the number of Aboriginal people who died was around 100, although official record keeping made the deaths of Aboriginal people largely invisible. At the conclusion of martial law, Windradyne walked from Bathurst to Parramatta to attend a feast held by the Governor, accompanied by 130 other warriors (Dortins, 2018). Governor Brisbane was relieved of his post on the same day by Earl Bathurst, who was unhappy with how martial law had been declared and carried out.

Reports of massacres and other atrocities led the British Government to establish a Senate Committee to examine the situation of Aboriginal people in Australia and make a number of proposals that formed the genesis of the Stolen Generations framework. A system of 'protection' and segregation was subsequently established, which was designed to corral Aboriginal and Torres Strait Islander people to 'self-sufficient agricultural communities on reserved areas modelled on an English village', with the underlying advantage of enabling the expansion of the land holdings of others in the colony (HREOC, 1997, p. 23). This system collapsed by the 1850s and Aboriginal people faced continued insecurity:

> Forced off their land to the edges of non-Indigenous settlement, dependent upon government rations if they could not find work, suffering from malnutrition and disease, their presence was unsettling and embarrassing to non-Indigenous people. Government typically viewed Indigenous people as a nuisance.
>
> (HREOC, 1997, p. 23)

The prevailing assumption was that Aboriginal people would 'die out', based on the racist notion that Aboriginal people were a distinct 'race' with inherent fragilities. At this time, missionaries were intensifying their efforts to lobby the government to establish reserves.

In NSW, a Protector of Aborigines was appointed in 1881, who recommended that reserves be created throughout NSW to house Aboriginal people (HREOC, 1997, pp. 2, 3). As a result, Chief Protectors were appointed to take responsibility for the welfare of Aboriginal people and move people onto reserves – dedicated land for use by Aboriginal people. The Protectors, who were often police, exercised enormous power over the lives of Aboriginal people, including assuming parental rights.

The NSW Aborigines Protection Board was subsequently established in 1883, charged with controlling the lives of Aboriginal people in NSW and managing the reserves. By 1939, over 180 reserves were in existence (HREOC, 1997, p. 34). While the Board did not possess the legal power to remove children, it contributed to this outcome in indirect ways. It set up a facility to house children at Warangesda (near Griffith) but relied on unofficial means such as enticements and bullying to fill it with children. For example, the parents who allowed their children to stay at the dormitory were allowed to stay on the reserve; free rail passes were offered to the parents who left their children at the dormitory and returned home; and families were warned that children may face prosecution under the *Neglected Children and Juvenile Offenders Act 1905* (NSW) if they were removed (Read, 1981, p. 7). Seeking to formalise these practices, the Board advocated that Parliament legislate to furnish it with the powers to remove children permanently. Thus, lobbying by the Aborigines Protection Board secured the passage of the *Aborigines Protection Act 1909* (NSW) and the *Aborigines Protection Amending Act 1915* (NSW).

The government next shifted its focus onto an increasing 'mixed descent population' and how to 'merge' this cohort. The government felt that this 'mixed descent population' could be a source of cheap labour to feed a growing Australian economy. Severing the bond of these children of 'mixed descent' with their Aboriginal families continued to be a key aim of government initiatives:

> Unlike white children who came into the state's control, far greater care was taken to ensure that [Aboriginal children] never saw their parents or families again. They were often given new names, and the greater distances involved in rural areas made it easier to prevent parents and children on separate missions from tracing each other.
>
> (van Krieken 1991, in HREOC, 1997, p. 24)

The 'Aborigines Protection' legislative framework was chiefly relied upon to remove Aboriginal children from their families in NSW. This was because the general child protection legislation required demonstrating that there was some sort of neglect to justify removal.

The *Aborigines Protection Act 1909* (NSW) is framed in humanitarian terms: 'An Act to provide for the protection and care of aborigines [sic]'. Section 11 of the Act outlines the Board's ability to apprentice young children aged between 14 and 18 years. However, the Act required the Board to seek the consent of the courts before removal could occur (HREOC, 1997, p. 3). This proved to be an obstacle to the removal of Aboriginal and Torres Strait Islander children from their families. The Board also faced difficulties associated with proving that a child was neglected. As a result, the Board campaigned for expanded powers, which were delivered by the *Aborigines Protection Amending Act 1915* (NSW). Under Section 4 of this amending legislation, the Board was given the power to 'assume full control and custody of the children of any aborigine [sic]' without having to establish negligence in a court hearing. Moreover, the age threshold was abolished, meaning that there was no minimum age for apprenticeship.

In NSW, the 'mixed descent' children were sent to training institutions to prepare for work. The Board established the Kinchela Training Institution for Aboriginal Boys in 1918 and the Cootamundra Domestic Training Home for Aboriginal Girls in 1911 (HREOC, 1997, p. 34). The policies were intended to 'control the reproduction of Indigenous people' and girls were targeted for this purpose, removed and given exhausting work with the aim of curbing reproduction (HREOC, 1997, p. 25). Indeed, 81% of all children removed up until 1921 were girls (HREOC, 1997, p. 37; see also Goodall, 1990, p. 44). According to Goodall, the sexuality of Aboriginal women was seen as a threat by the Board (Goodall, 1990, p. 44).

The increasing scope of these child removal practices led to resistance and protest. The 'Australian Aborigines Progressive Association' was formed in 1925 to protest the forced removal of Aboriginal children. This resistance resulted in greater scrutiny of the operations of the Aborigines Protection Board, including by a number of NSW parliamentary inquiries (HREOC, 1997, p. 38).

Assimilation became the national focus from 1937, described as a 'socio-cultural' model by the National Inquiry that attributed no value to Aboriginal cultures. The Aborigines Welfare Board replaced the Protection Board. For NSW, this meant that after 1940, Aboriginal children were subject to the same child welfare laws as non-Aboriginal children in terms of removal although after removal Aboriginal children became wards of the Board, unlike non-Indigenous children (HREOC, 1997, p. 39). Although the same grounds for removal applied to both Aboriginal and non-Indigenous children, courts were more likely to find Aboriginal children to be 'neglected', 'destitute' and 'uncontrollable' – factors that warranted their removal. In the view of the National Inquiry, there were two main drivers of this. First, the judgement that poverty was the same as neglect meant that more Aboriginal children were removed because, at the time, Aboriginal people were not able to access social security benefits and so did not have the same access to the safety net as non-Aboriginal families (HREOC, 1997, p. 27). Second, Aboriginal families were subject to higher levels of surveillance, meaning that they were more visible to the authorities. The same agencies – police and welfare staff – enacted removal before and after 1940. Yet after removal, different processes applied to Aboriginal and non-Aboriginal children. The increasing numbers of Indigenous children removed under the assimilation policies meant that institutions became full and Aboriginal children were placed with foster families who were non-Aboriginal, to expedite assimilation (HREOC, 1997, p. 28).

The Aborigines Welfare Board also established 'homes for the reception, maintenance and training of wards' (HREOC, 1997, p. 39). Those who left these homes were considered to have committed an offence and were punished in the Children's Court. Aboriginal parents whose children had been removed were then prohibited from contacting their children and could be punished for doing so. The Aborigines Protection Board were unable to cope with the significant number of Indigenous children being removed and had to come up with a new system. As a result, Aboriginal children deemed 'uncontrollable' – that is, refusing to attend school (Carrington & Pereira, 2009, p. 9) – were the responsibility of the Child Welfare Department and sent to other facilities such as the Parramatta Girls Home (HREOC, 1997, p. 41). The Aborigines Welfare Board was abolished in 1969, after which time all wards were transferred to the Child Welfare and Social Welfare Department, whose practices have been described as 'overt denial but covert recognition and denigration of Aboriginality' by historian Dr Heather Goodall (HREOC, 1997, p. 42; see Wootten, 1989, p. 26).

The 1970s saw the gains of many decades of Aboriginal activism take effect, with self-determination becoming a central policy platform of governments and the formal establishment of Aboriginal-led organisations advocating against the removal of Aboriginal children and placement with non-Aboriginal families. The organisation Link-Up was established in NSW to trace and reunite Aboriginal families, and in the early 1980s, the Secretariat of National Aboriginal and Islander Child Care (SNAICC) emerged (now known as SNAICC – National Voice for our Children). These organisations worked to establish the Aboriginal Child Placement Principles, which were officially incorporated into NSW legislation via the *Children (Care and Protection) Act 1987* (NSW). Davis (2019) has suggested these principles remain poorly understood and implemented despite being required by legislation.

The National Inquiry documents some of the impacts of the policies and practices around the forcible removal of children from their families and some of the consequences of institutionalisation, poor access to education and child labour. The harms of forced removal have been compounded by racism, experiences of sexual and physical assault, rejection and destruction of Aboriginal cultures, deceit and punishment. This has led to high rates of post-traumatic stress disorder (PTSD) and other trauma, poor physical and mental health, increased risk of alcohol or drug addiction to ease pain and further institutionalisation of Aboriginal and Torres Strait Islander peoples (HREOC, 1997, pp. 170–173). Parents of removed children felt guilt and despair and, due to the significant role played by wider family members in Aboriginal and Torres Strait Islander cultures, this impact was particularly acute (HREOC, 1997, p. 181). In the words of the *Bringing Them Home* Report, 'families and whole communities suffered grievously upon the forcible removal of their children' (1997, p. 185). These impacts have resonated through subsequent generations. In relation to the contemporary care and protection environment, the National Inquiry concluded:

> There is also a general recognition that the underlying causes of the overrepresentation of Indigenous children in welfare systems include the inter-generational effects of previous separations from family and culture, poor socio-economic status and systemic racism in the broader society. These causes combine to produce cultural differences between welfare departments and Indigenous communities, substance abuse, violence, poor nutrition, alienation from social institutions including the education system, family services and the criminal justice system, limited and poor housing options and a loss of hope, particularly among younger people.
>
> (HREOC, 1997, p. 374)

At the time of the release of the National Inquiry report, Indigenous children in NSW comprised 2.1% of the total population but 7.7–9% of all child protection notifications for the 1991–1992 to 1995 period and just over 21%

of children in care (HREOC, 1997, p. 381). At the same time, NSW had the highest number of Indigenous young people in detention and that over-representation was higher for Aboriginal girls (46%) than for Aboriginal boys (36%) (HREOC, 1997, p. 435). Aboriginal children were also in the criminal justice system at a much younger age than non-Indigenous children (HREOC, 1997, p. 436). These statistics have worsened since this time. In 2020/2021, 43% of children in OOHC in NSW were Indigenous, and 40% of children in detention were Indigenous (Productivity Commission, 2022).

A range of factors causing the over-representation of Indigenous young people in custody were identified by the National Inquiry. These included discriminatory policing practices, a lack of diversionary options for young Aboriginal people, high remand rates and an overall lack of engagement with Indigenous peoples on matters such as diversion and the impact of colonisation on Indigenous families. Subsequent research has confirmed that Indigenous young people are less likely to receive diversionary options such as cautions and more likely to be in custody when sentenced (Cunneen & McDonald, 1997; Luke & Cunneen, 1995; McGrath, 2016; Warner et al., 2021).

In NSW, the death of two children in state care sparked a major inquiry in 2008. The inquiry, conducted by Justice Wood, investigated all aspects of the child protection system (Wood, 2008). In a three-volume report, Wood made specific recommendations about, among other things, assessment of children entering OOHC, and the relative role of state government agencies and non-government organisations in caring for these children. The over-representation of Aboriginal children was particularly noted, with a specific recommendation about strengthening the capacity of Aboriginal families to provide foster and kinship care.

A major report by the Australian Law Reform Commission (ALRC) handed down in 2017 confirmed the increasing disparity in incarceration rates between Indigenous and non-Indigenous people in Australia. The ALRC was explicit in linking the child protection system, juvenile justice and adult imprisonment, finding that 'child removal into out-of-home care and juvenile detention could be considered key drivers of adult incarceration' (ALRC, 2017, p. 34). These links have been exacerbated by the drastic increases in the imprisonment of Indigenous women documented in the ALRC report. A number of recommendations were made to address the problems identified. Predominant among these was that the considerable funds devoted to incarceration should be reinvested in community-based and localised programs to address the drivers of crime and incarceration. In a similar manner, the 1997 National Inquiry's findings turned on the importance of realising self-determination:

> Our principal finding is that self-determination for Indigenous peoples provides the key to reversing the over-representation of Indigenous children in the child welfare and juvenile justice systems of the States and

> Territories and to eliminating unjustified removals of Indigenous children from their families and communities.
>
> (HREOC, 1997, p. 15)

Other countries that have been impacted by British colonisation have moved in this direction. Canada, for example, has devolved much of the child welfare and criminal justice system to Aboriginal nations (HREOC, 1997, p. 503). In the United States, the *Indian Child Welfare Act 1978* ensures that tribal courts have exclusive jurisdiction over child welfare proceedings involving First Nations children. The *Bringing Them Home* Report concludes that while Australia's arrangements can be described as 'paternalistic … in which limited powers are delegated and functions are performed with inadequate resources, often in adverse circumstances', the US and Canadian settings have demonstrated a capacity to 'depart from the culture of control' (HREOC, 1997, p. 505).

The question of how Aboriginal over-representation in care should be responded to was subsequently considered in the *Family is Culture* report (Davis, 2019), which made some 125 recommendations addressing the factors unique to Aboriginal and Torres Strait Islander children in care. Although these recommendations were diverse and wide-reaching, overall a key recommendation was to increase the agency of Indigenous people in the care system and, in particular, build the self-determination of Indigenous people and communities to make decisions about how their children should be cared for. The need for the Department of Communities and Justice to establish an Aboriginal Quality Assurance Unit to address the problems identified in the report was highlighted by Davis.

Juvenile justice and child protection

Running alongside this history, the 19th and 20th centuries saw children who were perceived as 'wayward, ungovernable, or delinquent' become the focus of government attention. Kociumbas (1997, p. 22) estimates that between 1788 and 1868, 15% of prisoners transported to Australia were children (in Carrington & Pereira, 2009, p. 24). Much of the treatment of juveniles at the time was racialised. In England, 'Arab boys' became the focus, as immigrants did in urban Sydney (Carrington & Pereira, 2009, p. 10). Juvenile delinquents were taken to training centres that were more akin to gaols. Certain populations were targeted for control as authorities were concerned that they might commit crime (Platt, 1977, p. xxvii in Carrington & Pereira, 2009, p. 11). 'Child saving' became the movement to save delinquent children via re-training institutions, which aimed to discipline and punish children in conditions that were harsh. Criticisms of the institutions, and a preference for family-like settings that were seen as more likely to be successful, led to a greater reliance on fostering. This inherent belief in the nuclear family continues today and is emblematic of the current preferences underpinning OOHC (Carrington & Pereira, 2009).

In NSW, children were treated in the same way as adults until the introduction of the *Neglected Children and Juvenile Offenders Act 1905* (Carrington, 1993). The policy and legislative frameworks of welfare and punishment continued to overlap until the latter half of last century. As Carrington and Pereira (2009, p. 26) write, 'the separation of the Children's Court from adult courts has been commonly identified as the point at which a welfare model was grafted onto the administration of juvenile justice'. The focus shifted to individual children and their families and needs assessments. The appetite for further intervention expanded and children were punished for non-criminal behaviour and institutionalised. Many who were committed to such institutions reported mental, physical and sexual abuse. Some were sentenced to longer periods of detention than they would have been had they committed a crime (Carrington & Pereira, 2009, p. 28). Carrington and Pereira (2009) refer to this as decision-making driven by a deficit discourse. Deficit discourse is a framework critiqued by Indigenous scholars in juxtaposition to a strengths-based approach. A deficit discourse is a:

> discourse that represents people or groups in terms of deficiency – absence, lack or failure. It particularly denotes discourse that narrowly situates responsibility for problems with the affected individuals or communities, overlooking the larger socio-economic structures in which they are embedded.
>
> (Fogarty et al., 2018, p. vi)

This change to the administration of juvenile justice also led to a focus on homogenising all children 'before the courts into a unitary category of maladjusted or delinquent youth in need of prescribed treatment of one kind or another' (Carrington & Pereira, 2009, p. 29).

Care and protection and juvenile justice matters in NSW are now handled separately in different parts of the Children's Court. This has occurred via the *Children (Criminal Proceedings) Act 1987* and the *Children (Care and Protection) Act 1987*. This reform reduced the number of children in detention but also decreased the age of young people coming into the care and protection system (Carrington & Pereira, 2009, pp. 22, 34). While this reduced some of the driving forces characteristic of a penal welfare model, as we explore in this book, some of its tenets, and impacts, remain. In the next section, we review existing literature on child removal and its impact to situate our NSW case study on the criminalisation of care-experienced children.

Research evaluating the impact of care experience

In this section, we consider research showing the impact on the child when a decision is made to remove them from their family. This is a topic that has been of longstanding interest to researchers. Early research focused on the effect of being raised in an orphanage. Although the methodological strength of these studies varied considerably, three overall conclusions emerged. First, children raised in institutions such as orphanages were vulnerable to a range of harms that could persist across their lives. Second, the degree of physical, cognitive and emotional problems suffered by children raised in orphanages very much depended on the degree of deprivation they experienced. Third, where children were taken out of orphanages at an early age (at less than one year of age), there was evidence of considerable catch-up in the areas in which they had experienced problems (Johnson et al., 2006; Woodhouse et al., 2018). The Romanian orphanage study is probably the best-known and most rigorous of these studies. Following the fall of the Ceausescu regime in 1989, a large number of children raised in very poor conditions in Romanian orphanages were adopted in the United Kingdom. They had all entered institutional care at an early age but differed in how long they had spent there. Although there was evidence of recovery for those who had spent less than six months in the orphanages, among those children who had been institutionalised for longer than this, there were considerable long-term maladaptive psychological sequelae impacting behavioural patterns and cognitive functioning (Rutter, 1998; Rutter & Sonuga-Barke, 2010).

The literature examining the impact of the care experience more broadly, like the orphanage studies, provides considerable evidence of resilience, particularly where children enter care at an early age and experience stable placements (Rutter et al., 1998; Tarren-Sweeney & Goemans, 2019). Nevertheless, a large body of literature shows that being raised in the care system can lead to educational, health and social problems (Baidawi & Piquero, 2021; Fernandez, 2019; Gypen et al., 2017; Malvaso et al., 2018; O'Higgins et al., 2017). A key concern of this book is the link between children in the care and justice systems.

Links between the care and justice systems

Research from both Australian and international jurisdictions shows that young people in OOHC, particularly those in residential care, are over-represented in the criminal justice system. In Australia, studies have found that placement in OOHC is associated with increased involvement with the criminal justice system (Gerard et al., 2019; Malvaso & Delfabbro, 2015; McFarlane, 2010, 2017; Ringland et al., 2015). Just over 50% of all children under youth justice supervision in Australia between 2018 and 2019 had been in the child protection system in the previous five years (AIHW, 2020). Further, girls under youth justice supervision were more likely to receive child protection services than boys (AIHW, 2020).

Several Australian studies have used file review methodology to investigate the question of whether children in the care system are more likely to come into contact with the criminal justice system. Although these studies relied on small samples and the estimates derived from them are not as reliable as population-level studies, they consistently found a strong relationship between the care and justice systems. In a study based on reviews of 111 files of children appearing in the NSW Children's Court between June and December 2009, McFarlane (2010) observed that 34% of her sample had recently been in care, with a further 22.5% judged to have been 'extremely likely' to have been in care (McFarlane, 2010, p. 346). In a later study examining 160 court files of young people who had appeared before the same court between 2008 and 2010, she found further evidence of substantial over-representation of care children in court, with the care children also found to be younger at entry to the criminal justice system and more likely to have been in remand custody (McFarlane, 2017). More recently, Baidawi and Sheehan (2019) reviewed 300 court files of cross-over children appearing in the Victorian Children's Court between 2016 and 2017. The children had experienced high levels of maltreatment and suffered from a range of physical and mental health conditions. Just under a half (41%) were less than 14 when first charged by police, with a similar number (42%) spending time in remand custody, and 12% receiving custodial sentences. These figures were substantially higher when compared to the data for all other children dealt with by the court. Multivariate analyses found neglect and maltreatment to be strongly related to earlier charge dates, with age, male gender, experience of parental death, early police charges, substance misuse and being in residential care for longer than 18 months all linked to total number of charges. Indigenous status was excluded in this study due to large amounts of missing data.

Other Australian studies have used administrative data to understand the overlap between the care and justice systems. In a study of 392 juvenile offenders under community supervision in NSW, 14.5% (n = 57) were found to have a history of placement in OOHC (Weatherburn et al., 2007). Kenny et al. (2007) identified that approximately a quarter of young people under both community and custodial supervision in NSW had experience of care. In a study of 17,638 young people coming into contact with the criminal justice system in NSW, Ringland et al. (2015) found that approximately 10% of their sample (9.1% of males and 12.5% of females) had previous OOHC placements.

In England and Wales, similar patterns of over-representation have been observed. The Taylor Review (2016) found considerable over-representation of care-experienced young people in various forms of detention and explained this in terms of a combination of individual-level risk factors and systemic problems in the management of care homes. The Laming Report (2016) similarly concluded that some 50% of children in custody had been in OOHC at some stage of their life. In the literature review prepared for the Laming Report, Staines argues that there are two competing explanations for the care–crime link: the risk factor approach and the adverse environment approach (Staines, 2016). In the first of these, factors preceding the young person entering care, such as a history of trauma (Felitti et al., 1998), are seen as the most important determinants of contact with the criminal justice system. The second of these approaches argues that it is instead the care environment that criminalises children through factors such as over-policing of relatively minor disciplinary infractions, and unstable and poorly run accommodation (Gerard et al., 2019; Shaw & Greenhow, 2021). The Howard League found that children in residential care were over 15 times more likely to have been subject to a final warning or reprimand during the year compared to children in the general population. Children in other forms of care (such as foster or kinship) were about four times as likely to come to the attention of authorities compared to the general population (Howard League, 2017). Similarly, Carnie and Broderick (2015), in a survey of Scottish prisoners, found that 26% of their prisoner respondents had been in OOHC and 16% had been in care at the age of 16.

An important study examining the relationship between care and crime was conducted by Claire Taylor, who interviewed 39 young people with experience of care (Taylor, 2006). Taylor argues that the notion of attachment is key to understanding the experiences and perceptions of young people in care. In her research, she combines insights from criminology in the form of Hirschi's social control theory (Hirschi, 1969) and the life-course criminological perspective (Sampson & Laub, 1993, 2003) with insights from psychology in the form of Bowlby and Ainsworth's attachment theory (Ainsworth et al., 2015; Bowlby, 2005). Taylor's theoretical approach allows psychology's understanding of the individual and their experiences of attachment to be combined with criminology's interest in the social determinants of attachment as well as turning points across the lifespan to help explain the complex interactions between young people's experiences of care and their life outcomes. A number of important themes emerged from participants' accounts of their care experiences. First, similar to the orphanage studies, experiences of care varied dramatically, with some individuals experiencing relatively stable foster placements and others having a very unstable history of placements. Second, the care environment was described by interview respondents as mayhem, particularly in relation to residential care. Respondents reported experiences of bullying, self-harm and violence in a context where staff were often unmotivated or, indeed, unable to address these problems. Third, while only a few respondents reported having close relationships with their carers, many spoke of the importance of having a caring presence in their lives, and the benefits of a safe and secure environment. Fourth, education was seen as key for building skills but also self-esteem in children whose lives had been marked by a lack of love and care. Finally, successful management of leaving care was found to be a critical determinant of the subsequent life outcomes of cared-for children, yet often this critical transition was poorly handled.

In a recent book from the England and Wales, Shaw and Greenhow (2021) investigate the 'criminalisation and exploitation' (p. 1) of children in care through an examination of multi-agency work, and the specific case of Multi-Agency Safeguarding Hubs (MASH), which are the first point of contact for all referrals to children's services in England and Wales. These authors conducted focus groups with a total of 36 participants, drawn from four MASH teams, one fostering agency and one group of senior social work managers. In relation to the criminalisation of children in care, familiar themes emerged, including the: role of the residential care environment; problems arising from the privatisation of care, in particular the desire to reduce costs leading to lower staff wages and lower staff–child ratios; policing of minor behavioural infractions in care; and, unstable placements. Multi-agency practice was perceived as having the potential to improve outcomes for these vulnerable young people, although effective implementation requires improvements in resourcing, education and planning.

Research in the United States has been characterised by large, well-conducted longitudinal studies, and these too have observed a robust relationship between the care and justice systems. Ryan and Testa (2005) found children with a history of care had approximately twice the odds of engaging in offending behaviour between the ages of 14 and 16 compared to those not in care, in a sample of 18,676 children born in Cook County, Illinois. They also found that placement instability was an important predictor of offending, with those in more unstable placements having higher odds of offending (Ryan & Testa, 2005). Another important study of outcomes for children in OOHC from the United States is the Midwest Evaluation of the Adult Functioning of Former Foster Youth (Courtney & Dworsky, 2006; Courtney et al., 2001). In a longitudinal study of 603 children in care, 28% of the sample had been arrested and approximately 20% had spent at least one night in custody (Courtney & Dworsky, 2006). Turning to other international jurisdictions, nearly 45% of females and 75% of males in a Swedish study of 700 young people with experience of OOHC who were placed in care for behavioural reasons had committed a crime by the age of 24, compared to 3.2% of females and 15.7% of males from the general population (Vinnerljung & Sallnäs, 2008). In summary, although estimates of the degree of over-representation vary according to jurisdiction, methodology and sample, it is clear that young people in OOHC comprise a sizable proportion of those coming into contact with the criminal justice system.

In Aotearoa New Zealand, Stanley (2017) explored the criminalising trajectory from care to custody based on a comprehensive review of 105 case files and interviews with 45 participants. She concluded that children in state care are far more likely to enter custody as a result of maltreatment, multiple care placements, damaging institutional cultures, social disadvantage, psychological harms and differential treatment in the criminal justice system. She found that children's involvement in the criminal justice system is closely associated with exposure to processes of both criminalisation and victimisation. Stanley's book, *The Road to Hell*, documents in detail a toxic mix of dysfunctional and abusive families, institutionalised racism and state violence in describing the experiences of 105 people removed from their families as children and placed in care (Stanley, 2016). She identified evidence of sexual abuse in care, from both workers and other children (16 of the care-experienced contributors reported abuse from workers and 48 from other children); physical abuse; criminalisation (47 out of 105 contributors came into contact with the criminal justice system) and various other forms of physical, social and emotional harm suffered by her contributors.

Like Australia and Aotearoa New Zealand, ongoing forms of colonialism and child removal policies in Canada have resulted in the over-representation of Indigenous children in the OOHC environment. The history of Canadian child removal through mandatory government policy dates back to the late 1800s, with ongoing discoveries of unmarked graves exposing the atrocities suffered by Indigenous children across Canada. Census data from 2016 reveal that Indigenous children (aged 0–14 years) make up 7.7% of all children in Canada but represent 52.2% of the children in care. Indigenous young people in Canada are eight times more likely to be incarcerated than their non-Indigenous counterparts (Corrado et al., 2014). Cesaroni et al.'s (2018) study investigated the perceptions of Indigenous young people from the Anishinaabe, Haudenosaunee and Métis communities about why Indigenous youth are over-represented in the Canadian criminal justice system. Five themes emerged from their analyses: the impact of colonisation and residential schools; the loss of Indigenous histories, traditions, cultures and ceremonies; the destruction of Indigenous families; racism and the loss of Indigenous identities (Cesaroni et al., 2018). The results revealed that the reasons for the over-representation of Indigenous youth in the Canadian criminal justice system are multilayered and complex, with one clear conclusion from the Indigenous Elders consulted being that solutions lie within Indigenous communities, where the connection to culture needed to heal their young people can be fostered.

Conclusion

Our book responds to the literature reviewed here and provides a contextual analysis of the contemporary links between the care and criminal justice systems in NSW, Australia. It is based on a research program stretching over five years in which we interviewed key respondents in these systems, observed court proceedings involving children in the care system and conducted court file reviews to better understand the intertwining relationship between children's involvement in the care and justice systems. Taylor's book gives valuable theoretical insights into this relationship; however, as it is based on interview data from England and Wales, it cannot provide an account of the significant role of colonisation within the NSW (and, indeed, Australian) context. Stanley's book is a vivid historical account of the experiences of a group of New Zealanders caught up in the care system, and while it is certainly of interest and relevance to contemporary policy makers and researchers both domestically and internationally, it does not speak directly to the current policy and research environment. The aim of our book is to examine the factors underlying the criminalisation of children in OOHC using an innovative mixed-method approach. We will examine, in turn, the role of trauma and abuse in this relationship, the residential care environment itself, how children in care are policed in contemporary NSW, the role of lawyers in advising care-experienced children, how the Children's Court deals with these children, and gender and care. And finally, we will seek to identify innovations partly informed by our case study on policy and practice responses in England and Wales. Throughout, we consider the relationship between Indigenous people and the care system, focusing on the legacies of colonisation.

References

Aborigines Protection Act 1909 (NSW). http://www.austlii.edu.au/au/legis/nsw/num_act/apa1909n25262.pdf

Aborigines Protection Amending Act 1915 (NSW). http://www.austlii.edu.au/au/legis/nsw/num_act/apaa1915n2321.pdf

Ainsworth, M. D. S., Blehar, M. C., Waters, E., & Wall, S. N. (2015). *Patterns of attachment: A psychological study of the strange situation.* Psychology Press.

Australian Institute of Aboriginal and Torres Strait Islander Studies [AIATSIS]. (2022, 27 January). *The stolen generations.* https://aiatsis.gov.au/explore/stolen-generations

Australian Institute of Health and Welfare [AIHW]. (2020). *Young people in child protection and under youth justice supervision 2018–19.*

Australian Institute of Health and Welfare [AIHW]. (2021). *Child Protection Australia 2019–2020* (Vol. 78).

Australian Law Reform Commission. (2017). *Pathways to justice: An inquiry into the incarceration rate of Aboriginal and Torres Strait Islander peoples.*

Baidawi, S., & Piquero, A. R. (2021). Neurodisability among children at the nexus of the child welfare and youth justice system. *Journal of Youth and Adolescence, 50*(4), 803–819. https://doi.org/10.1007/s10964-020-01234-w

Bedford, N. (2019). Storytelling in our legal system: Healing for the stolen generations. *Australian Feminist Law Journal, 45*(2), 321–331.

Bowlby, J. (2005). *A secure base: Clinical applications of attachment theory* (Vol. 393). Taylor & Francis.

Buti, A. (2004). The removal of indigenous children from their families: US and Australia compared. *University of Western Sydney Law Review, 8*, 125.

Carnie, J., & Broderick, R. (2015). *Prisoner Survey 2015* (Vol. 15). Scottish Prisoner Service.

Carrington, K. (1993). *Offending girls: Sex, youth and justice.* Allen and Unwin.

Carrington, K., & Pereira, M. (2009). *Offending youth: Sex, crime and justice.* Federation Press.

Cesaroni, C., Grol, C., & Fredericks K. (2018). Overrepresentation of Indigenous youth in Canada's criminal justice system: Perspectives of Indigenous young people. *Australian & New Zealand Journal of Criminology. 52*(1), 111–128. https://doi.org/10.1177/0004865818778746

Children (Care and Protection) Act 1987 (NSW). https://legislation.nsw.gov.au/view/whole/html/inforce/2001-07-02/act-1987-054

Children (Criminal Proceedings) Act 1987. https://legislation.nsw.gov.au/view/html/inforce/current/act-1987-055

Corrado, R. R., Kuehn, S., & Margaritescu, I. (2014). Policy issues regarding the overrepresentation of incarcerated aboriginal young offenders in a Canadian context. *Youth Justice, 14*(1), 40–62. https://doi.org/10.1177/1473225413520361

Courtney, M. E., & Dworsky, A. (2006). Early outcomes for young adults transitioning from out-of-home care in the USA. *Child & Family Social Work, 11*(3), 209–219. https://doi.org/10.1111/j.1365–2206.2006.00433.x

Courtney, M. E., Piliavin, I., Grogan-Kaylor, A., & Nesmith, A. (2001). Foster youth transitions to adulthood: A longitudinal view of youth leaving care. *Child Welfare, 80*(6), 685–717.

Cunneen, C., & McDonald, D (1997). Keeping Aboriginal and Torres Strait Islander people out of custody, a evaluation of the implementation of the recommendations of the royal commission into aboriginal deaths in custody, ATSIC, Canberra.

Davis, M. (2019). *Family is Culture: Review report.* Independent Review of Aboriginal Children in OOHC.

Dortins, E. (2018). *The lives of stories.* Canberra: ANU Press.

Evans, J., & Fluence, T. (2013). Securing the settler polity: Martial law and the aboriginal peoples of Van Diemen's Land. *Journal of Australian Colonial History, 15*, 1–22.

Felitti, V. J., Anda, R. F., Nordenberg, D., Williamson, D. F., Spitz, A. M., Edwards, V. et al. (1998). Relationship of childhood abuse and household dysfunction to many of the leading causes of death in adults: The adverse childhood experiences (ACE) study. *American Journal of Preventive Medicine, 14*(4), 245–258. https://doi.org/10.1016/S0749-3797(98)00017-8

Fernandez, E. (2019). Working towards better education for children in care: Longitudinal analysis of the educational outcomes of a cohort of children in care in Australia. *Oxford Review of Education, 45*(4), 481–501.

Fogarty, W., Lovell, M., Langenberg, J., & Heron, M-J. (2018). *Deficit discourse and strengths-based approaches: Changing the narrative of Aboriginal and Torres Strait Islander health and wellbeing.* The Lowitja Institute.

Gapps, S. (2021). *Gudyarra: The first Wiradyuri war of resistance—The Bathurst War, 1822–1824.* New South Publishing.

Geia, L., Hayes, B., & Usher, K. (2011). Editorial: A strengths based approach to Australian Aboriginal childrearing practices is the answer to better outcomes in Aboriginal family and child health. *Collegian, 18*(3), 99–100.

Gerard, A., McGrath, A., Colvin, E., & McFarlane, K. (2019). 'I'm not getting out of bed!': The criminalisation of young people in residential care. *Australian & New Zealand Journal of Criminology, 52*(1), 76–93. https://doi.org/10.1177/0004865818778739.

Goodall, H. (1990). 'Saving the children': Gender and the colonisation of aboriginal children in NSW, 1788 to 1990. *Aboriginal Law Bulletin, 2*(44), 6–9.

Grassby, A. J., & Hill, M. (1988). *Six Australian battlefields: The black resistance to invasion and the white struggle against colonial oppression* (pp. 160–161). Angus & Robertson Publishers.

Gypen, L., Vanderfaeillie, J., De Maeyer, S., Belenger, L., & Van Holen, F. (2017). Outcomes of children who grew up in foster care: Systematic review. *Children and Youth Services Review, 76*, 74–83. https://doi.org/10.1016/j.childyouth.2017.02.035

Hirschi, T. (1969). *Causes of delinquency*. University of California Press.

Howard League. (2017). *Ending the criminalisation of children in residential care*. Howard League.

Human Rights and Equal Opportunity Commission [HREOC]. (1997). *Bringing Them Home: Report of the national inquiry into the separation of Aboriginal and Torres Strait Islander children from their families*. Commonwealth of Australia.

Jacobs, M. (2009). *White mother to a dark race: Settler colonialism, maternalism, and the removal of children in the American West and Australia 1880–1940*. University of Nebraska Press.

Johnson, R., Browne, K., & Hamilton-Giachritsis, C. (2006). Young children in care at risk of institutional harm. *Trauma, Violence & Abuse, 7*(1), 34–60. https://doi.org/10.1177/1524838005283696

Kenny, D. T., Nelson, P. K., Schreiner, I., Lennings, C. J., & Butler, T. (2007). *Young offenders on community orders: Health, welfare and criminogenic needs*. Sydney University Press.

Kociumbas, J. (1997). *Australian childhood: A history*. Allen & Unwin.

Kostal, A. (2005). *Jurisprudence of power: Victorian empire and the rule of law*. Oxford: Oxford University Press.

Laming, H. (2016). *In care, out of trouble: How the life chances of children in care can be transformed by protecting them from unnecessary involvement in the criminal justice system*. Prison Reform Trust.

Lonne, B., Flemington, T., Lock, M., Hartz, D., Ramanathan, S., & Fraser, J. (2021). The power of authenticity and cultural safety at the intersection of healthcare and child protection. *International Journal on Child Maltreatment: Research, Policy and Practice, 3*(4), 393–408. https://doi.org/10.1007/s42448-020-00053-7

Luke, G., & Cunneen, C. (1995). *Aboriginal over-representation and discretionary decisions in the NSW juvenile justice system*. Juvenile Justice Advisory Council.

Malvaso, C. G., & Delfabbro, P. (2015). Offending behaviour among young people with complex needs in the Australian out-of-home care system. *Journal of Child and Family Studies, 24*(12), 3561–3569. https://doi.org/10.1007/s10826-015-0157-z

Malvaso, C. G., Delfabbro, P. H., Day, A., & Nobes, G. (2018). The maltreatment–violence link: Exploring the role of maltreatment experiences and other individual and social risk factors among young people who offend. *Journal of Criminal Justice, 55*, 35–45. https://doi.org/10.1016/j.jcrimjus.2018.01.006

Mann, T. (2017) *Australian Legal Dictionary*. Oxford: Oxford University Press.

McFarlane, K. (2010). From care to custody: Young women in out-of-home care in the criminal justice system. *Current Issues in Criminal Justice, 22*, 345–353.

McFarlane, K. (2017). Care-criminalisation: The involvement of children in out-of-home care in the New South Wales criminal justice system. *Australian & New Zealand Journal of Criminology, 51*(3), 412–433. https://doi.org/10.1177/0004865817723954

McGrath, A. (2016). Intersections of Indigenous status, sex and age in sentencing decisions in the New South Wales Children's Court. *Australian & New Zealand Journal of Criminology, 49*(1), 90–112. https://doi.org/10.1177/0004865814551614

Moore, C. (2017). *Crown and Sword*. Canberra.

Neglected Children and Juvenile Offenders Act 1905 (NSW). http://www5.austlii.edu.au/au/legis/nsw/num_act/ncajoa1905n16368.pdf

O'Higgins, A., Sebba, J., & Gardner, F. (2017). What are the factors associated with educational achievement for children in kinship or foster care: A systematic review. *Children and Youth Services Review, 79*, 198–220. https://doi.org/10.1016/j.childyouth.2017.06.004

Pihama, L., Smith, L. T., Evans-Campbell, T., Kohu-Morgan, H., Cameron, N., Mataki, T. et al. (2017). Investigating Māori approaches to trauma informed care. *Journal of Indigenous Wellbeing, 2*(3), 18–31.

Platt, A. M. (1977). *The child savers: The invention of delinquency*. University of Chicago Press.

Priest, N., Mackean, T., Davis, E., Briggs, L., &Waters, E. (2012). Aboriginal perspectives of child health and wellbeing in an urban setting: Developing a conceptual framework. *Health Sociology Review, 21*(2), 180–195.

Read, P. (1981). *The stolen generations: The removal of Aboriginal children in New South Wales 1883 to 1969*. New South Wales Department of Aboriginal Affairs.

Ringland, C., Weatherburn, D., & Poynton, S. (2015). Can child protection data improve the prediction of re-offending in young persons? *NSW Crime and Justice Bulletin* (Vol. 188). Sydney: NSW Bureau of Crime Statistics and Research.

Roberts, D. (1995). Bells falls massacre and Bathurst's history of violence: Local tradition and Australian historiography. *Australian Historical Studies, 26*(105), 615–633.

Rutter, M. (1998). Developmental catch-up, and deficit, following adoption after severe global early privation. *Journal of Child Psychology and Psychiatry, 39*(4), 465–476.

Rutter, M., Giller, H., & Hagell, A. (1998). *Antisocial behavior by young people*. Cambridge University Press.

Rutter, M., & Sonuga-Barke, E. J. (2010). Conclusions: Overview of findings from the ERA study, inferences, and research implications. *Monographs of the Society for Research in Child Development, 75*(1), 212–229.

Ryan, J. P., & Testa, M. F. (2005). Child maltreatment and juvenile delinquency: Investigating the role of placement and placement instability. *Children and Youth Services Review, 27*(3), 227–249. http://dx.doi.org/10.1016/j.childyouth.2004.05.007

Salisbury, T., & Gresser, P. J. (1971). *Windradyne of the Wiradjuri: Martial law at Bathurst in 1824* (No. 4). Wentworth Books.

Sampson, R. J., & Laub, J. H. (1993). *Crime in the making: Pathways and turning points through life*. Harvard University Press.

Sampson, R. J., & Laub, J. H. (2003). Life-course desisters? Trajectories of crime among delinquent boys followed to age 70. *Criminology, 41*(3), 555–592.

Shaw, J., & Greenhow, S. (2021). *The criminalisation and exploitation of children in care: Multi-agency perspectives*. Routledge.

Smith, L. T. (1999). *Decolonising methodologies*. Zed Books.

Staines, J. (2016). *Risk, adverse influence and criminalisation: Understanding the over-representation of looked after children in the youth justice system*. Prison Reform Trust.

Stanley, E. (2016). *The road to hell: State violence against children in postwar New Zealand*. Auckland University Press.

Stanley, E. (2017). From care to custody: Trajectories of children in post-war New Zealand. *Youth Justice, 17*(1), 57–72. https://doi.org/10.1177/1473225416669145

Tarren-Sweeney, M., & Goemans, A. (2019). A narrative review of stability and change in the mental health of children who grow up in family-based out-of-home care. *Developmental Child Welfare, 1*(3), 273–294.
Taylor, C. (2006). *Young people in care and criminal behaviour.* Jessica Kingsley Publishers.
Taylor, C. (2016). *Review of the youth justice system in England and Wales.* Ministry of Justice.
van Krieken, R. (1991). *Children and the State: Social control and the formation of Australian child welfare.* Sydney: Allen and Unwin.
Vinnerljung, B., & Sallnäs, M. (2008). Into adulthood: A follow-up study of 718 young people who were placed in out-of-home care during their teens. *Child & Family Social Work, 13*(2), 144–155. https://doi.org/10.1111/j.1365–2206.2007.00527.x
Warner, B., Spivak, B., Ashford, L., Fix, R., Ogloff, J., & Shepherd, S. (2021). The impact of offender–victim cultural backgrounds on the likelihood of receiving diversion. *Criminal Justice Policy Review.* https://doi.org/10.1177/08874034211046313
Weatherburn, D., Cush, R., & Saunders, P. (2007). Screening juvenile offenders for further assessment and intervention. *Crime and Justice Bulletin, 109.* Sydney: NSW Bureau of Crime Statistics and Research.
Wood, J. (2008). *Report of the Special Commission of Inquiry into child protection services in NSW* (Vols. 1 and 2). Department of Premier and Cabinet (NSW).
Woodhouse, S., Miah, A., & Rutter, M. (2018). A new look at the supposed risks of early institutional rearing. *Psychological Medicine, 48*(1), 1–10.
Wootten, H. (1989). Report of the inquiry into the death of Malcolm Smith, Royal Commission into aboriginal deaths in custody. AGPS, Sydney.

2 Care-experience, trauma, abuse and the criminal justice system

Trauma

The word trauma is derived from the Greek τραύμα (travma), which means wound. Originally, the word in English referred to a serious physical injury, but the meaning of trauma has since extended to include psychological and emotional reactions to adverse life experiences (Horwitz, 2018). The American Psychological Association (APA) incorporates the traditional notion of trauma as 'any serious physical injury, such as a widespread burn or a blow to the head' in its definition but emphasises the psychological aspect of this phenomenon as:

> any disturbing experience that results in significant fear, helplessness, dissociation, confusion, or other disruptive feelings intense enough to have a long-lasting negative effect on a person's attitudes, behaviour, and other aspects of functioning. Traumatic events include those caused by human behaviour (e.g., rape, war, industrial accidents) as well as by nature (e.g., earthquakes) and often challenge an individual's view of the world as a just, safe, and predictable place.
>
> (APA, 2019)

Trauma as a reaction to the experience of combat has been noted since Homer's *Iliad.* Adverse psychological reactions to the experience of war were observed following the American Civil War, and both World Wars I and II. Following the Vietnam War, observations of the effects of exposure to combat led to the development and recognition of a new psychological condition, post-traumatic stress disorder (PTSD). This condition first appeared in the third edition of the *Diagnostic and statistical manual of mental disorders* (DSM), published in 1980 (Friedman et al., 2011). In the most recent edition of the DSM (*Diagnostic and statistical manual of mental disorders: DSM-5*, 2013), PTSD is diagnosed where the individual has been exposed to actual or threatened death, serious injury or sexual violence and suffers at least one intrusive symptom (such as distressing memories, dissociative reactions, psychological distress), at least one avoidance symptom,

DOI: 10.4324/9781003093367-3

at least two arousal or reactivity symptoms (such as negative self-beliefs, negative emotional states, distorted cognitions) and at least two cognitive and mood symptoms (such as irritability and anger, hypervigilance, sleep disturbances). The ability of PTSD to capture the impact of historical and cumulative trauma across generations has been questioned by Indigenous scholars, as explored below (Yellow Horse Brave Heart, 2003).

Indigenous Australians have suffered trauma as a direct impact of the ongoing forms of colonisation they have experienced since the establishment of a British settlement at Sydney in 1788. Indigenous peoples in Australia have experienced trauma through the dispossession of their land, language and culture and the forced removal of their children (now known as the Stolen Generations). This has led to the disruption of the cultural kinship systems that underpin an Indigenous person's identity, spirituality and sense of belonging. These ongoing cycles of trauma have been transferred from one generation to the next in a process referred to as intergenerational trauma, or 'the continued cycle of trauma and poor social and emotional well-being that continues to contribute to the disadvantage and poor outcomes for Aboriginal and Torres Strait Islander peoples' (Hampton & Toombs, 2013, p. 227). Intergenerational trauma has been found to be associated with a range of symptoms, including 'feelings of shame, anxiety, depression, anger, helplessness, vulnerability and sadness' (Hampton & Toombs, 2013, p. 227). It continues to play a pivotal role in the violence and abuse experienced by Indigenous family and community dysfunction (Atkinson et al., 2010). It should be distinguished from transgenerational trauma, where a victimised child can become the perpetrator of sexual and physical violence against others, therefore perpetuating a cycle of abuse (Purdie et al., 2010). Our participants did not always recognise this distinction, and in the remainder of this book, we refer to intergenerational trauma only. Trauma also has gendered impacts, which we explore in this chapter and also in Chapter 7 in relation to our findings.

Adverse childhood experiences and complex trauma

While it is certainly possible that children in care can suffer from PTSD, the more common approach in the literature has been to investigate how different kinds of ACEs are related to health and other outcomes (including offending) in young people (Cook et al., 2005; Copeland et al., 2007; Harris & Fallot, 2001b). Ten separate ACEs have been identified in the research: emotional abuse, physical abuse, sexual abuse, emotional neglect, physical neglect, violent treatment of mothers, household substance abuse, household mental illness, parental separation or divorce and household criminal activity and incarceration. The original ACE study was conducted in San Diego (US), using a sample of 9,508 adults completing standardised medical evaluations (Felitti et al., 1998). In addition to the medical evaluation, the participants also completed a questionnaire measuring experiences of childhood abuse and household dysfunction. More than half the sample had experienced at least one type of ACE, and 6.2% reported more than four. The most common type reported was substance abuse in the house, while the least common reported was criminal activity/incarceration in the household. Exposure to childhood risk factors was strongly related to a range of adverse physical and mental health conditions in adulthood, including a higher risk of smoking, alcoholism, use of illegal drugs, obesity, inactivity, depression and suicide attempts. In a later study, Anda et al. (2006) argued that childhood maltreatment causes a range of neurological dysfunctions, which, in turn, are linked to specific health and social outcomes across the lifespan. They tested this using an expanded data set from the ACE study (N = 17,337). Just as in the original ACE study, Anda et al.'s study found that increased levels of ACEs were linked to a greater likelihood of a range of mental and physical health problems in adulthood, as well as increased risk of alcoholism, smoking and illicit drug use. As ACEs increased, so did comorbid outcomes in adulthood in a linear manner.

Data from our study were consistent with these findings. In our file reviews, we found evidence that 50% of the children with care experience had some experience of abuse and trauma compared to 11.4% of the children with no care experience (McGrath et al., 2020). Interview respondents also reported that children in their care had been the victims of a range of abuses, including sexual and physical assault by parents and carers, neglect and parental mental illness and drug use (OOHC1, OOHC12, M9, L4&L5, JJ7). Many examples were given in the interviews, including that of a child who had been kept in a dog choker (JJ1), a number of young women who had been the victims of sexual abuse as children (OOHC1, JJ7) and one young person whose mother had died by suicide when she was 11 (L4 & L5). One carer we spoke to characterised young people in care as suffering from 'severe trauma', with resulting drug and alcohol abuse and mental health disorders (OOHC1). In the words of one interview respondent, 'generally, they've got a fairly strong history of trauma' (JJ1).

Complex trauma

This pervasive pattern of trauma among care-experienced children has led some to argue that PTSD does not capture the full impact of exposure to developmental maltreatment. A group of child trauma specialists from the United States reviewed the relevant literature and suggested that children with histories of abuse could best be thought of as suffering from complex trauma, which could manifest itself in diagnoses of PTSD but also in a range of other conditions including depression, attention deficit hyperactivity disorder (ADHD), anxiety disorders, eating disorders and oppositional defiant disorder (ODD; Cook et al., 2005). In this regard, our findings revealed mental health disorders to be a key feature of children in the care and justice systems. Our file review data showed that 63.6% of care-experienced children suffered from mental health disorders compared to 20% of non-care children. In our detailed file reviews, there was evidence of young people in care who suffered from bipolar disorder, anxiety and depression. In some cases, we read descriptions of children being scheduled under Section 22 of the *Mental Health Act* NSW and forcibly taken to hospital by police. Interview respondents noted that mental health problems were a key feature of traumatised children in care. One magistrate commented: 'usually there are obvious mental health issues when the young people are coming to Court, especially if they're in out-of-home care because they're usually traumatised kids in the first place' (M13). Juvenile justice workers recounted how children in their care 'self-medicate their mental health through drug and alcohol use' (JJ6) and service providers also described the difficulties in obtaining appropriate mental health care for children in their care (OOHC12).

Cook and her colleagues identified seven domains of complex trauma: attachment, biology, affect regulation, dissociation, behavioural regulation, cognition and self-concept. As we have previously discussed, deficits in attachment relationships are a key characteristic of children in care (see Chapter 1; and Taylor, 2006). Psychological researchers have argued that early caregiving relationships form the basis of a child's subsequent beliefs about themselves, others and relations with others. Where there is abuse or trauma in these relationships, the attachment relationship is very much impacted. As might be expected, research shows that 80% of maltreated children are insecurely attached to their carers (Cook et al., 2005), resulting in heightened vulnerability to stress, problems with regulating emotions and help-seeking dysfunction.

Attachment dysfunction was a key theme emerging from our interview data. Many respondents identified this as the major challenge facing young people in the care and justice systems. Juvenile justice officers, care providers, lawyers, magistrates and police all provided examples of the lack of close attachments in these young people's lives. A police officer commented, 'but the family that they had – I think, they feel like they've been abandoned; they don't have an attachment to any family' (OP5); and a lawyer respondent observed, 'they don't have an attachment to anybody, anything, any place' (L13). One juvenile justice officer told us of a young man who had been the victim of extreme abuse:

> His mum passed away, he was raised by a stepbrother who was abusive, didn't feed him, like it's – all that stuff. He was five, I think, when his mum passed away. So that's so deep-seated. His earliest memories of life have been based around trauma and hurt. And so he's learned to survive through standing up for himself, being aggressive, being physical, but at the same time he doesn't even know – like his attachments are all over the place. And I think you see that a lot. There's a lot of attachment disorders with these kids.
>
> (JJ1)

Some children remain attached to their biological parents regardless of the trauma they have experienced at home. In one file we reviewed in detail, a 12-year-old boy, who was removed from home because of his mother's drug use and the physical harm and neglect he experienced, was apprehended by police on a train returning to his mother. There were notes on the file indicating that this was a frequent occurrence, and we found that he had had 25 missing persons' reports for the previous 12 months. Later, he was present during an interview in which Family and Community Services (FACs) workers openly discussed the lack of options available to him for accommodation placement, including home placement, despite his clear preference to stay with his mother. He then threw a chair at a carer and was charged by police. Police removed him in a highly distressed state by force and took him to hospital. We noted that he subsequently spent some three weeks in custody as no safe accommodation was available for him.

Complex trauma can also lead to biological changes in brain development. In younger children, this manifests in a lower capacity to regulate emotions, and later, a reduced ability to deal with stress as well as feelings of helplessness, confusion and anger. In middle childhood and adolescence, deficits in prefrontal brain development can lead to problems with self-regulation and an inability to understand the perspectives of other people. A key problem suffered by traumatised children relates to affect regulation, or the ability to understand and express emotions in a safe manner. These children are often emotionally labile, with extreme reactions to relatively minor stressors (Cook et al., 2005).

There were certainly vivid examples of these sequelae of complex trauma in our data. One young woman with a history of trauma was described as ranging 'from a really calm state to a very angry and escalated, erratic state within 30 seconds, and it could be anything, whether it's external influences, or things to do with her family' (JJ6). Many of the interview respondents involved in caring for these children commented on their problems with emotional regulation. For some, this was the key difficulty they faced in their day-to-day interactions with young people. One caregiver described their work as follows: 'I'm working with children in out-of-home care, [with] extensive trauma histories, that have issues around emotional regulation and developmental trauma … [they are] very distressed, upset, angry young people, a lot of the time' (OOHC2). Another said, 'most of them … like I said, have behavioural issues, and that's like anger regulation and expression' (JJ7). As we argued in our previous work, a key problem resulting from these difficulties with behavioural regulation is increased criminalisation, as police are often called to residential homes to deal with minor behavioural infractions arising from problems with behavioural regulation (see Gerard et al., 2019, for further examples). Multiple respondents also perceived this to be the case:

> because often their behaviours in the house are just symptomatic of underlying issues … often they self-medicate their mental health

> through drug and alcohol use, and they have an outburst when they are drug-affected...and the kids, particularly aggressive behaviour, like that's symptomatic of a deeper issue: hurt, rejection, abandonment, underlying trauma, sexual abuse, assault – that's generally what the issue is.
>
> (JJ1)

Dissociations, or alterations in consciousness, are also observed in maltreated children. These can take three forms: first, behaviour is automatised (that is, occurs without conscious control); second, painful memories are compartmentalised; and third, there is a detachment from both emotions and the self. Problems with behavioural regulation can also manifest in both over-controlled (such as compulsive compliance with routine and adult requests) and under-controlled (such as aggression and ODD) behaviour. In many ways, these behaviours serve to protect the child from the memory of traumatic experiences, and in some cases, they can be interpreted as attempts to gain a sense of control over their lives, while also avoiding emotional arousal and intimacy with other people.

Finally, abused children demonstrate impairments in cognitive functioning and self-concept. Neglected and abused children show difficulties in language development. There is also clear evidence that maltreated children perform poorly at school compared to other children and are also more likely to leave school early. In our study, we found evidence on file that 54.5% of the care-experienced children had significant problems with education (truancy, poor grades, school suspension) compared to 27% of non-care children. The interview respondents also noted this. One commented:

> they've got like a fairly strong history of trauma, so they've been disengaged from the educational system, disengaged from, like, pro-social support services, it's generally fairly likely they're not achieving very strongly academically – which is not necessarily to mean that they are not capable' (JJ1). Another commented, 'but we have got our kids, when they go to school, because of their behaviours, they are easily suspended from school.
>
> (JJ3)

One magistrate also perceived a strong relationship between care, offending and lack of engagement with education:

> so you've got kids from dislocated backgrounds being with kids from dislocated backgrounds and often that can be a pretty ordinary recipe...school is a huge thing. What's the number of kids involved in the crime jurisdiction and indeed to some extent the care jurisdiction that don't go to school?
>
> (M9)

Although establishing causation is difficult, these links have certainly been made in previous research as well (Fernandez, 2019). In addition, from an early age, traumatised children view themselves differently and are more likely to have a negative self-image, viewing themselves as imperfect and unlovable.

Trauma and Indigenous peoples

The impact of trauma on Indigenous children is exacerbated by systemic racism (Blagg et al., 2019; Dudgeon et al., 2017). Childhood experiences of trauma have a significant influence on the social and emotional well-being of Indigenous Australian children and, in particular, on their health and educational outcomes. Further, Indigenous Australian children are over-represented in suicide statistics compared to their non-Indigenous counterparts (National Children's Commissioner, 2014). Suicide rates among Indigenous Australians are some of the highest in the world, and even more concerning are the findings from the *Inquiry into Aboriginal Youth Suicide in Remote Areas* indicating that there is a strong correlation between Aboriginal children leaving the care environment and suicide rates (LAWA, 2016). Another factor that significantly affects Indigenous children's cognitive ability and emotional regulation is Foetal Alcohol Spectrum Disorder (FASD). FASD is characterised by a range of cognitive problems caused by the exposure of a foetus to alcohol during pregnancy. Indigenous children who are born with FASD experience numerous cognitive and developmental delays, such as behavioural difficulties and problems with the regulation of emotions, all of which have a significant impact on their ability to link actions to consequences (Douglas, 2010). These factors contribute, at least in part, to the sobering statistic that Indigenous children in Australia aged 10–16 years are 26 times more likely to be in a youth detention facility compared to their non-Indigenous counterparts of the same age (AIHW, 2016).

Our lawyer respondents recognised this complex interplay of factors in their Indigenous clients to a certain extent. When asked about their clients' characteristics, two of the lawyers spoke of 'mental health issues, history of abuse, neglect, unresolved trauma, homelessness … drug and alcohol I think is connected' (L4 & 5). Magistrates also recognised the existence of 'very evident cultural differences in terms of how Indigenous people engage with the Court' as well as 'really serious social and economic issues in their background' (M14). Nevertheless, it was noteworthy that across all the interviews we conducted, the word 'racism' was not used once. We, therefore, concluded that a change in culture is required across all government and non-government services associated with the care system that allows for recognition of Indigenous trauma as well as the impact of the history of colonisation on Indigenous peoples in Australia. This theme also emerged from our findings on intergenerational trauma.

We introduced the concept of intergenerational trauma earlier in this chapter and outlined the specific impact this has had on Indigenous peoples in Australia. Indigenous scholars in a number of colonised countries have argued that PTSD as a diagnosis is unable to capture the impact of historical trauma, the 'cumulative emotional and psychological wounding, over the lifespan and across generations, emanating from massive group trauma experiences' (Yellow Horse Brave Heart, 2003, p. 7). This trauma manifests in a number of ways, through various forms of psychopathology, suicide, anger and drug and alcohol abuse, but perhaps most notably in the form of unresolved grief (Yellow Horse Brave Heart, 2003). Historical trauma occurs in diverse ways in different colonised countries but includes genocide, ethnocide, forced removal of children, confiscation of land and medical experimentation (Atkinson et al., 2010; Pihama et al., 2017; Wirihana & Smith, 2019). A recent systematic review makes it clear that the pathways between experiences of historical trauma and adverse health effects are complex; nevertheless, the findings from the 19 studies reviewed showed statistically significant relationships between experiences of historical trauma and one or more negative health outcomes (Gone et al., 2019). Research examining different communities, including African Americans, Indigenous populations, Japanese Americans and immigrant communities, has begun to identify evidence of intergenerational transmission of trauma (Comas-Díaz et al., 2019). For instance, Yehuda et al. (2016) found evidence of epigenetic alteration in both Holocaust survivors and their offspring.

While research such as this remains in its infancy, it is clear that intergenerational trauma is of the utmost importance for understanding the experiences of Indigenous peoples, and their families, in care. Indeed, some of our interview respondents recognised the importance of this. One magistrate respondent, when asked about Indigenous children in the care and justice systems, told us:

> Look, it's a product of [intergenerational] trauma. It's absolutely without any question that, and we see young people whose parents are traumatised, whose grandparents are traumatised and probably their great grandparents were if they were still alive but of course most of those are dead because they died at an early age as a result of their trauma. So parents are usually unable to care for their children. It's often drugs but it's sometimes pure and basic neglect, not knowing how to parent and that's got to be something that's not been passed down in terms of their parenting and what they experience themselves.
>
> (M9)

This quote was unusual in that of all our interview respondents, this magistrate was one of the few to refer explicitly to intergenerational trauma and its role in bringing children before court. A caregiver also recognised this: 'so the children who have got those high behaviours, and that's all of our kids, all of our kids have got a diagnosis of complex or [intergenerational] trauma' (OOHC12). Other magistrate respondents also recognised the impact of intergenerational factors, yet without specifically linking this to trauma. One commented, 'but, for instance, I, regrettably, have been in the job long enough to be dealing with the children that were removed from their own parents and that generation is now having babies, as to whether we remove those' (M12). One of our lawyer respondents talked of seeing three generations of women in court (L13). Similar comments relating to intergenerational offending were made:

> you're getting intergenerational stuff for that. Like, it's not very common where we have an Indigenous client where his aunties, uncles, dad, wasn't in Gaol, or brothers, sisters, it's – I could probably almost say I haven't had one that hasn't had some kind of relative or close relationship with someone that was in gaol.
>
> (JJ5)

Overall, however, we concluded that there was little evidence of awareness of the importance of intergenerational trauma among our respondents. Although it is true that we did not explicitly ask about this, we did ask respondents to comment more generally about the factors relevant to Indigenous Australians in the care and criminal justice system. While there was certainly an understanding of the multigenerational enmeshment of Aboriginal people in the care and justice systems, less understanding was in relation to the historical factors driving this. We will return to this when we consider the tenets of trauma-informed care and how caregivers could incorporate understandings of intergenerational trauma into the provision of such care.

Trauma and gender

A recent literature review investigating the relationship between care and custody among girls found the gendered impact of ACEs to be a key theme (Fitzpatrick et al., 2019). The authors argued the common occurrence of trauma among young women in the care system leads to greater criminal justice system involvement (Fitzpatrick et al., 2019, p. 12). Other studies reviewed by Fitzgerald et al. showed the heightened impact of adversity on females compared to males (Fitzpatrick et al., 2019, p. 12). This was because girls in care have experienced greater adversity, are more likely to have experienced sexual assault and exploitation and have 'higher rates of extreme and complex trauma than boys' (Fitzpatrick et al., 2019, p. 12).

It has long been argued by feminist scholars that females and males have very different pathways to crime. For instance, Daly argues that there are five categories of female offender who come into contact with the courts, and their pathways to court reflect circumstances particular to women, such as interpersonal violence at the hands of partners and sexual victimisation (Daly, 1992). Hannah-Moffat (2009) argues that women's criminogenic needs differ greatly from men's, but that they are often characterised as categories of risk rather than need. Female offenders are also more likely to have experienced abuse and neglect in childhood, and violence perpetrated by women is often a response to abusive adult relationships (Holtfreter & Cupp, 2007).

Fitzpatrick et al.'s review came to similar conclusions. The evidence they reviewed suggested that vulnerability and adversity is more likely to contribute to violent offending by girls compared to boys (McAra & McVie, 2010). Further, the abusive experience experienced by girls accelerates their offending until they 'catch up' with boys (Fitzpatrick et al., 2019, p. 12). Family breakdown and domestic violence increase the likelihood of girls being arrested as adults, with each 'additional childhood risk factor' increasing by 21% the probability of arrest.

Fitzpatrick et al. concluded that there was a lack of research on the intersection of gender, ethnicity, care experience and justice system involvement. Since the publication of this review, some research has addressed this gap in knowledge. One recent study from the United States examined the impact of a trauma-informed care program for care and justice involved young women (N = 109, 63% African American). The research evaluated an intervention program delivering specific trauma-informed strategies, collaborative problem solving and self-care (Crosby et al., 2019). The program was designed to reduce trauma symptoms and prevent the criminalisation of trauma responses. After participants completed the program, a statistically significant reduction in their trauma symptoms was observed, although contrary to predictions, this did not vary by race. Further, Salceda et al. (2020) tested how dialogic feminist gatherings helped strengthen protective factors for adolescent girls living in OOHC as a result of needing to escape gender-based violence. Fifteen girls participated in the research, engaging in guided conversation and reflections intended to improve their competence in relationships. Salceda et al. concluded that preventive socialisation mechanisms such as the dialogic feminist gatherings may assist in reducing gender-based violence for care-experienced girls (Salceda et al., 2020).

Links between trauma and the criminal justice system

Whilst the majority of people who experience trauma do not become involved in the criminal justice system, young people with histories of trauma and ACEs are over-represented in the criminal justice system (Malvaso et al., 2021). Children in the criminal justice system are far more likely to have been exposed to traumatic experiences. In a study of 64,329 juvenile offenders in Florida, 27.4% of males and 45.1% of females had experienced five or more ACEs (Baglivio et al., 2014). The most common ACE for both genders was exposure to family violence; but females were far more likely to have been the victim of both physical and sexual abuse. Compared to the original ACE study by Felitti et al. (1998), 2.8% of the juvenile offenders in the Florida study reported no ACEs (compared to 36% of Felitti et al.'s sample), and 50% of the juveniles in the later study had four or more ACEs in contrast to only 13% of the original study sample. In another study (Baglivio et al., 2015), high ACEs were associated with early arrest and greater offending trajectories through mid to late adolescence, and youths with five or more ACEs were more likely to begin offending early in life. Similar findings have been observed in Australia and the United Kingdom (Craig et al., 2017; Malvaso et al., 2019).

Although studies such as these make it clear that some traumatised children will become involved in the criminal justice system, it is also the case that the majority will not. This was demonstrated clearly in well-known American longitudinal studies that investigated this relationship. In the Rochester Youth Development Study, a longitudinal study of 1,000 young people in New York State that used both self-reporting and official data, Smith and Thornberry (1995) found that 45% of the participants who had been maltreated had a criminal record, compared to 31.7% of non-maltreated participants. Therefore, while these findings reveal maltreatment to be a predictor of delinquency, and in particular of more serious forms of delinquency, it is by no means inevitable that maltreated youths will come into contact with the criminal justice system. Widom (1989) observed similar findings in a study of 908 juveniles with histories of abuse and neglect. Overall, she found that 28.6% of these young people had adult criminal records compared to 21.1% of a matched control group, again demonstrating that while a history of trauma is related to later involvement in the criminal justice system, this is true for only a minority of abused children. A more recent meta-analysis identified a relatively modest difference in delinquency of 11% between maltreated and non-maltreated youths (Braga et al., 2016).

In the light of findings such as these, researchers have become interested in the factors that make it more (or less) likely for abused children to come into contact with the criminal justice system. In a recent review of 124 studies examining the maltreatment-offending nexus, Malvaso et al. (2021) investigated the relationship between abuse, trauma symptoms and offending, testing whether abused children with trauma symptoms were more likely to offend compared to those who did not suffer from these symptoms. The maltreatment–offending pathway was concluded to be a result of an interplay of 'individual, social, and contextual risk and protective factors' (Malvaso et al., 2021, p. 9). Similar conclusions emerged from an earlier review of 33 studies by Braga et al. (2016). Overall, it can be concluded that more ACEs raise the likelihood of offending although it is by no means inevitable that traumatised children will be arrested or taken before court. Physical and sexual abuse is related to a greater likelihood of aggression. Further, girls are more likely to be the victim of this type of abuse; however, this has no clear impact on their offending (Braga et al., 2016).

While it is clear that more needs to be known about these complex relationships, our findings indicate that exposure to the residential care environment itself could be a factor that raises the likelihood of traumatised children coming into contact with the criminal justice system. In our previous work, we argued that the criminalisation of children in care is a result of a range of factors that include a care environment where minor disciplinary infractions are dealt with by police and undertrained and underqualified staff are unable to manage these problems in-house (Gerard et al., 2019). In the Rochester studies conducted by Thornberry and colleagues (Ireland et al., 2002; Smith & Thornberry, 1995), it was observed that childhood-only abuse was not a predictor of later offending, whereas abuse continuing into adolescence was. This finding is relevant to the situation of children who find themselves in the criminalising environment of residential care, and who then face the re-traumatisation that results from contact with police and courts. In this regard, one of our interview respondents commented, 'and then the removal from care causes as well – we've found some significant trauma related to that, with particularly the older kids – kids that are removed at an older age in the spectrum' (JJ4). Clinicians have long argued that appropriate care for traumatised children should recognise their histories of abuse and focus on this rather than their immediate behaviour. This approach, known as trauma-informed care, has been recommended as best practice for the care of children with histories of trauma and abuse (Harris & Fallot, 2001a). In the next section, we will briefly describe the principles of trauma-informed care. We will then consider how trauma-informed care could incorporate knowledge about historical and intergenerational trauma. Finally, we will consider what a trauma-informed criminal justice system would look like.

Trauma-informed care

Trauma-informed care practices refer to service delivery models that aim to change care practices across entire organisations. Organisations need to have a common trauma lexicon and ensure that all aspects of their services are tailored to meet the needs of the trauma victim (Harris & Fallot, 2001a). The aim of trauma-informed care practices is to help individuals feel safe, reduce re-traumatisation, assist in the trauma recovery and realign the individual's developmental trajectory. Rather than view childhood trauma victims as uninterested or uncooperative and, therefore, requiring disciplinary action, these practices see the child's problematic behaviour as a trauma symptom and focus on building trust with the child. The use of these practices has been argued to benefit staff as well as cared-for children.

The NSW Therapeutic Care Framework (TCF) has trauma-informed care at its centre. This framework aims to 'guide NSW service providers, caseworkers, carers and other stakeholders to provide the best possible individualised Therapeutic Care for children and young people'. The extent to which the principles of this framework were evident in practice across NSW was unclear in our study. Respondents from FACS were of the view that the framework would 'very much improve the care that the children receive, but also ensure that the trauma and abuse is addressed, and then they'll have a better future life outcome' (FACS 3). Further, it would 'translate the clinical input into the day-to-day interactions that the carers, the residential care workers have with the children and how well they [the children] are supported in a clinical framework' (FACS 2). The service providers interviewed stated that their care for young people was informed by trauma-informed care principles. One told us:

> we use an ARC [Attachment, Regulation, Competency] model which is attachment, regulation and competency, that's a well-evidenced model ... but we added a C to that, so it's ARCC for us which is about community because we thought it was really important to connect our kids in residential care, either to the communities that they come from, and that then includes their families and whatever is in with that community, or the community they land in here; it might be a bit of both.
>
> (OOHC12)

The ARC model is a well-recognised trauma-informed care program developed in the United States (Kinniburgh et al., 2005).

However, a key conclusion drawn from our interviews with a range of informants (juvenile justice officers, legal aid lawyers, police, magistrates, OOHC service providers) was that there is an overwhelming focus on managing the immediate day-to-day behaviour of young people in care, with punitive disciplinary practices and reports to police a common feature of residential care homes in particular. There were many examples of this shared in the interviews (see Gerard et al., 2019, for more examples), but the following account from a lawyer respondent is of particular interest given the young person's history of trauma:

> the one that I've done this week, it almost seems so trivial, it seems ridiculous, but it's also – so this young girl, she's a victim of sexual assault. She can't live at home, she's not in state care ... and she just wants – because of her past, she's not comfortable with male workers, she's asked if she could have her own medication – she's got some new medication – her psychiatrist apparently said it's fine for her to have seven days at a time in her room and administer to herself. Usually they keep medication in a locked cabinet and the staff would give it out, but she doesn't want to get it from the male staff members and, so, they came up with this agreement that she could have seven days [of medication] in her room as long as she did certain things like, kept her room locked, kept it

> in blister packs, filled out a medication form; all quite reasonable things that she was willing to agree to and it's a psycho-risk management thing. Then they also wanted her to sign to say that if another resident broke into her room or got hold of her medication, then she'd be responsible for the consequences of that.
>
> (L3)

Although, as the lawyer noted, this seemed a trivial matter, we did note the lack of recognition and understanding of this girl's history of trauma and the legalistic insistence on her taking responsibility for things arguably outside her control. As Harris and Fallot (2001a) note, there are three key principles to trauma-informed care: first, *understanding trauma*; second, *understanding the survivor* and third, *understanding services*, to return the survivor's sense of control and autonomy. While we acknowledge the difficulties faced by care staff in managing the behaviour of abused and traumatised children, in our view, the evidence from our study shows a wide gap between policy and practice in this regard.

We also found a similar gap in discourse in relation to the care of Indigenous children. There were many references to the over-representation of Indigenous children, in both the care and justice systems; but as we previously argued, while there was some recognition of the types of caring practices that might increase the criminalisation of young people, concerns were also expressed about the cultural safety of the care environment and the cultural competence of carers (Gerard et al., 2019). As we have discussed in this chapter, we did find some degree of awareness among our interview respondents of the significance of historical trauma, yet this was limited. Indigenous scholars have proposed care principles informed by an understanding of historical and intergenerational trauma. In this regard, the Australia-based We Al-li program aims to 'train the trainer' and address historical trauma at a community-wide level (Atkinson et al., 2010). Successful completion of the training involves overviewing five different counselling techniques and considering how best to combine them; developing skills in deep listening, conversation and facilitating group discussions; learning about unresolved trauma and its effect on individuals and communities and learning about trauma and abuse within communities. In Aotearoa New Zealand, Pihama et al. (2017) have developed a framework for trauma-informed care that is designed to heal the collective impact of historical and intergenerational trauma and recognises the limitations of care programs based on individualistic western philosophies. Key to these Māori-specific programs is understanding the impact of historical and intergenerational trauma and focusing on communities rather than individuals. In relation to the care of Indigenous children in NSW, the principles of the We Al-li program provide valuable guidance, particularly in teaching carers about historical trauma and its effects and ensuring community is at the centre of the care system. This is consistent with the recommendations of the *Family is Culture* report, particularly in relation to prioritising Indigenous self-determination in the care system (Davis, 2019).

Trauma-informed care and the criminal justice system

As we have discussed, the central tenet of trauma-informed care is a focus on understanding and responding to the trauma suffered by the young people in care rather than their immediate behaviour. In the care context, there are validated programs that can be adopted, and as we have seen, these frameworks can incorporate notions of historical and intergenerational trauma when led by Indigenous peoples and communities. Guiding policy for care in NSW requires a trauma-informed approach. But given the clear nexus between the care and justice systems, the question arises as to the extent to which trauma is considered in the criminal justice system, and indeed, what a trauma-informed criminal justice system should look like.

To consider the first question, we found little evidence in our study to indicate that histories of trauma and abuse were considered in any real sense in the operation of the criminal justice system. In the cases, we observed in the Children's Court, the care status of the child was only mentioned in six out of 134 matters. We contrasted this with the file review data, which provided evidence of care experience in 24% of the files we reviewed. Further, as previously discussed, we found evidence on file of possible trauma and abuse for half of the care-experienced children but only 11% of the non-care children. In addition, in a number of matters, we observed we only became aware of the care background of the child upon reading the file. So, overall, we concluded that it was not unusual for the care and abuse background of the child to be overlooked in court proceedings.

In a series of interviews with magistrates, we asked about the factors they considered when sentencing the children appearing before them. Many magistrates reflected on contemporary factors when describing how children in care came to be brought before court. Mental health was one such factor, with many magistrates discussing the use of sections 32 and 33 of the *Mental Health (Forensic Provisions) Act 1990* (NSW). Under the section 32 provisions, where an offence was committed by an offender who was mentally ill, or developmentally disabled, the matter can be adjourned, the offender bailed or the charge can be dismissed and the offender discharged unconditionally, into the care of a responsible person or into an appropriate treatment facility. Under section 33, magistrates have the power to order defendants apparently suffering from mental illness to be taken to an appropriate treatment facility for assessment and detention. In general, the magistrates and lawyers we interviewed found this to be a good alternative to custody. One lawyer respondent commented that 'if a kid wouldn't be going into custody you've got a pretty good argument that it's better to go down a path of diversion under medical help rather than that path' (L10). Magistrate and lawyer respondents also saw these orders as valuable in keeping mental health problems out of court: 'I am of the view that section 32 applications are quite useful in this context, so I am generally particularly attentive. They tend to arise more frequently in the kids in out-of-home care environments' (M6). Across the magistrate responses, there was also a distinct focus on behaviour rather than traumatic histories: 'How do they end up in court? Lots and lots of violence within their placements and lots and lots of damage, general acting out behaviour within their placements which is generally what [brings] them before the court' (M10). Magistrates highlighted drug use and sexual behaviour: 'and there was another one who was in care and just kept absconding and would shack up with any male that she could find, I think. She was only 12 or 14' (M3). This magistrate went on to comment:

> And whenever young people come before the court where alcohol or illicit drugs have been an element of the offending, I always reiterate to them or try and impress on them the damage that the alcohol or the illicit drugs is doing to development of their brain. And I speak to them as if this may be the first time they've ever heard it. And I tell them that on a daily basis I see people, adults appearing before me, where cannabis use or alcohol abuse has been a feature of their lives and it's just ruined their lives and the lives of their families. So if you want to avoid that then you don't touch alcohol until you're an adult.
>
> (M3)

While mental health and drug use are certainly legitimate factors to focus on, these comments indicate that magistrates are very much focused on the behaviour in front of them when dealing with young people in court. It is true to say that this is the key task of the criminal justice system. However, a criminal justice system that aims to be trauma-informed ought to give equal or even greater consideration to the histories of the young people who come before court. In principle at least, it seems that magistrates do recognise the significance of these histories; however, we observed little evidence of this in practice. This was also true of the police officers we interviewed. A key theme emerging from our interviews with police was frustration with the necessity of dealing with the behavioural infractions of children in care. Some police explicitly rejected the idea that they should take into account the young person's background:

> But a lot of young people, I think, want to be the victim, when it comes to sentencing. They know that – they don't necessarily know that the – they know they've done the wrong thing, that's why they're there – that's why they've got convictions. They know they've done the wrong thing. But they're quick to blame, oh, it's my upbringing – it's my upbringing – it's my upbringing – their mum wasn't around and dad's a druggie or mum's in Gaol or whatever. So – so – so what? To me that doesn't matter.
>
> (OP4)

In the file reviews, we observed clear examples of re-traumatising policing practices. In one, a young Indigenous woman with care experience was living under the care of the Minister in a motel. The young person assaulted and threatened her carer and the motel manager. The file noted that she threatened suicide. The notes went on: 'The accused YP [young person] commenced making a number of threats to harm herself and kill herself and stated she just wanted to die. The accused YP was searched and placed into the rear of a police caged vehicle'. She was subsequently taken to hospital as an involuntary patient. Later, the same young woman was charged with behaving in an offensive manner and resisting arrest. The police facts read:

> police took hold of the accused [when] she began to violently thrash around and kick out at police. She was taken to the ground and handcuffed however continued to yell, scream and violently thrash around. Police attempted to use the YP's case worker and family to calm her down to no avail. The YP was placed in the juvenile justice cells before being placed in a caged police truck and transported to … police station. Upon arrival the YP had calmed down and apologised for her behaviour at the courthouse.
>
> (File Note 60/90)

Conclusion

Although we acknowledge the frustrations experienced by police, we also argue for the need to avoid the ongoing criminalisation of young people in care and to commit to the principles of trauma-informed care at all levels of the criminal justice system. In practice, this means that only the most patently criminal behaviour should be referred to police. Further, police training should incorporate thorough information about trauma and abuse among young people and how best to respond. This training should be ongoing, reflective and monitored as part of performance review processes. When children are brought before the court, their status as care children and their history of trauma should always be made known to magistrates. As Harris and Fallot (2001a, p. 3) write:

> Systems *serve* survivors of childhood trauma without *treating* them for the consequences of that trauma; more significant, systems serve individuals without even being aware of the trauma that occurred. This lack of awareness can result in failures to make appropriate referrals for trauma services. It can also result in inadvertent retraumatisation when a service system's usual operating procedures trigger a reemergence or an exacerbation of trauma symptoms.

We saw evidence of all these harms in our research. Moreover, Harris and Fallot's work does not consider notions of historical and intergenerational trauma, which puts young Indigenous people in care at even greater risk of re-traumatisation. In our view, recognition and understanding trauma should be at the heart of the criminal justice system's response to young people in care.

References

American Psychiatric Publishing. (2013). *Diagnostic and statistical manual of mental disorders: DSM-5* (5th ed.).

American Psychological Association. (2019). *APA dictionary of psychology.*

Anda, R. F., Felitti, V. J., Bremner, J. D., Walker, J. D., Whitfield, C., Perry, B. D. et al. (2006). The enduring effects of abuse and related adverse experiences in childhood. *European Archives of Psychiatry and Clinical Neuroscience, 256*(3), 174–186. https://doi.org/10.1007/s00406-005-0624-4

Atkinson, J., Nelson, J., & Atkinson, C. (2010). Trauma, transgenerational transfer and effects on community wellbeing. In P. Dudgeon, M. Wright, Y. Paradies, D. Garvey, & I. Walker (Eds.) *Working together: Aboriginal and Torres Strait Islander mental health and wellbeing principles and practice* (pp. 135–144). Australian Institute of Health and Welfare.

Australian Institute of Health and Welfare. (2016). *Youth detention population in Australia 2016.*

Baglivio, M. T., Epps, N., Swartz, K., Huq, M. S., Sheer, A., & Hardt, N., S. (2014). The prevalence of adverse childhood experiences (ACE) in the lives of juvenile offenders. *The Journal for Juvenile Justice, 3*(2), 1.

Baglivio, M. T., Wolff, K. T., Piquero, A. R., & Epps, N. (2015). The relationship between adverse childhood experiences (ACE) and juvenile offending trajectories in a juvenile offender sample. *Journal of Criminal Justice, 43*(3), 229–241. https://doi.org/10.1016/j.jcrimjus.2015.04.012

Blagg, H., Tulich, T., & May, S. (2019). Aboriginal youth with foetal alcohol spectrum disorder and enmeshment in the Australian justice system: Can an intercultural form of restorative justice make a difference? *Contemporary Justice Review, 22*(2), 105–121.

Braga, T., Gonçalves, L. C., Basto-Pereira, M., & Maia, Â. (2016). Unraveling the link between maltreatment and juvenile antisocial behavior: A meta-analysis of prospective longitudinal studies. *Aggression and Violent Behavior, 33*, 37–50. https://doi.org/10.1016/j.avb.2017.01.006

Comas-Díaz, L., Hall, G. N., & Neville, H. A. (2019). Racial trauma: Theory, research, and healing – Introduction to the special issue. *American Psychologist, 74*(1), 1.

Cook, A., Spinazzola, J., Ford, J., Lanktree, C., Blaustein, M., Cloitre, M. et al. (2005). Complex trauma in children and adolescents. *Psychiatric Annals, 35*(5), 390–398.

Copeland, W. E., Keeler, G., Angold, A., & Costello, E. J. (2007). Traumatic events and posttraumatic stress in childhood. *Archives of General Psychiatry, 64*(5), 577–584. https://doi.org/10.1001/archpsyc.64.5.577

Craig, J. M., Piquero, A. R., Farrington, D. P., & Ttofi, M. M. (2017). A little early risk goes a long bad way: Adverse childhood experiences and life-course offending in the Cambridge study. *Journal of Criminal Justice, 53*, 34–45. https://doi.org/10.1016/j.jcrimjus.2017.09.005

Crosby, S. D., Day, A., Baroni, B. A., & Somers, C. (2019). Examining trauma-informed teaching and the trauma symptomatology of court-involved girls. *The Urban Review, 51*(4), 582–598. https://doi.org/10.1007/s11256-019-00533-2

Daly, K. (1992). Women's pathways to felony court: Feminist theories of law breaking and problems of representation. *Southern California Review of Law and Women's Studies. 2*(1), 11–52.

Davis, M. (2019). *Family is Culture: Review report.* Independent Review of Aboriginal Children in OOHC.

Douglas, H. (2010). The sentencing response to defendants with foetal alcohol spectrum disorder. *Criminal Law Journal, 34*(4), 221–239.

Dudgeon, P., Calma, T., & Holland, C. (2017). The context and causes of the suicide of Indigenous people in Australia. *Journal of Indigenous Wellbeing, 2*(2), 5–15.

Felitti, V. J., Anda, R. F., Nordenberg, D., Williamson, D. F., Spitz, A. M., Edwards, V., Koss, M., & Marks, J. (1998). Relationship of childhood abuse and household dysfunction to many of the leading causes of death in adults: The adverse childhood experiences (ACE) study. *American Journal of Preventive Medicine, 14*(4), 245–258. https://doi.org/10.1016/S0749-3797(98)00017-8

Fernandez, E. (2019). Working towards better education for children in care: Longitudinal analysis of the educational outcomes of a cohort of children in care in Australia. *Oxford Review of Education, 45*(4), 481–501.

Fitzpatrick, C., Hunter, K., Staines, J., & Shaw, J. (2019). *Exploring the pathways between care and custody for girls and women: A literature review.* Nuffield Foundation.

Friedman, M. J., Resick, P. A., Bryant, R. A., & Brewin, C. R. (2011). Considering PTSD for DSM-5. *Depression and Anxiety, 28*(9), 750–769.

Gerard, A., McGrath, A., Colvin, E., & McFarlane, K. (2019). 'I'm not getting out of bed!': The criminalisation of young people in residential care. *Australian & New Zealand Journal of Criminology, 52*(1), 76–93. https://doi.org/10.1177/0004865818778739

Gone, J. P., Hartmann, W. E., Pomerville, A., Wendt, D. C., Klem, S. H., & Burrage, R. L. (2019). The impact of historical trauma on health outcomes for indigenous populations in the USA and Canada: A systematic review. *American Psychologist, 74*(1), 20–35. https://doi.org/10.1037/amp0000338

Hampton, R., & Toombs, M. (2013). Culture, identity and Indigenous Australian people. In R. Hampton, & M. Toombs (Eds.) *Indigenous Australians and health: The wombat in the room* (pp. 3–23). South Melbourne: Oxford University Press.

Hannah-Moffat, K. (2009). Gridlock or mutability: Reconsidering gender and risk assessment. *Criminology & Public Policy, 8*, 209.

Harris, M., & Fallot, R. D. (2001a). Envisioning a trauma-informed service system: A vital paradigm shift. *New Directions for Mental Health Services*, 89, 3–22. https://doi.org/10.1002/yd.23320018903

Harris, M., & Fallot, R. D. (2001b). *Using trauma theory to design service systems.* Jossey-Bass.

Holtfreter, K., & Cupp, R. (2007). Gender and risk assessment. *Journal of Contemporary Criminal Justice, 23*(4), 363–382. https://doi.org/10.1177/1043986207309436

Horwitz, A. V. (2018). *PTSD: A short history.* Johns Hopkins University Press.

Ireland, T. O., Smith, C., & Thornberry, T. P. (2002). Developmental issues in the impact of child maltreatment on later delinquency and drug use. *Criminology, 40*(2), 359–400. https://doi.org/10.1111/j.1745-9125.2002.tb00960.x

Kinniburgh, K. J., Blaustein, M., Spinazzola, J., & Van der Kolk, B. A. (2005). Attachment, self-regulation, and competency. *Psychiatric Annals, 35*(5), 424–430.

Legislative Assembly, Parliament of Western Australia. (2016). *Learnings from the message stick*. The report of the Inquiry into Aboriginal Youth Suicide in Remote Areas, Legislative Assembly. Committees. Education and Health Standing Committee [Report 11]. Parliament of Western Australia.

Malvaso, C. G., Cale, J., Whitten, T., Day, A., Singh, S., Hackett, L., Delfabbro, P. H., & Ross, S. (2021). Associations between adverse childhood experiences and trauma among young people who offend: A systematic literature review. *Trauma, Violence, & Abuse, 0*(0). https://doi.org/10.1177/15248380211013132

Malvaso, C. G., Delfabbro, P. H., & Day, A. (2019). Adverse childhood experiences in a South Australian sample of young people in detention. *Australian & New Zealand Journal of Criminology, 52*(3), 411–431. https://doi.org/10.1177/0004865818810069

McAra, L., & McVie, S. (2010). Youth crime and justice: Key messages from the Edinburgh study of youth transitions and Crime. *Criminology and Criminal Justice, 10*(2), 179–209. https://doi.org/10.1177/1748895809360971

McGrath, A., Gerard, A., & Colvin, E. (2020). Care-experienced children and the criminal justice system. *Trends and Issues in Crime and Criminal Justice No. 600*. Australian Institute of Criminology.

National Children's Commissioner. (2014). *Children's rights report 2014*. Australian Human Rights Commission.

Pihama, L., Smith, L. T., Evans-Campbell, T., Kohu-Morgan, H., Cameron, N., Mataki, T., Te Nana, R., Skipper, H., & Southey, K. (2017). Investigating Māori approaches to trauma informed care. *Journal of Indigenous Wellbeing, 2*(3), 18–31.

Purdie, N., Dudgeon, P., & Walker, R. (2010). *Working together: Aboriginal and Torres Strait Islander mental health and wellbeing principles and practice*. Commonwealth of Australia.

Salceda, M., Vidu, A., Aubert, A., & Roca, E. (2020). Dialogic feminist gatherings: Impact of the preventive socialization of gender-based violence on adolescent girls in out-of-home care. *Social Sciences, 9*(8), 138.

Smith, C., & Thornberry, T. P. (1995). The relationship between childhood maltreatment and adolescent involvement in delinquency. *Criminology, 33*(4), 451–481. https://doi.org/10.1111/j.1745–9125.1995.tb01186.x

Taylor, C. (2006). *Young people in care and criminal behaviour*. Jessica Kingsley Publishers.

Widom, C. S. (1989). Child abuse, neglect, and violent criminal behavior. *Criminology, 27*(2), 251. https://doi.org/10.1111/j.1745–9125.1989.tb01032.x

Wirihana, R., & Smith, C. (2019). Historical trauma, healing and well-being in Māori communities. *MAI Journal, 3*(3), 197–210.

Yehuda, R., Daskalakis, N. P., Bierer, L. M., Bader, H. N., Klengel, T., Holsboer, F., Holsboer, F., & Binder, E. (2016). Holocaust exposure induced intergenerational effects on *FKBP5* methylation. *Biological Psychiatry, 80*(5), 372–380. https://doi.org/10.1016/j.biopsych.2015.08.005

Yellow Horse Brave Heart, M. (2003). The historical trauma response among natives and its relationship with substance abuse: A Lakota illustration. *Journal of Psychoactive Drugs, 35*(1), 7–13. https://doi.org/10.1080/02791072.2003.10399988

3 The residential care environment

Introduction

> So it's a house, obviously, and it has got other – I think there's usually ranging from about four young people living in the house, and they have – I think they try to implement … as if you're in a normal, functioning family with rules, and routines, and this is the time you wake up. Okay, you've got to get ready for school. These are the rules of the house. Everybody has a night to cook. You do your Saturday chores, and it's obviously staffed 24/7, so it's bringing some structure and routine for the young person. Obviously, there's a lot of troublesome kids living in there – so the staff are faced with a lot of challenging behaviours with young people, whether it be absconding, outbursts, property damage, just things like that.
>
> (JJ6)

The above quote is a description of a residential care home provided by a Juvenile Justice worker. Residential care is where children under the protection of the government are placed in group homes with paid carers. Of the 46,000 children in OOHC in Australia in 2019–2020, approximately 7% were in residential care (AIHW, 2021). Children in residential care are older than those in home-based care (AIHW) and, as we previously argued, have a higher likelihood of coming into contact with the criminal justice system. In NSW, while FACS is responsible for placing children in care, the majority of residential care is provided by non-governmental and private sector organisations contracted by the Department and accredited by the Office of the Children's Guardian, NSW, in reference to the NSW Child Safe Standards for Permanent Care. These Standards are based on the legal obligations set out in *Children and Young Persons (Care and Protection) Act NSW* (1998) and the *Children and Young Persons (Care and Protection) Regulation NSW* (2012). Renewed attention was placed on these standards and the accreditation process following a hearing before the NSW Legislative Council Standing Committee in 2017, at which it became evident that three

DOI: 10.4324/9781003093367-4

of the fifteen districts administered by FACS did not meet the accreditation standards (NSW Legislative Council General Purpose Standing Committee, 2017). At the time of our fieldwork, FACS was implementing the Quality Assurance Framework to address these concerns. Since the completion of our fieldwork, the Child Safe Standards have been updated (Office of the Children's Guardian, 2020).

For many children, care is a positive experience that takes them away from dangerous home environments. Research from the United States involving interviews with 180 children in care, aged 9–11, found that these children had both positive and negative perceptions of being in care. While 76 of the children (42%) thought that their lives would have been better if they had stayed with their families, 95 (53%) thought that their lives in care were about the same or better (9 children did not answer this question). The children thought that the most helpful things about care included having a better home environment and being away from their biological parents. However, when examined by type of care, a clear majority of children in residential care reported that their lives would have been better had they stayed with their families (Dunn et al., 2010).

This chapter focuses on residential care and provides evidence that contextual factors unique to the residential care environment contribute to the criminalisation of care-experienced children. In this regard, we define context widely, to include the regulatory environment, the professionals who come into contact with care homes (such as police) and the care homes themselves. We start by describing the regulatory environment and interrogating the relationship between the Department of Communities and Justice and the various care providers, based on our interviews with departmental officers and residential care providers. We then turn to consider the residential care environment itself. Taylor's book *Young People in Care and Criminal Behaviour* describes residential care as 'mayhem' (Taylor, 2006). Drawing on our interviews and fieldwork, we consider whether this is the case in NSW. Specifically, we seek to answer the question, what is residential care like for the young people who reside there, as well as for care workers and other professionals? A key question we had in this regard related to the cultural safety of the care environment for young Indigenous people and the extent to which the Aboriginal Child Placement Principles governing the placement of Indigenous children are observed in the residential care sector.

A significant area of conflict that emerged in our research involved the interaction between police and residential care homes. In Chapter 4, we describe police perceptions of this relationship. However, in this chapter, we focus on the policing of care-experienced children from the perspective of the care homes, asking, to what extent is the management of what is perceived as problematic behaviour delegated to police, and is there any evidence of the Joint Protocol (see below) in action? Staffing of care homes also emerged as a key point of contention, and the next section of the chapter examines perceptions and findings concerning staffing. Finally, we consider the general implications of our findings for the residential care system, contextualising these in relation to the recommendations and findings of previous research.

Our research was undertaken before and after the implementation of the NSW Government's Joint Protocol to Reduce the Contact of Young People in Residential Care with the Criminal Justice System in 2016. The Joint Protocol was designed: to reduce the frequency of police involvement in residential care; to promote diversion; to promote the safety, welfare and well-being of those in residential care; to improve relationships, inter-agency communication and information sharing; to promote an early intervention approach and to support victims in residential care (NSW Ombudsman, 2019). The guiding principles of the Joint Protocol are to foster a trauma-informed approach and use law enforcement as a last resort. The Joint Protocol sets out joint and individual responsibilities of agencies – FACS, OOHC service providers and police – and establishes a state-wide governance process. FACS has responsibility for the implementation and training aspects of the protocol, and a comprehensive review is due every three years (Joint Protocol, p. 20). The most recent iteration, in 2019, included consultation with Aboriginal stakeholders (Joint Protocol, p. 2).

We have previously analysed some of the benefits and challenges of the Joint Protocol, based on respondent views from our pilot study (McFarlane et al., 2019). The impetus for the state-wide Joint Protocol came from the inter-agency work of the Western Sydney Residential Providers Forum, which included stakeholders from police, OOHC service providers, FACS and Legal Aid (NSW Ombudsman, 2019). The iterative development of the Joint Protocol, its adaptation from a UK model that had reportedly reduced unnecessary criminalisation and the momentum it provided augured well for reducing unnecessary police contact. Our interviews with police respondents, OOHC service providers, lawyers and FACS respondents, which took place before the Joint Protocol was announced, underscored the need for a joint protocol to reduce police contact. Research findings obtained subsequent this will help determine the efficacy of the Protocol in the absence of a more thorough-going evaluation.

The regulatory environment for residential care

While foster and formal kinship care have long been provided through the means of a formal contract with the state, the transition of residential care service provision from the government to the private and not-for-profit sectors accelerated following the recommendations of the Wood Commission (Wood, 2008). These recommendations aimed to improve outcomes for children consistent with the belief that the non-government sectors are better placed to provide care in more cost-effective ways. Although it is difficult to determine how much the provision of care to young people costs the government, almost AU$7.5 billion was spent on child protection services nationally in 2020–2021 (Productivity Commission, 2022). In NSW, this translated into $1,436 per year for every child in the state aged 0–17 years. Given the magnitude of this expenditure, it seems reasonable to question the rationale for why care is contracted out to the non-government and private sectors. Scholars in England and Wales have also expressed concerns about marketisation and the for-profit model for care (Carey, 2019; Shaw & Greenhow, 2021). In this section, we examine the contracting of residential care from the perspective of the contracting agency and the service provider.

The processes around contracting out care and the oversight and monitoring of care facilities were seen as very important by our respondents. At the time we conducted our interviews, many facilities were renegotiating contracts with FACS. Some of our interview respondents were involved in this process, which meant we were able to explore problems that had arisen prior to the process being undertaken, opportunities for improvement in the contracting process and respondents' perceptions of the contracting and re-contracting process.

From the perspective of our FACS respondents, the contracting process was deficient, particularly in the ways in which the contracts had previously been drafted: 'our contracts unfortunately were incredibly flexible and didn't specify a lot when they were first written' (FACS2). Similarly, one Juvenile Justice respondent commented: 'I think once the contract's handed over, that a lot of the responsibility and the monitoring of the service provision is sort of disappeared' (JJ2). Further, the process allows for little focus on the provision and oversight of quality, appropriate care:

> So we contracted with those existing providers and basically the view was taken that if you have accreditation that was the mark of quality and basically we were locked into those contracts … for the last few years it's been a supply-driven market place where we've got a set number of residential care facilities and it's all about trying to fit the children in – the young people into the various properties and premises where they are, rather than designing the system to meet the children's needs. So, one of our things we'll try to build in is some flexibility so we're not locked into configurations.
>
> (FACS1)

Consequently, a key aspect of the re-contracting process has been a focus on ensuring that staff hired to care for children are appropriately qualified and experienced or are given the opportunity to gain experience with proper supervision and training. The current Standards state that staff must have 'appropriate qualifications' (Standard 7) but do not specify what these qualifications are. Further, the therapeutic care framework (TCF) for managing the behaviour of children in OOHC has been implemented across many facilities in response to concerns about a lack of understanding of how children with trauma backgrounds should be cared for. We discuss this in greater detail in Chapter 2; however, the framework is certainly relevant to a discussion of the residential care environment. Training on trauma-informed care is provided via online modules hosted by the Association of Child Welfare Agencies (ACWA) and is part of the training expected of carers per Standard 7 (Office of the Children's Guardian, 2020).

We were concerned to hear about the lack of oversight of children in care by FACS. As one interview respondent put it, 'some of the services are good, but what services that aren't so good, because we're locked into these contracts, sometimes we're not as – well, it's our own fault as well, we should have been much clearer about what our expectations were' (FACS1). This seemed to us to represent a fundamental problem in the contracting-out process. Children who are taken from their families are the responsibility of the state, and by proxy, of the relevant minister. The state has a clear duty of care towards these children, even if their care is provided by private and not-for-profit organisations; therefore, justifying inadequate care on the basis of deficient contracts is clearly unsatisfactory. If the contracting out of care is to continue, more effective monitoring and oversight by the contracting agency is essential, with the ability to break contracts in cases where standards are not met, as well as contingency plans for the care of children receiving suboptimal care. In short, the contracting out of care should not be seen as discharging the state's responsibility for the well-being of these vulnerable young people.

While there was recognition that criminalisation occurs in the residential care environment, respondents from the department attributed this to a few substandard providers, or to inadequate contracts:

> The issues at the moment are basically that there isn't consistency. Some service providers and staff in residential homes are really good at responding appropriately on the ground, at a day-to-day level, with handovers and understanding trauma. And using discretion when there's kids getting upset. Not calling the police first instance. But that's not consistent across the state. So it's about giving these kids the chance to be treated equitably, no matter where they are, in a kind of home-like environment, where the parents aren't calling the police in the first instance.
>
> (FACS 3)

For our participants, problems in the OOHC system were a result of inadequate contracts, with the re-contracting process seen as the solution. The implementation of the therapeutic care framework was also viewed as leading to improved responses by carers, which would address criminalisation. The general perspective was one of optimism, with a belief that existing problems could be solved. A similar view was expressed in relation to the implementation of the Joint Protocol. We were more sceptical in this regard, and in our fieldwork, we observed many examples of problematic practice.

Further, many of the initiatives relied upon to improve practice lacked proper evaluation in our view (Commissioner for Children and Young People, Victoria, 2021; Davis, 2019).

The NSW Legislative Council (General Purpose Standing Committee No. 2), in a wide-ranging inquiry into the care system, considered questions around the privatisation of residential care and the resulting contracting out process. The committee commented:

> it is clear that there is room for improvement to existing contracting arrangements. The committee considers it important that the government learn from findings of the Auditor-General, and feedback from the wider sector, and develop a contracting model that supports better outcomes for children and young people in out of home care. Enhanced visibility of these outcomes and the 'quality' of services actually being delivered is critically important. In this regard, the committee agrees that implementation of a quality assurance framework will be instrumental for both government and non-government providers in the future. Putting that quality assurance framework in place must be made a first order priority. (p. 123)

The General Purpose Standing Committee recommended that the NSW Auditor-General be given legislative power to 'follow the money' and the ability to audit all non-governmental services providing care to children via contracts with the state (p. 123). Evidence from our study supports this call. The Auditor-General has subsequently examined the contracting out of the Permanency Support Program (a component of OOHC services) and Specialist Homelessness Services by FACS and found that FACS could not demonstrate that the non-government organisations (NGOs) contracted were delivering community services effectively and efficiently (Audit Office of NSW, 2019). A similar examination of the provision of residential care in NSW would be of great benefit.

The residential care environment

A key question that arose from our research was whether residential care is a safe environment for children. Governmental and judicial inquiries in Australia and the United Kingdom have found evidence of unsafe care placements, both in the residential care setting (Davis, 2019; Laming, 2016; Wood, 2008) and in foster care (Queensland Family and Child Commission, 2016). Recent research with care-experienced children has revealed evidence of sexual assault and harassment, some of which was perpetrated by carers (Death et al., 2021; Shaw & Greenhow, 2020).

The research of Death and colleagues (2021) for the Australian Royal Commission into Institutional Responses to Child Sexual Abuse provides first-hand accounts of sexual assault in residential care perpetrated by co-residents, carers and people from outside the home. While some participants reported staff responses to be supportive, and helpful in acknowledging and managing their sexuality, at other times, staff were viewed as facilitating the abuse. The respondents in our research similarly reported instances of sexual assault and harassment of children occurring in residential care homes, by both other residents and carers. Our Juvenile Justice respondents recounted the experience of a girl reporting both physical and sexual assault by other young people in her residential home. They told us that carers encouraged her not to make a complaint. When this young woman returned to her residential care facility following these offences, she found that her room had been set on fire (JJ13). Like the participants in Death et al.'s research, we found evidence that carer responses to incidents of sexual assault were not always appropriate and, in some cases, led to further victimisation in the form of reprisals for reporting abuse. While it is difficult to determine how widespread these types of incidents are based on our data, our findings are consistent with other studies in suggesting that residential care is not always a safe environment, particularly for young women.

Criminal offences do occur in residential care environments, and when charges are laid, this has potentially serious consequences for both the offender and victim. Often, the immediate response is removal of either the victim or offender from the home, and this can have serious ramifications for both. If there are no other suitable placements available, these young people can be left without safe accommodation or remanded in custody, or the victim and alleged offender may be forced to remain living in the same environment.

We saw evidence of this in our observations of Children's Court proceedings. In one matter, a girl who had been charged with violent offences against another child at a residential care home applied to be allowed to stay at the same residence as the victim (Day 5, Case 14). The dilemma facing the magistrate was over whether to refuse to allow the girl to reside at her usual place of residence, thereby leaving her in unstable accommodation, or whether to leave the victim and alleged perpetrator living together. There was evidence that the offender suffered from psychological disorders as she had previously been sentenced under provisions relating to mental health conditions (section 32 of the *Mental Health (Forensic Provisions) Act 1990* (NSW) – see Chapter 7 for further discussion in this regard). In this case, the defence lawyer requested a variation to the Apprehended Domestic Violence Order (ADVO) and bail conditions to allow her to stay at the same residence as the victim. The choice before the magistrate was, therefore, either to cause further upheaval in this girl's life or let her remain in the same residence as the victim. Removal was risky given secure housing is a protective factor against involvement in the criminal justice system (Baidawi & Sheehan, 2019; McFarlane, 2018; Shaw, 2016; Taylor, 2006). In this regard, research has shown that a lack of suitable accommodation results in children being denied bail and kept in custody, or even being granted bail but still kept in custody because of a lack of suitable accommodation (Bartels et al., 2015, p. 37). Remand custody can also limit the options available to a magistrate at sentencing, such as the ability to use supervision in the community as opposed to custodial orders (Baidawi & Sheehan, 2019). Ultimately, the application succeeded in this case, and the magistrate allowed the young person to stay at her residence with the victim. We can see many good reasons for making this determination; however, it is clear that balancing the safety of the victim with the desire to avoid further criminalisation of the offender in an environment where accommodation options are limited is an ongoing challenge, and one that should be of concern to care authorities.

While in this case we thought that the magistrate was right to try to avoid further criminalisation of the young woman accused of the assault, we also recognised the potential for further trauma and stress for the victim in being forced to remain in the same house as the alleged offender. Situations such as these have the potential to exacerbate existing trauma, particularly because many children enter care as a result of being removed from violent family situations. The possibility of re-traumatisation is high, and this is something that should be avoided as a priority (Mendes et al., 2019; Tregeagle et al., 2019). The care environment should always be safer than the one from which a child has been removed.

Culturally safe care and Indigenous children

On 30 June 2021, there were 6,829 Indigenous children in care in NSW (compared to 9,066 non-Indigenous children), a rate of 59.5 per 1,000 children (against 5.4/1,000 for non-Indigenous children). Two hundred and twenty-three of these Indigenous children were in residential care, compared to 325 non-Indigenous children. Indigenous children are over-represented in care, and this extends to residential care facilities. There is legislation in place that aims to ensure cultural safety for Indigenous children in care, perhaps most notably the Aboriginal Child Placement Principles (ACPP). The principles are designed to improve communication between government and community and emphasises the importance of appropriate care and self-determination (Tilbury et al., 2013). The well-recognised patterns of over-representation in care described above reinforce the need for care environments to be culturally safe (Davis, 2019).

Providing a culturally safe environment means that Indigenous children in care should be able to express their cultural and spiritual beliefs in a supportive environment, in which their identity and culture are fully acknowledged and respected (SNAICC, 2021). Williams (2008) defines cultural safety as arising from 'an environment that is safe for people: where there is no assault, challenge or denial of their identity, of who they are and what they need. It is about shared respect, shared meaning, shared knowledge and experience, of learning, living and working together with dignity and truly listening' (Eckerman, 1994, as cited in Williams, 2008). While there is no consensus on the best approach to caring for Indigenous children, Indigenous peoples have specific collective rights that incorporate their traditional laws and customs. Ramsden (2002) argues that cultural safety requires 'setting up systems which enable the less powerful to genuinely monitor the attitudes and services of the powerful to comment with safety, and ultimately, to create useful and positive change' (p. 121). In a care system that takes the principles of cultural safety seriously, Indigenous people provide strategic organisational leadership in relation to care practices and policies relating to Indigenous children (Ball & Baidawi, 2021; Krakouer et al., 2018).

The interpretation of cultural safety and culturally safe practices for Indigenous peoples is often contested by service providers. Organisations continue to find it difficult to define what culturally safe care is, and this lack of clarity can result in Indigenous children being placed in environments that cause cultural dislocation and harm. Davis (2019) has identified a number of examples of poor practice in this regard, including failures to accurately record Indigenous heritage, failures to place Indigenous children in accordance with the recognised SNAICC principles, failures to put in place proper cultural plans, failures to consult with extended family about removals and failures to comply with legislative requirements.

Indigenous children in OOHC have known vulnerabilities including experience of trauma that impact on their well-being (Raman et al., 2017). Further, connection to Country and connection to culture are important factors in the health and well-being of Indigenous Australian children (Lohoar et al., 2014). Indigenous cultures traditionally focused on kinship and connection to culture to provide supportive and caring environments for children. As a result of the disruption and harms of colonialism and child removal, these traditional practices were interrupted, and for many families, these important connections were lost for generations.

Despite clear policies and even legislation designed to promote and ensure culturally safe care, self-identified Indigenous respondents in our interviews perceived that the needs of Indigenous children in care cannot be met without more Indigenous identified positions among staff and more resources to facilitate greater connection to culture. A Juvenile Justice participant in an Aboriginal-identified position provided an example of the need for more cultural resources and education for staff working with children across the child welfare and criminal justice systems. When running a Sorry Day activity with Indigenous children in detention, he was 'talking about tribes and totems and kids were just all over me, just thirsty for knowledge. And that was just going in there for a day. So I don't think there's enough of that' (JJ9). This respondent told us, 'just on the Aboriginal side of things culturally out-of-home care kids aren't getting their needs met' (JJ9). He went on:

> now if you're going to put a white person, no disrespect, with an Aboriginal person that's got no idea about cultural issues, how that kid is

> then treated for the rest of his time in FACS has a detrimental effect on that young person big time. And I've seen it time and time again. It was a bit like the kid I was telling [you about] a minute ago. First time I met that kid, here he's got these white workers who probably destroyed half of what happened and then they put an Aboriginal person in and the young person can't deal with it. Culturally he's got no idea and then you're taken off your parents and then you're put through 17 different foster homes. Not one of them is Aboriginal.
>
> (JJ9)

Our respondents from the OOHC sector recognised the importance of culture for Indigenous children in their care: 'There are places for them to go, like, try and get all the Indigenous kids to practise their culture and they see someone and wanted some of the Elders to teach them what's wrong and what's right, and act as a role model for these Indigenous kids' (OOHC10). But more resources need to be devoted to this: 'I think that we need to maybe fund some of our money to those type of areas where they can focus more on the Indigenous kids and get them to learn their culture, and then slowly from there we can improve the kids' behaviour' (OOHC10). Another OOHC provider told us, 'we work intensively with other Aboriginal organisations, [to address] the needs of the young Aboriginal children in terms of knowing their culture, where they came from and where they are going and their sense of belonging' (OOHC 13). But in many of our interviews with OOHC respondents, the topic of Indigenous children in care did not arise. And although we note that some service providers did recognise the importance of cultural safety, their somewhat complacent comments are in stark contrast to the raw anger of one of the Indigenous people we spoke to:

> Well they're [the workers] not Aboriginal. So rarely do you really know what's going on with Aboriginal people … honestly, what would you know? You don't know nothing. You haven't lived in [their] shoes, what's culturally appropriate for [them]. So that's a big dilemma as well. Like, I've had out-of-home care kids, just making me think of all this stuff because I've been here for that long, is that we've had out-of-home care kids as young as 11, 12 and 13 placed … down here … they've kicked them out, they got nowhere to go and they end up here. Well they've assaulted someone at the centre where they're at, then they are here and they don't want them back. Why the fucking hell did you take them … in the first place, please?
>
> (JJ10)

In our interviews, we asked respondents about the demographics of children in care without specifically referring to Indigenous children. While most respondents recognised the over-representation of Indigenous children in the criminal justice and care systems, many did not reflect on the specific vulnerability of Indigenous children, the provision of culturally safe care practices, the complexities of intergenerational trauma and the need for culturally competent care practices. More broadly, the provision of staff professional development in relation to cultural safety and cultural competency needs to be at the centre of organisational responses (Mendes et al., 2019). We note that up until the writing of this book, there had been a failure to implement Davis's (2019) recommendations and to ensure that change is implemented by and with Indigenous communities (Gerard et al., 2019).

There is global recognition across colonised nations such as Australia, Canada and Aotearoa New Zealand that the removal of Indigenous children from their families results in systemic harm and intrinsically links the care environment and the criminal justice system (Blackstock et al., 2020; Davis, 2019; Stanley, 2017). As the ACPP make clear, when Indigenous children need to be removed from their family home, they should be placed in culturally safe environments, and residential care for Indigenous children should be run by organisations controlled by Indigenous communities. However, despite clear evidence of the harms resulting from removal, many Indigenous children are placed in OOHC, often in locations far removed from their families and communities. Developing capacity to facilitate specialised forms of cultural care requires organisations to engage with Indigenous stakeholders to guide culturally appropriate care practices for Indigenous children. Organisations providing out-of-home care characteristically have a range of tactical strategies to prepare staff to work with Indigenous peoples and communities across the care sector. However, what is less characteristic is the care system's ability to effectively consult with Indigenous communities and implement recommendations in organisational practice, including at a very basic level, through the employment of Indigenous staff (Davis, 2019; Mendes et al., 2019).

Policing children in residential care

We discuss in Chapter 4 the frustration police experience through their interactions with residential homes. Here, we consider this fraught relationship from the perspective of the residential care sector. Our earlier research showed how staff in care homes use police as a way of managing minor behavioural infractions (Gerard et al., 2019). Our subsequent findings add further depth to this picture. Many OOHC staff in our study expressed frustration that children did not take advantage of existing support structures and failed to recognise how their current behaviour could affect their future lives. While we understand this frustration, placing the responsibility for poor behaviour and lack of foresight onto traumatised children with little family support is in our view unfair as well as inconsistent with the principles of trauma-informed care:

> My biggest issue at the moment is just engagement of young people. So I have a lot of kids that need a lot of help, but not engaged in anything to want to do anything. So I've got one kid that has been gone for two

> months almost, in and out. You'll see her occasionally, you'll speak to her occasionally, but she's just not there. You can't get her into school. You can't get her to the doctors. You can't do anything with her. And then some kids that are in house blatantly refusing to do stuff, that's always the biggest issue that you'll have.
>
> (NGO6)

As evident in the above comment, in direct contrast to the tenets of trauma-informed care, carers thought it important that children should face the consequences of their behaviour. There were clear examples in our data of police being called to residential care homes for this reason, with many calls related to minor infractions such as not being home at curfew time. One carer told us:

> but if it starts to be a problem, if they're doing it on purpose, if they're smashing stuff when they're really angry, we can have them charged but because they're underage it's normally just a warning, but it's good for them to know that if you – once you get into the real world, if you do something wrong, the cops are going to come, and you are going to get in trouble.
>
> (NGO11)

Another said, 'but if there's any property damage like that, there's no tolerance to it. It's automatically call the police and it's a police matter. They'll be charged with property damage as a strategy to try and stop that property damage because obviously there's only so much funding that we have as a service' (NGO5). This comment also seems in clear conflict with the provisions of the Joint Protocol, which stipulate that calling police must be a last resort: 'I guess for us in our protocol we've stated very clearly that calling police should be used as a last resort' (L1). Others in the OOHC sector did recognise the problems around calling the police:

> One of the kids came back to me one day; they had done some property damage. It was not very significant but it was property damage, and then one of the staff members called the police for them, and then when I came into the house, I said, 'One day you told me that this is like home, this is a family'. And I said, 'Yeah, that's it', and she said, 'But if it was your own children, if they – would you call the police?', and I said, 'What happened? Tell me what happened?' So she explained that she was angry, she was not being listened to and the only way that she thought she could be listened to was by doing that.
>
> (NGO13)

This respondent told us that they had only called the police after the third incident: 'the third one is deliberate' (NGO13). Another agreed: 'Well, within our organisation the police don't get called until the last straw really with the young person if there's an incident. Unless it's quite a severe matter, if there's been an assault or something like that where the police [must] be called' (NGO4). A third respondent also thought that calling the police was a last resort, in accordance with the Joint Protocol:

> But when you've got a young person in the house who is continuously doing those things, like, repetitively over and over again, staff in the house and us as an organisation really don't have much room to move, like, we don't have much power and we're restricted in what we can do a lot, so we call the police.
>
> (NGO5)

While the interview respondents from FACS recognised the potential for children to be criminalised through poor behaviour management practices, some attributed this to individual providers rather than systemic practices:

> there's one particular service I'll give as an example of where it's shabby – what I would consider to be shabby behaviour and I think they may have stopped this because actually in a meeting I got glares from various people. But I'm not going to apologise for bringing it up, but one of our practices used to be if the children broke curfew, even if they knew where that child/young person was – so in this particular example the young fellow had a bit of a developmental issue and he was addicted to being on the internet – he was at the internet café – they'd phone up the police and report him missing even though they knew that 9 times out of 10 he'd be down at the local internet café. So, I mean, that's what I would consider really shonky, shabby behaviour.
>
> (FACS1)

Consistent with our earlier findings, we found no evidence of any sense of accountability on the part of FACS, with the blame being placed on 'bad' providers rather than a lack of appropriate oversight'. As one FACS respondent observed:

> we're all collectively aghast at the fact that going into out-of-home care means you're more likely to come in contact with police because – as a response to your behaviour.
>
> (FACS2)

Another FACS respondent suspected that 'it suits them that the children or young people clear out because they go, "Well that's easy; I don't have to worry about them being in the house and having to manage them"' (FACS1). However, there was clear recognition about the role of police: 'But the general principle is that obviously you don't get the police involved – the principle I would operate on is if it was your own child would you be calling the police?' (FACS1).

While most participants in this study agreed that calling the police should be a last resort for care providers, perceptions about whether this was really the case varied greatly. People working in the OOHC sector, while acknowledging that police were sometimes called for relatively minor offences, almost universally were of the view that in their homes, the policy and practice were to only call the police for serious offences. The police respondents viewed this very differently, with at least one police officer telling us that they went to care homes every day they were on duty (P5). The magistrates in our study also thought that police were called as 'a first rather than last resort' (Magistrate focus group), a view echoed by the lawyers and FACS respondents. In any event, police involvement in responding to minor offending in OOHC facilities was almost universally acknowledged to be a significant driver of the criminalisation of care-experienced children, and one of the main reasons for the high incidence of police call-out was that staff in residential homes are not properly trained and qualified and are consequently unable to manage problematic behaviour in-house. The next section of this chapter considers the dilemmas related to the staffing of residential homes.

Staffing: low pay, high turnover

The challenge of employing and training suitable staff was a key theme to emerge from our research. The previous Child Safe Standards for Permanent Care which were in force at the time of our research stated 'people who work with and care for children and young people have appropriate training for their role and are provided with opportunities for professional development' (Office of the Children's Guardian, 2015, Standard 20). However, the Standards did not set specific minimum qualifications. The new standards hold staff should be equipped with the knowledge, skills and awareness to keep children safe, through continual education and training (Office of the Children's Guardian, 2020, Standard 7). One of our FACS respondents advised that when advertising for staff for one of the few facilities that is still directly run by the Department, there are minimum education standards: 'we say we want a Cert. III (technical and further education certificates in NSW range from level 1 to 4' (Level 3 is directed at "a competent self-managed employee, TAFE NSW, 2021) '...and a first-aid certificate and then we buddy up our workers, we buddy them and we train them and we offer training, on the job training to them and we also do six to eight weekly group debriefing and training" (FACS2). This participant also noted that this minimum qualification expectation was not consistent across the care sector: 'other agencies take a more mish mash melange approach, if it's a way I can describe it'.

Some of our respondents (L13, M7, M8) perceived deficits in staff quality to be a direct result of the contracting out of care: 'the NGO [role in the]

OOHC system [is] … a real failure and … warped I think' (M8). Because of the low salaries available, attracting appropriate staff was seen as particularly difficult. One respondent working in the OOHC sector told us that 'recruitment retention is a huge problem, because the majority – they're paying so low wages' (NGO1). Another OOHC manager linked this with the qualifications and experience of staff:

> I'm not saying that you need to have university or TAFE or whatever, but it is helpful. So there seems to be a drop in the quality of staff. And the burnout is higher and the turnover rate, I would say, is higher as well. So for it to be successful you actually need a consistent team for a long time period. So if there's a massive change all the time, there's not consistency, and that will also impact the client.
>
> (NGO2)

Even so, this OOHC manager perceived that there had been improvements in the quality of staff: 'Your staff may not be – staff qualifications may not be up to scratch but it has gotten a lot better than what it was' (NGO2). One of our FACS respondents (FACS2) thought that teachers, nurses or early childhood educators would be suitable carers although the significantly lower pay in the OOHC makes the employment of these professionals unlikely. One of our respondents, an OOHC facility manager (NGO1), noted that given that the job involves shift work at relatively low pay, retaining staff was a challenge. He provided the following illustration of the problems in retaining staff:

> I would have care workers who would come in and do eight-hour shifts in the house: morning shifts, afternoon shifts, and night shifts. They're going in to work with five young people who are going to constantly all day abuse them, spit at them, throw food at them, threaten to beat them up, you get no reward for trying to help them, and then you're paying them $21 an hour.
>
> (NGO1)

This comment clearly illustrates the challenges of attracting and keeping well-qualified, experienced staff to work in a low-paying job where they are expected to provide a sophisticated level of support, and manage and respond to problematic, sometimes criminal behaviour, while being at risk of harm and abuse themselves. In England and Wales, Narey (2016) has similarly identified the difficulty of recruiting high-quality staff who are asked to do a difficult job in unrewarding circumstances for low pay.

Staff inexperience can also lead to court supervision plans not being complied with. For instance, one Juvenile Justice respondent supervised a young woman in an OOHC placement who had an extensive court-mandated plan to help her transition to living independently, which included programs to develop her communication skills. However, the program was not implemented, and as a result, this young woman left care without these necessary skills for independent living. The Juvenile Justice worker attributed these problems to the 'inconsistency and mismanagement of staff, [and the] high turnover of staff at this placement' (JJ2). Other Juvenile Justice respondents perceived OOHC staff as struggling to manage the complexities of care with little support and resources: 'They don't know what to do, and they are kind of – the strong ones kind of are resilient and they manage to pull through, but often, yeah, they are just really – they are just not well supported, I think. They are under-staffed, I think, for what the – like the intensity of the kids presenting behaviours, they probably can do with extra support. And then they just probably feel overwhelmed a lot of the time' (JJ1). It is, thus, clear that the provision of competent and well-qualified staff is an ongoing challenge for the residential care sector.

Education and training for OOHC staff

How might this situation be improved? What does a well-trained and qualified OOHC sector look like? There are three relevant aspects to this: the education that staff receive prior to obtaining employment in the sector, ongoing professional development and on-the-job experience.

Our interview respondents were critical of the experience and education level of staff working in residential care. A police participant noted that staff in some residential care facilities are only a few years older than the children they are caring for – 'people who are two or three years older … that have no life experience' (P5) – and she believed that these children need experienced carers who can assume a parenting role. A FACS participant highlighted some of the problems that arise when young people are hired as carers: 'They're not youth workers, they are carers because I'm expecting that if you're working in a home and there are 12 or 13 year olds … you're not being their friend, you're caring for them in a de facto role like a parent would' (FACS2). These comments highlight the difference between providing the basic supervision provided by simply having an adult in the house and what Day (2017) calls the 'gold standard' of parenting, which is providing emotional and aspirational support to help a child thrive rather than just survive.

No clear view emerged from our interviews with respondents working in the OOHC sector about the standard of training and education among staff in their facilities, with some perceiving that staff were better trained than previously, whereas others thought that there had been a decline. One participant was of the view that even though staff may not have the training and expertise needed, previously, the situation was worse: 'Your staff may not be – staff qualifications may not be up to scratch but it has gotten a lot better than what it was' (OOHC4). However, others felt differently: 'From what I can see there has been a slight drop in the quality of staff, so there's less people with qualifications ... so there seems to be a drop in the quality of staff. And the burnout is higher and the turnover rate, I would say, is higher as well' (OOHC3).

As noted in the above section, FACS's re-contracting process was being undertaken at the time we interviewed that cohort, and FACS was in the process of implementing the TCF (see Chapter 2). There was an acknowledgement that a consistent trauma-informed approach to care had not been employed previously in both government and contracted care facilities. The FACS interview respondents were clear that it is important for carers to be trained in using therapeutic responses to trauma-informed behaviour and that therapeutic approaches should be embedded in policy and practice guidelines. Implementation of the framework was expected to be coupled with training and support for carers and providers, and an evaluation process was to be part of this implementation: 'We would think they'd very much need additional training and support ... what we are proposing is joint training around trauma and abuse, and that will touch on the therapeutic care. But, at the same time, when funded services go through the recommissioning process, they will need to demonstrate that all staff are going to be trained in therapeutic care' (FACS3). Since this interview, the training on the TCF has become available via a series of modules on the ACWA website. The new child safety standards explicitly identify experiences of trauma as a factor that relevant organisations need to be aware of and that staff must be trained to respond to. Standard 7 requires that staff are equipped with 'the knowledge, skills and awareness to keep children safe, through continual education and training', but it does not mandate what form this training should take (Office of the Children's Guardian, 2020). There has been some debate about whether mandatory minimum qualifications should be introduced (Narey, 2016), with no consensus emerging. At present, the onus for training staff is placed very much on the organisation. Given the problems identified here relating to staff training and qualifications, we think there should be some measure of oversight of this.

Conclusion

Our findings raise significant concerns about the contracting out of residential care and question whether residential care is a safe environment for young people. FACS clearly needs to have greater oversight of the contracting process, the provision of care and the training and qualifications of staff working in care homes. The Joint Protocol was introduced during this research project and was seen as a potential solution to the criminalisation of children in residential care. Although our study is in no way an evaluation of this protocol, we failed to observe any evidence of it in action. In any event, we await a thorough evaluation of the program, which we hope will lead to a reduction in the criminalisation of children in residential care.

References

Audit Office of New South Wales. (2019). *Contracting non-government organisations.* NSW Auditor-General.

Australian Institute of Health and Welfare. (2021). *Child protection Australia 2019–20* (Vol. 78).

Baidawi, S., & Sheehan, R. (2019). 'Crossover kids': Offending by child protection–involved youth. *Trends and Issues in Crime and Criminal Justice*, 582, 1–23.

Ball, R., & Baidawi, S. (2021). Aboriginal crossover children's characteristics, service needs and service responses: The views of Australian key stakeholders. *Children and Youth Services Review, 129,* 106176. https://doi.org/10.1016/j.childyouth.2021.106176

Bartels, L., Bolitho, J., & Richards, K. (2015). Indigenous young people and the NSW children's court: Magistrates' perceptions of the court's criminal jurisdiction. *Australian Indigenous Law Review, 19*(2), 34–44. https://doi.org/10.3316/informit.574136187604513

Blackstock, C., Bamblett, M., & Black, C. (2020). Indigenous ontology, international law and the application of the Convention to the over-representation of Indigenous children in out of home care in Canada and Australia. *Child Abuse & Neglect, 110,* 104587. https://doi.org/10.1016/j.chiabu.2020.104587

Carey, M. (2019). Some ethical limitations of privatising and marketizing social care and social work provision in England for children and young people. *Ethics and Social Welfare, 13*(3), 272–287.

Children and Young Persons (Care and Protection) Act NSW. (1998). https://legislation.nsw.gov.au/view/html/inforce/current/act-1998-157

Children and Young Persons (Care and Protection) Regulation NSW. (2012). https://legislation.nsw.gov.au/view/html/inforce/current/sl-2012-0425

Commission for Children and Young People. (2021). *Out of sight: Systemic inquiry into children and young people who are absent or missing from residential care.*

Davis, M. (2019). *Family is Culture*: *Review report.* Independent Review of Aboriginal Children in OOHC.

Day, A. (2017). Hearing the voice of looked after children: Challenging current assumptions and knowledge about pathways into offending. *Safer Communities, 16*(3), 122–133.

Death, J., Moore, T., McArthur, M., Roche, S., & Tilbury, C. (2021). Young people's perceptions of sexual assault in residential care: 'It does happen a lot'. *Journal of Child Sexual Abuse, 30*(1), 4–20. https://doi.org/10.1080/10538712.2020.1715521

Dunn, D. M., Culhane, S. E., & Taussig, H. N. (2010). Children's appraisals of their experiences in out-of-home care. *Children and Youth Services Review, 32*(10), 1324–1330. https://doi.org/10.1016/j.childyouth.2010.05.001

Gerard, A., McGrath, A., Colvin, E., & McFarlane, K. (2019). 'I'm not getting out of bed!': The criminalisation of young people in residential care. *Australian & New Zealand Journal of Criminology, 52*(1), 76–93. https://doi.org/10.1177/0004865818778739

Krakouer, J., Wise, S., & Connolly, M. (2018). 'We live and breathe through culture': Conceptualising cultural connection for Indigenous Australian children in out-of-home care. *Australian Social Work, 71*(3), 265–276. https://doi.org/10.1080/0312407X.2018.1454485

Laming, H. (2016). *In care, out of trouble: How the life chances of children in care can be transformed by protecting them from unnecessary involvement in the criminal justice system*. Prison Reform Trust.

Lohoar, S., Butera, N., & Kennedy, E. (2014). *Strengths of Australian aboriginal cultural practices in family life and child rearing*. Child Family Community Australia.

McFarlane, K. (2018). Care-criminalisation: The involvement of children in out-of-home care in the New South Wales criminal justice system. *Australian & New Zealand Journal of Criminology, 51*(3), 412–433. https://doi.org/10.1177/0004865817723954

McFarlane, K., Colvin, E., McGrath, A., & Gerard, A. (2019). 'Just another policy document?' Can a protocol end the criminalisation of kids in care? *Alternative Law Journal, 44*(1), 37–42. https://doi.org/10.1177/1037969x18795498

Mendes, P., Saunders, B., & Baidawi, S. (2019). The experiences of Indigenous young people transitioning from out-of-home care in Victoria, Australia. In V. Mann-Feder, & M. Goyette (Eds.) *Leaving care and the transition to adulthood: international contributions to theory, research, and practice* (pp. 149–171). Oxford University Press.

Mental Health (Forensic Provisions) Act NSW. (1990). https://legislation.nsw.gov.au/view/html/repealed/current/act-1990-010

Narey, M. (2016). *Residential care in England: report of Sir Martin Narey's independent review of children's residential care*. Department of Education.

New South Wales Legislative Council General Purpose Standing Committee. (2017). *General Purpose Standing Committee No. 2. Report.*

New South Wales Ombudsman. (2019). *Joint protocol to reduce the contact of young people in residential out of home care with the criminal justice system*. NSW Ombudsman.

Office of the Children's Guardian. (2015). *Child safe standards.*

Office of the Children's Guardian. (2020). *Child safe standards.*

Productivity Commission. (2022). *Report on government services*. Australian Government.

Raman, S., Ruston, S., Irwin, S., Tran, P., Hotton, P., & Thorne, S. (2017). Taking culture seriously: Can we improve the developmental health and well-being of Australian Aboriginal children in out-of-home care? *Child: Care, Health and Development, 43*(6), 899–905. https://doi.org/10.1111/cch.12488

Ramsden, I. (2002). *Cultural safety and nursing education in Aotearoa and Te Waipounamu* (Doctoral dissertation, Victoria University of Wellington).

Queensland Family and Child Commission. (2016). *When a child is missing: Remembering Tiahleigh – A report into Queensland's children missing from out-of-home care.*

Shaw, J. (2016). Policy, practice and perceptions: Exploring the criminalisation of children's home residents in England. *Youth Justice, 16*(2), 147–161. https://doi.org/10.1177/1473225415617858

Shaw, J., & Greenhow, S. (2020). Children in care: Exploitation, offending and the denial of victimhood in a prosecution-led culture of practice. *The British Journal of Social Work, 50*(5), 1551–1569. https://doi.org/ 10.1093/bjsw/bcz137

Shaw, J., & Greenhow, S. (2021). *The criminalisation and exploitation of children in care: Multi-agency perspectives*. Routledge.

SNAICC. (2021). https://www.snaicc.org.au/policy-and-research/child-safety-and-wellbeing/keeping-our-kids-safe/

Stanley, E. (2017). From care to custody: Trajectories of children in post-war New Zealand. *Youth Justice*, *17*(1), 57–72. https://doi.org/10.1177/1473225416669145

TAFE NSW. (2021). What qualification do I need? https://www.tafensw.edu.au/article/-/blogs/what-qualification-do-i-need-

Taylor, C. (2006). *Young people in care and criminal behaviour.* Jessica Kingsley Publishers.

Tilbury, C., Burton, J., Sydenham, E., Boss, R., & Louw, T. (2013). *Aboriginal and Torres Strait Islander child placement principle: Aims and core elements.* Secretariat of National Aboriginal and Islander Child Care.

Tregeagle, S., Moggach, L., Trivedi, H., & Ward, H. (2019). Previous life experiences and the vulnerability of children adopted from out-of-home care: The impact of Adverse Childhood Experiences and child welfare decision making. *Children and Youth Services Review*, *96*, 55–63. https://doi.org/10.1016/j.childyouth.2018.11.028

Williams, R. (2008). Cultural safety; what does it mean for our work practice? *Australian and New Zealand Journal of Public Health*, *23*(2), 213–214.

Wood, J. (2008). *Report of the Special Commission of Inquiry into child protection services in NSW* (Vols. 1 and 2). Department of Premier and Cabinet (NSW).

4 Policing children with care experience

Introduction

In the previous chapter, we looked at OOHC service provider respondents' perceptions of their relationships with police. In this chapter, we turn our focus to the perceptions of our police respondents. In the Australian context, the fraught relationship between police and those with care experience, particularly Aboriginal and Torres Strait Islander people, has a long history (HREOC, 1997). Police were on the frontline of administering the practices and policies of colonisation, including the forms of child removal that led to the Stolen Generations (Cunneen, 2001). Acute and painful historical continuities are reflected in the current OOHC system, including the involvement of police in removals (Davis, 2019). While young people in care might have contact with police as victims, witnesses and offenders, this chapter will primarily focus on interactions with police while children are in residential care.

The need to divert young Aboriginal people from the criminal justice system is acknowledged in the latest strategy for the NSW Police, *Aboriginal Strategic Direction 2018–2023* (ASD) (NSW Government & NSW Police Force, 2018). Preventing young people from coming into contact with the criminal justice system has been a recurring recommendation of royal commissions nationally and in jurisdictions across Australia (e.g. Australian Government, 2017; Johnston, 1991). Our study was able to capture some of the drivers of police contact and some potential ways to divert young people from involvement in the criminal justice system.

Previous research from the United Kingdom has shown how police perceptions of and responses to children in OOHC are significant factors in the criminalisation of these children in the criminal justice system and that a lack of multi-agency cooperation can compound this criminalisation (Howard League, 2017; Laming, 2016; Shaw & Greenhow, 2021). Our research reveals the same trends and provides additional examples of accelerants and inhibitors in the Australian context, supporting and expanding on work by Davis (2019) and Tillack et al. (2018). Further, we examine how the legacy of colonisation, and the involvement of law enforcement in the ongoing removal of Aboriginal children from their families, shapes the relationship between police and care-experienced children and influences the responses of both.

DOI: 10.4324/9781003093367-5

The history of policing in Australia is intrinsically linked to the history of colonisation. Rather than a grassroots community-based evolution of policing or policing of poverty in an age of industrialisation, as has occurred in England, policing in Australia was militaristic from the start and its first role was enabling and enforcing colonial practices (Cunneen, 2001). Police took on a more paramilitary-type role in early settler colonial history, enacting the militaristic style of policing seen in Ireland (Sturma, 1987). This involved the dispersal and removal of Aboriginal and Torres Strait Islander peoples to allow pastoralists to settle on unceded traditional lands. As tensions rose the frontier violence escalated, and police were heavily involved in suppressing uprisings and partook in massacres and violence against Aboriginal and Torres Strait Islander peoples. Police also took on an authoritarian role, governing Aboriginal people who were placed on missions and reserves, and were directly involved in the forced removal of Aboriginal children from their families. The legacy of the frontier violence, the paramilitary role of policing during colonisation and ongoing systemic racism have all resulted in fractured relationships between police and Indigenous peoples in Australia today (Cunneen, 2001; Finnane, 1994). The Royal Commission into Aboriginal Deaths in Custody (Johnston, 1991) provided several recommendations on how police could improve their relationship with Indigenous communities; however, current policing practices and engagement strategies can only be described as inconsistent in approach and effectiveness (Davis, 2019; Gillfeather-Spetere, 2019; New South Wales Parliament, 2014). Police contact with children in OOHC, a significant proportion of whom are Aboriginal and Torres Strait Islander children (Davis, 2019), is best understood in the context of this history.

This chapter draws primarily on our interview data with police, triangulated with the responses from our other interview respondents and the court observation data. Ten frontline serving NSW police officers were interviewed, and one police officer was interviewed twice, with 12 months between the two interviews. There were five respondents from regional areas and five from the Sydney greater metropolitan area. The respondents ranged in rank, with five being more junior officers and five more senior. Our other interview data, the court observation data and the file reviews provided additional context and perspectives to enrich the analysis of the police interview data. Our OOHC, Juvenile Justice, lawyer and magistrate stakeholders regularly had professional dealings with police in the residential care setting and when children with care experience were involved in the criminal justice system. First, this chapter explores how our police respondents characterised their involvement with children in OOHC and with OOHC service providers, and how this influenced their perceptions of and relationships with children and their carers. We then examine the consequences of police attitudes and expectations of children in OOHC, specifically how this contributes to criminalisation through inappropriate and inadequate responses to care-experienced children. We also consider what appropriate responses might look like. Last, we explore how these issues crystalise for children when they go missing from care.

Intense police involvement with residential care

One of the more notable findings of our interview data was the frequency and volume with which police came into contact with children in residential care. This contact did not just occur at the children's places of residence but also in public spaces. One police respondent noted that:

> they had 900 missing person reports from out-of-home care sites, in just that one LAC [Local Area Command]. So that's 450, which is more than one a day. And it was representing a large percentage of their total workload in attending out-of-home care sites.
>
> (P1) (Gerard et al., 2019)

The police respondents reported that carers called them primarily to respond to incidents of alleged offending or to report a child missing (P1, P2, P5, P6). It was clear from the interview data that police responses to matters involving children in residential care constituted a significant part of their day-to-day operational duties. P5 noted that responses to residential care home call-outs were such a large component of officers' work that they were likely to be called out 'there very early on in their career … you're probably out there day one on the job'. Comments about the frequency of call-outs to residential care facilities were coupled with a sense of frustration on behalf of the respondents, demonstrated by the following comment:

> We get very frustrated. You can just tell. I'm just, yeah; it's the same houses all the time. You hear the address… I've already – without being rude – I've already lost interest in you. I've already lost interest.
>
> (P5)

Police contact with children in OOHC was partially driven by the nature of the residential care environment itself (as unpacked in the previous chapter). However, our police respondents also believed that the children in residential care spent more time in public spaces than non-care-experienced children because many children in residential care feel unsafe in their group home. This is consistent with research that shows that children feel unsafe in residential care and that police are often aware of these feelings (Colvin et al., 2018; Moore et al., 2017).

> I chatted to one just the other day, because he wasn't at school. So not necessarily a victim or a witness, just was, that's how you come in contact with young people all the time.
>
> (P5)

Children in residential care may also self-place with family or friends and tend to move between residences. In addition, the lower school attendance rate seen among care-experienced children means that they are more often out in public during school hours, which makes them more visible to police (Gerard et al., 2019; Mendes et al., 2014). Increased exposure to police has been linked to criminalisation of young people (Cunneen, 2001; Howard League, 2017; Richards et al., 2019). This exposure is compounded for children from the residential care environment because of their increased tendency to be in public spaces (Gerard et al., 2019; Shaw & Greenhow, 2021).

For Indigenous children, there are several factors that influence the increased contact with police, including more surveillance (Cunneen, 2006) and carers reporting Indigenous children for behavioural indiscretions. While these factors are relevant to all children in OOHC, the over-representation of Indigenous children in the OOHC system exacerbates this reality. The Royal Commission into the Detention and Protection of Children in the Northern Territory (Australian Government, 2017) found that reform across youth justice was necessary to challenge the systemic failures that place Indigenous children at a higher risk of criminalisation than their non-Indigenous counterparts. Further, an Indigenous young person is more likely to be charged than given a caution under police discretionary powers (Cunneen, 2001; Warner et al., 2022).

In our study, children in OOHC were found to be less likely to receive the benefits of diversionary approaches. Our review of the files identified that care-experienced children are more likely to have been charged (as opposed to cautioned) by police previously. Of the 92 cases we reviewed, 36% of the care-experienced children had at least one previous charge compared to 17% of the non-care-experienced children ($p = 0.057$). In relation to cautions, among the 92 cases, only ten children (both with and without care experience) had previously been cautioned. Given the small sample size, any differences would be unlikely to reach statistical significance. However, it is worth noting that only one care-experienced child in the sample of files had been cautioned previously, compared to nine non-care-experienced children. The one care-experienced child was an Indigenous boy. Three out of the nine non-care-experienced children who received a caution were female, representing a slightly higher proportion than the overall numbers of female children in the sample. These figures suggest that care-experienced children are more likely to receive a punitive approach and less likely to receive the benefits of cautions and other diversionary mechanisms from police. Our findings confirm the observations of previous studies that diversionary approaches tend to be used for particular cohorts of children and not others, such as Indigenous children (see Davis, 2019; Luke & Cunneen, 1995) and those with care experience (see Hunter, 2022).

Although police clearly attend residential care facilities regularly, one senior police officer noted that this did not mean that the police response to the situation cultivated relationships, built trust or created a sustainable solution. Competing demands from other matters needing attention and police operational policies and procedures could impact the efficacy of their response:

> The police come, particularly busy commands, they've got a lot of work on, they're fairly abrupt, they're fairly impatient to get to the next, more pressing job, and yet they're supposed to sit down and reason with these children, who have trained professionals who have trouble dealing with it, so what chance does a second- or third-year constable, who doesn't have any of their own children, and might only be six or seven years older than the kid that they're talking to? It just is not a productive situation.
>
> (P1)

This type of policing task requires patience, which can be difficult to manifest when an officer believes that there are more urgent issues requiring their attention, particularly if they believe that the incident they are responding to should be managed 'in house', such as children being reported missing when they are only half an hour late or children engaged in minor behavioural infractions. Police who respond to call-outs are generally more junior police, who are often young, less experienced and have little knowledge of complex Indigenous community relationships (Cunneen, 2001; Davis, 2019). As the respondent above illustrates, the police are not 'trained professionals' when it comes to managing children's behaviour. Our respondents perceived that they were ill-suited to negotiating with children exhibiting problematic, and not necessarily criminal, behaviour. When considering the likelihood that the children police will be encountering have experience of trauma, the above comment highlights the inability of police to respond effectively to children in these situations.

NSW Government's Joint Protocol to Reduce the Contact of Young People in Residential Care with the Criminal Justice System is intended to reduce the frequency of reporting, as part of the broader measures designed to reduce criminalisation. An early iteration of protocol initiatives was commented on by P1, who noted that, in one geographical area, it had resulted in 'a minimum 40% saving in their resources' and in the time police spent at OOHC locations, 'and more cordial relationships with the workers and the managers of that site'. These results demonstrate the wider benefits of reducing criminalisation – the related reduction in both workload and resource drain for law enforcement and the criminal justice system.

Using police as a behaviour management tool

In the previous chapter, we discussed FACS and OOHC providers' perceptions of police involvement in residential care homes. The perspective of our police respondents was that they were used as a behaviour management tool, which was a clear source of frustration. Respondents from our other interview cohorts supported this view that police were used as a behaviour management tool rather than for legitimate criminal justice issues (JJ4, JJ6, L7). The police respondents were critical of service providers and their staff, noting the disparity between parenting approaches in the home and in OOHC:

> The carers ... it's a job to them. I don't think they necessarily put in the hard – you know, like as if it's a parent or a family member, you're going to push them or help them get to where they want to go; whereas these kids don't have that. Unless the child themselves wants to take opportunities that are given to them, if given to them. It would be hard to self-motivate yourself as a kid, you know.
>
> (P4)

The police interviewed expressed the view that they were called to group homes to manage behaviour as a result of the inability of service providers to perform their job adequately:

> There's so many people that provide a service and as soon as they become alarmed about what it is they're meant to be providing, they ring up the police to substitute that gap.
>
> (P1)

The police respondents echoed some of the challenges identified in the previous chapter around training, education and experience of OOHC staff, and how this impacted their law enforcement role. One respondent commented:

> They are not prepared. They are not experienced. It's very – it's a – from what I understand, it's very easy to get a job in these centres, as a carer. But these are kids that need role models and parenting figures, not people who are two or three years older, who have – are 18 or 21, that have no life experience, who don't have that persona, who don't have that confidence, who've never raised children, let alone raised children or young people that have issues.
>
> (P5)

These perceptions of our police respondents of OOHC staff and the practice of using police as a behaviour management tool gave rise to poor relationships between OOHC service providers and police. One of our police respondents described their relationship with OOHC service providers as 'fractured' (P2).

The OOHC service provider respondents also perceived that the quality of the relationship they had with local police influenced the interactions between police and children in OOHC. In this regard, positive relationships with police are understood to be key to supporting the complex needs of children in OOHC (Shaw & Greenhow, 2021). Some of the OOHC respondents supported this understanding:

> some of them won't know anything about us at all, and they don't understand what we're doing, what our roles are. And then there'll be police that know us, we have good relationships in some regions, and they're fantastic.
>
> (OOHC2)

Conversely, negative relationships impacted the way police felt about children and police responses to incidents in care homes. For instance, one officer noted poor relationships between police, children in OOHC and service providers:

> There would be complaints coming in from these places about the attitude of some of the police that attended, because they were just completely frustrated with going to these addresses at the same time, all the time, for the same reasons, having to do the same old thing for no different result. And that was leading to a breakdown in the relationship between the commands and the service providers.
>
> (P1)

Open dialogue and good communication were seen as a potential way to improve relationships:

> [One] Local Area Command was just completely open and honest and saying, 'We had a poor opinion of resi care workers'. And so it's part of the professionalisation between both saying, 'We want to actually improve our opinions of both of you and we want to understand how difficult it is for you but let's see us both committing to doing things differently', and that's changed the landscape a bit because they've built trust in each other and around the fact that they can choose to – they can manage that behaviour and they're not calling police as much, it's got the buy-in from police straightaway because it's like, we can see those results.
>
> (L1)

While functional and respectful inter-agency relationships can improve police attitudes towards carers and children and may also improve police responses to children, it is not necessarily a panacea to the criminalising effect of responses to care-experienced children. Shaw and Greenhow's (2021) extensive research into multi-agency responses to children in OOHC demonstrates that we should exercise caution in solely focusing on improving relationships between agencies who interact with children in OOHC as a means to reduce criminalisation. Adequate resourcing and professional development are also key factors (Shaw & Greenhow, 2021).

The police respondents viewed many of the incidents reported by residential care homes as minor and felt that police involvement served to escalate them. One police respondent recounted how many reports were received for behaviour that should not have been criminalised. Her view was that carers were not behaving as parents would when disciplining their child and were instead relying on police to perform this role:

> As a copper, don't ring me and say, such and such has been naughty and you want me to chastise them as a parent or an authority figure. You're the carer, that is your job. If you want them charged ring me. I'll happily do my job. But as a parent, that is your job.
>
> (P5)

As conveyed above, police are not parents – they are law enforcers and their response will be determined by any criminal behaviour perceived to have occurred, no matter how minor (Colvin et al., 2020; Gerard et al., 2019). Yet, police can also exercise discretion in these situations, although research has shown that children in OOHC and Indigenous children are less likely to receive the benefits of such discretion. Increased adoption of diversionary approaches is certainly consistent with the trauma-informed approach we discussed in Chapter 2 when police are called to respond.

Perceptions and attitudes: 'They need to stop putting shit kids in with shit kids in the youth care'

The above quote was provided by one of our junior police respondents and reveals highly negative perceptions of children in OOHC, in particular residential care, by many police officers. Some of the responses from police were based on generalised assumptions about children in care and populist notions of punishment (Deuchar et al., 2015; Richards et al., 2019). Six out of our ten police respondents made comments of this nature, exemplified below in a discussion held among several police respondents. One respondent in the group went so far as to support the reintroduction of corporal punishment: 'Oh, the kid's playing up, there must be something wrong, let's take him and do activities. It's a joke. They should cane them.' (P7) Another observed:

> They should have punishment of some kind, but we've got one youth care that they tried a punishment system where it was like no TV or no phone, but they act out more on that and then the carers just become at risk because then they start assaulting them and they start punching holes in the walls, they start throwing things at them, so there's no system.
>
> (P9)

These negative attitudes and the preference for punitive action were palpable among our junior police respondents, who were more involved in the day-to-day policing of OOHC. One of our senior police respondents contextualised these attitudes by explaining that junior police tend to choose formal interventions over discretion, to initiate AVOs or charges for property damage and assault or to arrest children and refuse bail:

> the system in relation to bail and AVOs for kids in out-of-home care and homeless, that's the only victory young coppers can get.
>
> (P1)

Children's perceptions of police mirror these tensions. Research by the CREATE Foundation, which supports children with care experience, has found that many children feel anxious when interacting with police, both as victims and offenders. There was a general consensus that police did not understand their histories of trauma or support their needs (Tillack et al., 2018). Some of the OOHC respondents gave examples that were consistent with Tillack et al.'s (2018) work. For example, the below quotes speak to the poor relationships between police and children:

> the cop on the street or in the car, who's actually constantly dealing with young people who are telling them to F-off, and causing problems, because those police then become quite cynical, and will just lock the kids up. And let's say, the relationship between those police and the young people doesn't repair; it just, again, it just reinforces what the young people believe about police and what they've been taught about police, and taught about how people of authority can control you.
>
> (OOHC 1)

> Because I've had police say, they're just out-of-home care kids, they're always a nuisance, they can't learn, that's why they're in there.
>
> (OOHC 3)

In contrast, there were some examples of good practice identified by our respondents. One OOHC staff member had had some success working with individual police:

> I had a male policeman – in the police force for about 30 years – and he used to come into my house sort of once a week; just call in. And one day, I was talking away to him, and he had pink nail polish on [laughs]. And I said, 'What on earth are you doing with that?' He said, 'Oh, the girls here just wanted to do my – they were doing their nails, so they've done mine.' That was building a rapport.
>
> (OOHC 1)

This police officer's actions are emblematic of the relationship building that is required to improve relationships with children in care and Indigenous communities (Davis, 2019; NSW Govt & NSW Police Force, 2018). Where the OOHC respondents offered positive examples of police interactions with children, they related them to building relationships and consideration of children's histories, which are both integral to a trauma-informed response (Bateson et al., 2020; Gillespie-Smith et al., 2020; Ko et al., 2008).

Children with care experience, particularly Indigenous children, may have complex and negative experiences of police from an early age, complicating their response to police. Indigenous communities have experienced generations of exposure to trauma and this generates distrust and fear of law enforcement figures (ALRC, 2018; Willis, 2011). This is intensified when children themselves experience removal and placement in the care system. Additionally, police may be involved in child protection and domestic violence interventions with children as victims and then later encounter these same children in care.

Police expectations of children's respect and 'manners'

The police respondents expected children to treat them with respect. This concept of respect seemed to relate more to social etiquette rather than not engaging in offending behaviour:

> The young person [needs to be] taught manners, taught how to dress appropriately, taught how to talk to somebody face-to-face.
>
> (P2)

One officer noted that bail conditions for children will often include a condition to follow the 'reasonable directions' of a parent or carer, and these could relate to curfews but also to demonstrating 'manners'. Failure to adhere to this condition could result in bail being breached and punitive consequences for the child:

> I don't care necessarily if you're in a group home or a normal home, the bail conditions would probably be the same. We just want someone in authority to take care of you, make sure you do the right thing. So if they're in a group home, you live at that group home, with that carer, and you obey the reasonable directions of the carer. So if they say make your bed – and I explain it to the young person – a reasonable direction – be home for dinner; a reasonable direction – make your bed, clean your room. I'll explain those exact same bail conditions to someone who was living at home with their parents. Obey your parents. If your mum says you need to be at school, you're at school. If your mum says I want you to make a sandwich for lunch, that's reasonable. Go and clean your room up, make your bed – same conditions. To me it makes no difference.
>
> (P5)

The examples of 'reasonable directions' given by this respondent include things like 'making a sandwich' and 'making their bed', but failure to do so can result in a breach of bail conditions. While this approach seems extreme, our previous research (Gerard et al., 2019) identifies clear examples of just this sort of escalation – for instance, a case where a child refused to follow the direction of a carer to get out of bed, so police were called and the child spent time in custody. In this example, we question whether the reasonable directions were, in fact, reasonable given the child's likely past exposure to trauma. Further, children may not be capable of following all directions, for example, where they have an intellectual disability or cognitive impairment (Greig et al., 2019). Given that many bail conditions or conditions attached to AVOs contain similar language, such as 'obey reasonable directions', this can escalate matters unnecessarily via the reporting of breaches.

Re-traumatising through police contact

The discussion so far has identified that the perceptions of the police respondents of children from OOHC are characterised by punitive attitudes and unrealistic expectations of children's behaviour. Juxtaposed with these responses and attitudes is that police frequently interact with children from residential care, as highlighted at the start of this chapter:

> Because even the most junior police officer has probably been out there very early on in their career … you're probably out there day one on the job, so you get a really good feel for them, right off the bat.
>
> (P5)

Where frequent contact is coupled with a lack of understanding, interactions with police may trigger trauma responses by children.

> You get some, you know, new constables that don't have any stripes yet who, sort of, don't have too much of an understanding of, you know, the trauma background … And so the police officers don't have too much knowledge around that which a lot of them don't, he blurted out in the conversation, 'So where's your mum and dad, mate?'
>
> (OOHC 5)

On this subject, the OOHC staff member noted the impact that a lack of police understanding about care-experienced children had on children's behaviour:

> what the police say to the young people can have a severe impact on their behaviours for the next few weeks.
>
> (OOHC 5)

Some of our police respondents did recognise the importance of understanding a child's history and being aware of their trauma background. One respondent not only showed a clear awareness but also highlighted the lack of support for police in these situations:

> Yeah, they definitely need ongoing counselling, and [*pause*] interaction with psychiatrists, I think, a lot of them, yeah. They need their problems spoken about and dealt with by professionals who can help them. Yeah, because they're put in these homes, and they just – they go a bit stir-crazy, and then we're the last stop to help them, and we're not trained in mental health or that side of things. We're not social workers. We only deal with the criminal side of whatever they've done. So, we only see them in a bad light; we can't help them with any psychological problems they've got.
>
> (P6)

Despite recognising the trauma backgrounds of children in OOHC, this respondent still did not feel equipped to respond appropriately to children and saw the prevalence of negative police attitudes towards such children. This suggests that trauma-informed policing needs to go beyond recognition of trauma – building relationships adds another layer to an effective trauma-informed response. While there are different opinions on what trauma-informed policing should look like, common themes emerge from the evidence base such as the importance of recognition and consideration of trauma backgrounds and building relationships (Bateson et al., 2020; Davis, 2019; Gillespie-Smith et al, 2020; Ko et al., 2008). Further, building relationships is required by the ASD.

It is clear from P6's above comment that he did not feel that police were adequately prepared when interacting with children with trauma backgrounds despite frequent contact. Our OOHC respondents, recognising this inadequacy, also felt that police needed more specific training on trauma-informed service provision:

> there should be specific trauma-informed care training for police officers who are on the frontline or custody managers who process these kids.
>
> (OOHC 5)

The ASD indicates that 'Working with Aboriginal Community Training' needs to include foundational knowledge for officers to better understand 'the trauma and intergenerational grief suffered by Aboriginal communities' (NSW Government & NSW Police Force, 2018, p. 14), especially among women and children. A key aim of the strategy is to reduce the over-representation of Aboriginal young people in custody and it recommends a number of actions, including providing resources to officers in relation to 'Indigenous mental health, youth suicide and child abuse' (NSW Government & NSW Police Force, 2018, p. 18) and improving the safety and well-being of Indigenous youth through targeted youth at risk programs. However, the ASD falls short in failing to recognise or commit to provide any formal training in relation to the underlying causes of and responses to Indigenous childhood trauma and cognitive impairments such as Foetal Alcohol Spectrum Disorder (FASD), or community-based intergenerational healing models like those outlined in the *Working together: Aboriginal and Torres Strait Islander mental health and wellbeing principles and practice* (Atkinson et al., 2014). Training for police also needs to include conceptualisations and mechanisms for trauma-informed practice, how to build relationships and how to account for trauma histories when interacting with care-experienced children. Policy development in this space could look at police agencies internationally that have taken a trauma-informed approach, such as the Ayrshire police division in Scotland (Gillespie-Smith et al., 2020).

Children missing from care

Our prior research findings indicate that inadequate or inappropriate police responses to children who go missing in care can have serious consequences (Colvin et al., 2018), and other recent research shows the problem persists (McFarlane, 2021; Queensland Family and Child Commission, 2016). A recent inquiry, the latest of many, found that there was still great concern around the high number of children going missing from care and the responses to missing persons reports (Commission for Children and Young People, Victoria, 2021). Australian Federal Police data reveal that although children in OOHC represent approximately 1% of the child population, over half of all missing children reports are from OOHC (McFarlane, 2021).

Our research demonstrates that police frustration with the OOHC population can lead to inaction or inappropriate responses to children going missing from care. One of our Juvenile Justice respondents exemplified this, recounting a particular area where children were experiencing increased contact with police because of frequent callouts for going missing, saying: 'Other (police) stations we have where their approach is pretty clear on enforcement only, and getting young people off the streets. That's probably the extent of their – I guess, their approach to the issue' (JJ4).

There are many reasons children go missing from care. For instance, it can be because they do not want to return to their placement, and often this is when children self-place back with family or kin. Yet, children who leave their residential care placement in an attempt to self-place with family or friends are seen as being without appropriate accommodation, leading to the court refusing bail or setting accommodation requirements pursuant to section 28 of the *Bail Act 2013* (NSW). In the absence of suitable accommodation being found, the child will remain in custody. One lawyer respondent gave the following example:

> We have another young person who just last week said, 'I don't want bail if you make me go back there', so he's in custody – no further offending. He just wants to live with his nan. He is refusing to go back to the placement and he said, 'I'll just stay in custody until you get me a different place', so there are kids that are completely disengaged from their placement. They don't want to go back there so it doesn't matter how good the placement is or how hard they work or what plans they've got in place – if the kid does not want to be there at all.
>
> (L6)

This child preferred to stay in custody rather than return to his OOHC placement. Yet, his desire to live with his nan could result in him being a flight risk for bail and being detained in custody. Clearly, this is not an appropriate reason for a child to be held in custody and contravenes key principles about incarceration as a last resort (as set out in the *Convention on the Rights of the Child*). For Indigenous children, a desire to return to Country and kin (Davis, 2019) results in frequent missing persons reports; AFP data reveal that one-third of children missing in OOHC were Indigenous. Additionally, 85% of all Indigenous missing children were in OOHC at the time (McFarlane, 2021). This places Indigenous children at increased risk of police contact and consequently of being in breach of bail conditions (Colvin et al., 2018; Richards et al., 2019).

Our research found that when care-experienced children went missing it was not uncommon for this to be perceived as offending behaviour by our police and OOHC respondents (Colvin et al., 2018). The challenge for policing practice is how to respond to missing children in a way that ensures their safety but does not result in criminalisation. While children may self-place or simply be absent from their placement for a time, they may come to harm during this period of absence from OOHC. Further, there are instances when children go missing because they are at risk of harm or have already been harmed. How police respond is crucial – interacting with children who have self-placed but are not immediately at risk of harm may lead to an unnecessary escalation of incidents; yet not responding at all may mean a child is not receiving help when it is needed. Successive inquiries in Australia (Commission for Children and Young People, Victoria, 2021; Queensland Family and Child Commission, 2016) and overseas (Jay, 2014) show that when children go missing from residential care there is often an inadequate or inappropriate response, and children have heightened exposure to the risk of criminal and sexual exploitation (Shaw & Greenhow, 2021). In the United Kingdom, Jay's (2014) *Independent Inquiry into Child Sexual Exploitation in Rotherham* into the serious abuse of children indicated that the inadequate response of agencies, including police, resulted in serious harm and death for children in OOHC. The inquiry found that almost two-thirds of children victimised had more than one missing person report and police had failed to act when children at risk were reported missing and often treated child victims with 'contempt' (p. 7).

In our court observations, we saw an example of how an inappropriate response to a young person going missing escalated to time spent in custody. Fourteen-year-old 'Lila' argued with her grandmother and subsequently went missing from her family home. The result of this missing persons report was Lila's appearance in court with charges of resisting arrest and assaulting a police officer. When Lila was found by police, she was taken to the police station and detained there for over an hour while her family were contacted. She tried to leave, but the police refused to let her go. She swore at the officer and pushed past to exit the room she was detained in, resulting in the charges. As a consequence of her being charged, her family advised police that they did not want her to come home and she, therefore, became homeless and entered the child protection system. The magistrate presiding over Lila's case was clear that this police response was inappropriate and questioned whether police had the right to detain her when she had not committed any offence at the time she was brought into the police station:

> These charges originally came before the court because she was a missing person. She came into police custody, waited a long time and went to leave. Police stopped her. In effect I am being asked to detain her because of that charge alone and because her parents have not taken responsibility for her or allowed anyone else to give her accommodation … It's not a concern under the Bail Act, I'm not even sure there has been an offence. Did police have an entitlement to detain her?
>
> (Case 9, Day 5)

This case also illustrated the difficulties missing children can face when attempting to secure bail. Parental consent is needed for children under 16 years of age to be placed in a youth refuge. This consent is not required if formal steps are taken to place the child in OOHC. Lila's family wished to 'teach her a lesson' by refusing to let her return home and refused her placement in a youth refuge. Lila spent one night in custody after being refused police bail and was then effectively homeless, facing continued time in custody under section 28 of the *Bail Act 2013* until appropriate accommodation could be found for her. When informed that FACS's intervention would be limited as the agency could do little in the two days before the matter was to return to court, the magistrate's response was unequivocal:

> That's crap, under the law they have a statutory responsibility, it's FACS's cheap way of getting out of situations … Because her parents failed her, I am granting unconditional bail. You are free to go.
>
> (Case 9, Day 5)

Police were responding to Lila as a missing child, but subsequent events resulted in her being charged with offences against police. The matter was adjourned to a later date and Lila was free to leave, though she was still without any accommodation.

Our magistrate respondents observed that breaches of court orders and bail often result from children going missing. As one magistrate commented:

> Most of the breach action that I take is for non-compliance with supervision orders. They ... go missing and hence don't attend the appointments.
>
> (M3)

The consequences of taking children into custody when they are self-placing or absent from their placement cannot be underestimated. In Lila's case, the consequences were severe, resulting in serious charges where she had no record of offending, time in custody and insecure housing previously.

Conclusion

This chapter presents the analysis of our data that focuses on police practice and police interactions with children with care experience. The punitive attitudes of police combined with their unrealistic expectations of children contributed to poor interactions and an escalation of criminal justice responses. Despite the frequency of call-outs to residential care, our data indicate that police do not have an adequate awareness of the trauma backgrounds of the children they interact with, even when they do show some awareness of the chaos of the residential care environment. Our analysis reveals that police are used as a behaviour management tool in the OOHC system and that this, coupled with the frequent call-outs, results in feelings of frustration towards the children and their carers. The consequence of using police as a behaviour management tool is an escalation from what should have been an appropriate response from carers to criminal charges, illustrating the processes of criminalisation. These incidents damage inter-agency relationships, further compounding the already poor communication between police and carers and negatively impacting police attitudes towards children and carers. These problems challenge the ability of police to develop positive relationships with children in OOHC – a factor that is key to a trauma-informed response. When children go missing from care, all these factors are crystallised, leading to children being criminalised for going missing and/or not receiving police assistance when needed. Despite the ASD setting out a clear pathway for appropriate policing of Indigenous children, our research demonstrates that these principles are not always adopted in policing practice. Criticisms of the ASD note that despite setting out these evidence-based principles, the document is not clear on how this is to be translated into practice through ongoing training and support for officers.

References

Atkinson, J., Nelson, J., Brooks, R., Atkinson, C., & Ryan, K. (2014). Addressing individual and community transgenerational trauma. In P. Dudgeon, H. Milroy, & R. Walker (Eds.) *Working together: Aboriginal and Torres Strait Islander mental health and wellbeing principles and practice* (pp. 289–306). Commonwealth of Australia.

Australian Government. (2017). *Royal Commission into the detention and protection of children in the northern territory: Final report.* https://www.royalcommission.gov.au/royal-commission-detention-and-protection-children-northern-territory

Australian Law Reform Commission. (2018). *Pathways to justice: Inquiry into the incarceration rate of Aboriginal and Torres Strait Islander peoples.* ALRC Report 133, 2018.

Bail Act 2013 (NSW). https://legislation.nsw.gov.au/view/html/inforce/current/act-2013-026

Bateson, K., McManus, M., & Johnson, G. (2020). Understanding the use, and misuse, of adverse childhood experiences (ACEs) in trauma-informed policing. *The Police Journal, 93*(2), 131–145. https://doi.org/10.1177/0032258X19841409

Colvin, E., Gerard, A., & McGrath, A. (2020). *Children in out-of-home care and the criminal justice system: A mixed-method study.* Australian Institute of Criminology.

Colvin, E., McFarlane, K., Gerard, A., & McGrath, A. (2018). 'We don't do measure and quotes': How agency responses criminalise and endanger the safety of children missing in care in New South Wales, Australia. *The Howard Journal of Crime and Justice, 57*(2), 231–249.

Commission for Children and Young People, Victoria. (2021). *Out of sight: Systemic inquiry into children and young people who are absent or missing from residential care.* State Government of Victoria.

Convention on the Rights of the Child. https://www.ohchr.org/en/instruments-mechanisms/instruments/convention-rights-child

Cunneen, C. (2001). *Conflict, politics and crime: Aboriginal communities and the police.* Allen and Unwin.

Cunneen, C. (2006). Racism, discrimination and the over-representation of Indigenous people in the criminal justice system: Some conceptual and explanatory issues. *Current Issues in Criminal Justice, 17*(3), 329–346.

Davis, M. (2019). *Family is Culture: Review report.* Independent Review of Aboriginal Children in OOHC.

Deuchar, R., Miller, J., & Barrow, M. (2015). Breaking down barriers with the usual suspects: Findings from a research-informed intervention with police, young people and residents in the west of Scotland. *Youth Justice, 15*(1), 57–75. https://doi.org/10.1177/1473225414530538

Finnane, M. (1994). *Police and government: Histories of policing in Australia.* Oxford University Press.

Gerard, A., McGrath, A., Colvin, E., & McFarlane, K. (2019). 'I'm not getting out of bed!': The criminalisation of young people in residential care. *Australian and New Zealand Journal of Criminology, 52*(1), 76–93 http://journals.sagepub.com/doi/full/10.1177/0004865818778739

Gillespie-Smith, K., Brodie, Z., Collins, K., Deacon, K., & Goodall, K. (2020). *Moving towards trauma-informed policing: An exploration of police officers' attitudes and perceptions towards Adverse Childhood Experiences (ACEs)*. Scottish Institute for Policing Research.

Gillfeather-Spetere, S. (2019). From pursuit to progress: Critical reflections on concepts of young people and crime in Australia. *Current Issues in Criminal Justice*, *31*(1), 111–121.

Greig, H., McGrath, A., & McFarlane, K. (2019). 'Taking the wheels off': Young people with cognitive impairment in out-of-home care. *Psychiatry, Psychology and Law*, *26*(6), 920–937. https://doi.org/10.1080/13218719.2019.1644249

Howard League. (2017). *Criminalisation of children in residential care should be 'a national concern'*.

Human Rights and Equal Opportunity Commission. (1997). *Bringing Them Home: Report of the national inquiry into the separation of Aboriginal and Torres Strait Islander children from their families*. Commonwealth of Australia.

Hunter, K. (2022). 'Out of place': The criminalisation of black and minority ethnic looked after children in England and Wales. *Prison Service Journal*, *258*, 13–18.

Jay, A. (2014). *Independent inquiry into child sexual exploitation in Rotherham 1997–2013*. Rotherham Metropolitan Borough Council.

Johnston, E. (1991). *Royal commission into aboriginal deaths in custody: National report, volume 1*. Australian Government Publishing Service.

Ko, S. J., Ford, J. D., Kassam-Adams, N., Berkowitz, S. J., Wilson, C., Wong, M., Brymer, M. J., & Layne, C. M. (2008). Creating trauma-informed systems: Child welfare, education, first responders, health care, juvenile justice. *Professional Psychology: Research and Practice, 39*(4), 396–404. https://doi.org/10.1037/0735-7028.39.4.396

Laming, H. (2016). *In care, out of trouble: How the life chances of children in care can be transformed by protecting them from unnecessary involvement in the criminal justice system*. Prison Reform Trust.

Luke, G., & Cunneen, C. (1995). *Aboriginal over-representation and discretionary decisions in the NSW juvenile justice system*. Juvenile Justice Advisory Council of NSW.

McFarlane, K. (2021). *Children and youth reported missing from out-of-home-care in Australia: A review of the literature and analysis of Australian police data*. Report for Australian Federal Police.

Mendes, P., Michell, D., & Wilson, J. (2014). Young people transitioning from out-of-home care and access to higher education: A critical review of the literature. *Children Australia, 39*(4), 243–252. https://doi.org/10.1017/cha.2014.25

Moore, T., McArthur, M., Death, J., Tilbury, C., & Roche, S. (2017). Young people's views on safety and preventing abuse and harm in residential care: 'It's got to be better than home'. *Children and Youth Services Review*, *81*, 212–219.

New South Wales Government & NSW Police Force. (2018). *Aboriginal strategic direction 2018–2023*. https://www.police.nsw.gov.au/safety_and_prevention/your_community/aboriginal_persons_and_communities/aboriginal_issues/aboriginal_strategic_direction

New South Wales Parliament. (2014). *Family response to the murders in Bowraville*. Legislative Council Standing Committee on Law and Justice.

Queensland Family and Child Commission. (2016). *When a child is missing: Remembering Tiahleigh*.

Richards, K., Cross, C., & Dwyer, A. (2019) Police perceptions of young people: A qualitative analysis. *Police Practice and Research*, *20*(4), 360–375. https://doi.org/10.1080/15614263.2018.1428899

Shaw, J., & Greenhow, S. (2021). Professional perceptions of the care-crime connection: Risk, marketisation and a failing system. *Criminology & Criminal Justice*, *21*(4), 472–488. https://doi.org/10.1177/1748895819877441

Sturma, M. (1987). Policing the criminal frontier in mid-nineteenth-century Australia, Britain and America. In M. Finnane (Ed.) *Policing in Australia: Historical perspectives* (pp. 15–34). New South Wales University Press.

Tillack, K., Raineri, T., Cahill, A., & McDowell, J. (2018). *Youth justice report: Consultation with young people in out-of-home care about their experiences with police, courts and detention*. CREATE Foundation.

Warner, B., Spivak, B., Ashford, L., Fix, R., Ogloff, J., & Shepherd S. (2022). The impact of offender–victim cultural backgrounds on the likelihood of receiving diversion. *Criminal Justice Policy Review*, *33*(3), 298–316. https://doi.org/10.1177/08874034211046313

Willis, M. (2011). Non-disclosure of violence in Australian Indigenous communities. *Trends and issues in crime and criminal justice*, *405*(January 2011), 4–10. Australian Institute of Criminology.

5 Lawyers, cultural competence and advising children with care experience

Introduction

Lawyers play a significant role in advising and representing Indigenous and non-Indigenous children with care experience who come into contact with the criminal justice system. This chapter analyses our interview, file review and court observation data to capture a small slice of how lawyers interact with children in care, many of whom are Aboriginal and Torres Strait Islander children. We interviewed 14 legal practitioners currently working in specialist youth and children's organisations responsible for delivering legal services to children in care or with care experience in NSW. In NSW, Legal Aid has a specialist Children's Legal Service (CLS) that can advise and represent children and young people on criminal matters and AVOs, and CLS lawyers are attached to some of the Children's Court locations around the state. Beyond the CLS, legal aid is provided to children through private solicitors or other community legal centres, and via the Aboriginal Legal Service (ALS) (NSW Legal Aid, 2019a). The ALS is a specialist legal service for Aboriginal people in NSW established by advocates to address racism and to embody self-determination (Green, 2020).

Although small, our interview cohort included respondents located in regional ($n = 2$), outer metropolitan ($n = 7$) and metropolitan ($n = 5$) NSW. None of our respondents identified as Indigenous. Only two of the lawyer respondents we interviewed were also representing children in care in matters we observed in the Children's Court. The bulk of respondents were recruited by contacting organisations and inviting participation in our study. Perhaps on account of this research design, we may have attracted interview respondents already knowledgeable about the involvement of those with care-experience in the criminal justice system. All our interview respondents demonstrated an acute awareness of the challenges facing children with care experience and the tense relationships between OOHC providers and police in the criminalisation process. The respondents we interviewed saw themselves as drivers of change and provided examples of how their interventions had ameliorated some of the challenges facing children in OOHC or with care experience. As we explore in this chapter, there was a disparity

DOI: 10.4324/9781003093367-6

between the understanding demonstrated during our interviews and what we observed of lawyers in Children's Court proceedings. In the matters we observed, lawyers often demonstrated a lack of sensitivity, cultural competence or understanding of the impact of trauma and offered incomplete and partial representations of a child's personal history. This is a pattern that emerged across all our analyses.

In this chapter, we start by outlining the concept of trauma-informed lawyering (Katz & Haldar, 2016) before moving to an exploration of lawyers' understanding of care-experienced children. We then analyse how trauma-informed approaches were conceptualised and implemented by the legal practitioners we spoke to and/or observed in Children's Court proceedings. Cultural competence is critical to trauma-informed lawyering in the Australian context. In our final section, we analyse the data collected on the cultural competence of legal professionals representing Indigenous care-experienced children in the criminal justice system. Cultural competence relates to a lawyer's professional capability to provide appropriate and effective legal representation for Indigenous children in the criminal justice system. We reiterate that Indigenous cultural competence is not a one-off learned skill. Rather, it constitutes a lifelong journey of informing one's professional capability to respond to the cultural difference of Indigenous peoples and communities (Ranzijn et al., 2008). Our findings highlight a lack of appropriate services for Aboriginal people and a dearth of culturally situated background information reaching those who are making decisions in the NSW Children's Court.

Lawyers and trauma

Many lawyers are exposed to trauma in their everyday work (James, 2020). As James writes, certain lawyers, including criminal lawyers, may be particularly affected due to their exposure to traumatised clients or fact-scenarios, and this can negatively affect their well-being and effectiveness. The concept of 'trauma-informed lawyering' is said to be having a significant impact on how lawyers deliver services to traumatised populations (see Katz & Haldar, 2016). Trauma-informed lawyering is about the client, the institution and it is also about the self-care of lawyers as practitioners (Katz & Haldar, 2016). Trauma-informed lawyering is defined by Katz and Haldar (2016, p. 361) as follows:

> 'Trauma-informed practice' is an increasingly prevalent approach in the delivery of therapeutic services, social and human services, and now legal practice. Put simply, the hallmarks of trauma-informed practice are when the practitioner … puts the realities of the clients' trauma experiences at the forefront in engaging with clients and adjusts the practice approach informed by the individual client's trauma experience. Trauma-informed practice also encompasses the practitioner

employing modes of self-care to counterbalance the effect the client's trauma experience may have on the practitioner.

Being trauma-informed involves understanding the impact of trauma and working to reduce the possibility of re-traumatisation (Katz & Haldar, 2016). On this basis, this approach lends itself to the context of working with care-experienced children. It is particularly relevant in the context of Australia where the continuing impact of colonisation has resulted in the prevalence of intergenerational trauma for Aboriginal and Torres Strait Islander people (see Atkinson et al., 2010).

Katz and Haldar (2016) and Katz (2019) explore what trauma-informed practice means for lawyers representing children in the child welfare system. While arguably the concept of trauma-informed practice has been more influential in occupations such as social work for some time, Katz (2019) notes that it is still relatively new for legal practitioners. It is argued by Katz and Haldar (2016, p. 362) that recognising the impact of trauma on clients' behaviour and actions is imperative to providing effective representation (see also American Bar Association, 2014; Patten & Kraemer, 2013). Both Peña (2019) and Katz and Haldar (2016) argue that trauma-informed lawyering should be taught to all law students and that ongoing education and resources for practising lawyers are needed.

Katz and Haldar (2016, pp. 359–360) identify four key aspects of trauma-informed lawyering: 'identifying trauma, adjusting client–attorney relationship, adapting litigation strategy, and preventing vicarious trauma'. A shift in legal practice is required, particularly in terms of the types of questions asked by legal counsel of their clients and an awareness of how trauma affects behaviour and responses to stressful situations, such as arrest and incarceration. Tailoring legal work to clients' specific needs can help advocates raise issues that may otherwise be ignored, such as why a client may have been in a heightened state during an incident related to the court hearing; or asking questions that highlight the underlying reasons for a problem, such as why a client may keep absconding from a residential care setting.

Advocacy work in the United Kingdom has examined the role that lawyers play in advocating for care-experienced children, particularly in police custody (Howard League, 2019). The Howard League released a step-by-step guide for lawyers representing looked-after children at police stations (Howard League, 2019). The guide provides information for lawyers of children with care experience, canvassing key statistical information, background to the criminalisation process, information about trauma and other relevant issues that may present in their clients and advice on how to interact effectively and positively with care-experienced children. The guide recognises that children in care may have experienced trauma and provides specific advice on their needs and alerts lawyers to the potential for unnecessary criminalisation.

Our research indicates that few resources exist in the NSW context in terms of materials to support lawyers representing care-experienced children in the criminal justice system. To illustrate, Callander et al. (2020) produced the *Care and protection: Working with children, a guide to best practice for legal representatives* for Legal Aid, an excellent guide on the impact of trauma and on relationship-building for lawyers working with children in the care and protection jurisdiction. An earlier report by NSW Legal Aid showed that criminal law solicitors were readily identifying the criminalisation of children in OOHC (Gough, 2011). The *Bugmy Bar Book* (2019), a guide for lawyers and judges, now contains a section on OOHC, but more resources and culturally situated supports for children are required. We return to this discussion below in the context of analysing data on cultural competence.

Our interviews with lawyer respondents did not ask about Katz and Haldar's four aspects of trauma-informed lawyering as we were not aware of these authors' work at the time of the interviews. As a result, in what follows, we put together our respondents' views on the characteristics of children in care in the criminal justice system and the factors contributing to their over-representation, alongside our file reviews and observations of Children's Court proceedings. While this will not speak directly to the anatomy of trauma-informed lawyering, it will provide a snapshot of the integration of some aspects of trauma-informed approaches in the NSW context.

Lawyers' understanding of care-experienced children and criminalisation

The lawyer respondents we interviewed provided many examples of trauma and complexity in the lives of their care-experienced clients. All lawyer respondents recognised that care-experienced children display challenging behaviour as a result of experiences of considerable trauma and disadvantage, including cognitive impairments. Most also articulated to us how a residential care environment exacerbates the already significant challenges facing children in care. As one respondent described:

> So, they have complex needs as a result of their exposure or their experience of very traumatic events in their life. So whether that be sexual assault or whatever and that comes with all the literature and social sciences around child adolescent behaviour and the impact that that has on attachment and of course that then, I guess – it's symptomatic then through all these very difficult or challenging behaviours that arise from their traumatic experiences. So it's that continuum… They're then all pumped out together and placed in a house with other strangers and those strangers will happen to have the same sort of complex needs as they do or challenging behaviours and then you're stuck in this resi care system where you've got workers who may not be that skilled. You've got a sector that's not that developed in terms of a therapeutic care framework.
>
> (L1)

This lawyer respondent referred to the underdeveloped therapeutic care framework, as is discussed in Chapters 2 and 3, and the significant impact of this that results in criminalisation. Other examples of trauma and trauma responses were described by our lawyer respondents and included sexual and physical assault, and drug and alcohol use (L6, L10, L11). Vividly, one lawyer respondent told us that 'it would be the exception that you saw a kid come in that didn't come from a background of horror' (L10).

In our interviews, the lawyer respondents demonstrated a significant understanding of trauma and how it impacts the behaviour and responses of children with care experience. Two of our legal respondents (interviewed together) explained:

> So, they're – a lot of them have probably diagnosed mental health problems. A lot of them have what I would call a behavioural disability, so that they're not just 'little shits', they actually have something which is really almost, or sometimes entirely beyond their control, but instead of being treated as somebody who needs support for a disability, or they need trauma counselling, or whatever, they're just sort of criminalised.
>
> (L4)

As this respondent observed, children are presenting with complex needs and are being criminalised for certain behaviours rather than receiving therapeutic support. The shorthand ascribed to their behaviour is 'little shits', which implies a dismissive approach and very little effort to understand the contextual factors impacting the child's behaviour.

It was felt by our lawyer respondents that it is important to understand trauma so as not to misrepresent this cohort as akin to any other group of young people who might be characterised as simply pushing boundaries (L1). This is a discrete cohort of young people with complex needs and problematic responses to them result in an escalation of legal issues and further criminalisation. A clear finding of our study relates to the use of police as a behavioural management tool (Gerard et al., 2019; see Chapter 4). The lawyer respondents we interviewed observed OOHC service providers using police to show care-experienced children that there are 'consequences' for their behaviour. For instance:

> We had a matter in court where the house manager has gone on record saying, 'We wanted to teach her consequences. Like, she needs to know consequences', and … she has a cognitive impairment. She's got a moderate intellectual disability. This is not teaching her a lesson. She had no prior criminal history up until residing in this particular house and so it's stuff like that. So it's this idea that we're going to teach consequences.
>
> (L1)

In this example, a child with cognitive impairment is brought into the criminal justice system and now has a police record. The behaviour of the OOHC service provider is seemingly benevolent – intended to help the child understand the consequences of their actions (in the form of legal consequences). As well as making clear the connection between residential care and processes of criminalisation, this example also highlights the stark vulnerability of children in OOHC. In contrast, a child who behaves similarly in their own home is unlikely to face the same 'legal' consequences. Moreover, this case demonstrates an unwillingness on the part of OOHC service providers to adjust their response to accommodate an identified cognitive impairment. The expectations for the child are inappropriate and ultimately harmful. Rather than rely on law enforcement, other mechanisms for teaching consequences should be utilised.

Another lawyer respondent recalled some of the clients he had represented and their complex needs and trauma backgrounds that played a role in bringing them into police custody:

> On Wednesday when there were those two kids who went into custody, the one kid had a list of conditions of schizophrenia, autism, bipolar, a cognitive impairment where his capacity was anything from – his mother thought between age three and seven, the carer thought maybe 10, and then … also anxiety and depression, that was his raft of issues. And the next kid that came in, also in custody, right after that was for – was a kid that suffered from foetal alcohol spectrum disorder and autism, I mean, those are probably the highest ends of it, the most clear cases but, yeah, I mean, trauma is in every kid that comes before our court.
>
> (L10)

As evident in other interview responses, this respondent attests to the high level of disability and trauma among the children coming into custody. The respondent went on to explain how factors such as intellectual disability compound the legal challenges facing children and can contribute to further victimisation and exploitation:

> So, let's just give you one example. So, she's got an intellectual disability. She was raped in primary school at 10 years of age by her teacher. She has been on the run with a mother who has autism and can't figure out how to get support services for her, mum doesn't have the skill set. She then got pregnant at 16/17 through sexual assault, had two children, both of them were removed to mum. She's not allowed to stay with mum because she's now moving with the methamphetamine crowd out here. Because she's got an intellectual disability she's a perfect courier and so she can't go home to mum because mum has got her children. She's got an intellectual disability, she can't read or write, she's being trafficked

> like a little drug mule around the local community, she's homeless, she's got her own addiction and I'm trying to link her into the NDIS [National Disability Insurance Scheme] system and I ring the lady and she says, 'Oh, she needs to fill in a form and I need a client number' … I end up getting the form filled out and the client number and then can't find her. She's now disengaged. The most vulnerable person I know in this community does not have an allocated case worker on the NDIS scheme.
>
> (L10)

The fraught context for the child and their family is plainly articulated by this lawyer. The victimisation and the inability to access support services – health, legal and other community supports – are mapped out. Ultimately, in this case, the lawyer respondent had to battle with administrative hurdles and, by that point, they had lost contact with a person with a significant need for the services offered by NDIS. As we know, children and adults with cognitive impairments are over-represented in the criminal justice system (Baldry et al., 2015). Further, women with cognitive impairment are more likely than men to have a criminal record (Fogden et al., 2016). Greig et al.'s (2019) study in NSW demonstrated that children with cognitive impairments living in OOHC are more likely to be vulnerable to criminal exploitation. Our research clearly illustrates how this occurs and how poorly services respond to people in need.

The lawyer respondents were also aware of 'huge amounts of transience and instability' (L6) among children with care experience, involving movement between multiple schools and placements (L11). A high number of placements has been found to be associated with involvement in the criminal justice system (Davis, 2019; Ryan & Testa, 2005; see also Baidawi & Sheehan, 2019), and an inability to access therapeutic services (Devlin et al., 2022). One lawyer respondent stated that children with care experience tend to form deep bonds with other children in care, whom they then go on to offend with (L6). Children with cognitive impairments living in OOHC are typically perceived as having a 'decreased ability … to engage productively in known protective factors' such as pro-social peer groups (Greig et al., 2019, pp. 925–926). For some lawyer respondents, institutional abuse compounded pre-existing trauma: 'The solutions [placing children in OOHC] have proved to be equally as damaging as the original trauma' (L11).

Our data included examples of lawyers being involved in house-level negotiation as a means of de-escalating situations and reducing the need to involve police (L1). For instance, in one case, this informal approach was thought to be having a significant positive impact:

> So this 13-year-old person I'm talking about – their [lawyer] worked directly with [their OOHC service provider] about how do carers

> respond to this young person when things happen with the LAC – so we set up a meeting with the LAC about this young person and the service provider about what's going on for him and how we can deal with him differently when things do arise in the care home. So you can imagine how significant an impact that would have. Then when he moved from – so that started to have an impact then he moved to the [suburban] LAC with [OOHC provider] and we started seeing him come back a few times because [suburb] wasn't aware of it, so then the [lawyer] started doing that all over again, you know – meet up with [suburban] LAC – talk to them about the young person – meet with the service provider – work on the big plan, and you can really start seeing it having an effect.
>
> (L6)

We note that this is an interventionist approach, which is not without its challenges. For example, it can be time-consuming and needs all parties to be willing to participate. However, other respondents agreed that having an independent advocate for young people to assist them to negotiate the challenges that arise when living in these institutions is of considerable value:

> I always think – and I thought it a lot when I was in criminal law, is that young people, when dealing with these services, whether it's FACS or NGOs, they need an advocate … doesn't have to be a legal advocate, just someone reasonable on their side because … the young people are often really badly behaved and so forth, they're not angels, but, the way that they're treated, it's passive aggressive and just the institutional mucking you around – different providers saying different things, told you can go and see your family on the weekend and then it's cancelled at the last minute and then someone else says you can go and then someone's – different things being said at different times and just messing with their minds.
>
> (L3)

The advocacy work described above was intended to manage the inconsistent approaches to children, establish behavioural management plans to support the child as well as manage the responses of some OOHC staff (L3). Another lawyer respondent reported a marked difference between the approach to a child's behaviour taken by regional managers of residential care services and house managers (L3). In particular, the regional managers, who were not involved with children at a day-to-day level, unlike house managers, tended to have a more theoretical understanding of behaviour management and to adopt a more trauma-informed approach. Yet, this was often not evident in the approach adopted by house managers, who have responsibility for the daily care of children.

While the lawyer respondents we interviewed were aware of the impacts of trauma on behaviour and how this led children into the criminal justice system, our observation of court proceedings found little evidence that this understanding was shared by legal practitioners in court. The next section will analyse the data collected from our file reviews and court observations.

Lawyers, care experience and court

Our file reviews and court observations revealed that it was not uncommon for the children appearing in the Children's Court to have several pages' worth of criminal history. Critically, most charges were linked to their care experience. As one lawyer respondent explained:

> It's really common that when you get these kids, they might have five or six pages of criminal history, and their prior criminal history is stuff that's occurred in and around this out-of-home care home. The whole – my whole experience of Children's Court, generally, it's really rare to get a client who comes from anything approaching a functional home.
>
> (L3)

The type of offending captured in the lengthy criminal records described above is linked to the residential care setting, marking a clear distinction between children with care experience and those from the non-care cohort. It is worth noting that prior criminal records can result in bail refusal and more serious criminal sanctions if the child is convicted of an offence. In this regard, our file reviews revealed that children with care experience had more extensive criminal records than their non-care counterparts.

We found a marked disparity between our lawyer respondents and the lawyers we saw represent children with care experience in court. In essence, the lawyer respondents interviewed demonstrated significant understanding of the challenges faced by care-experienced children, the nature of their offending and the process of criminalisation, in particular the impact of systemic responses that result in criminalisation. The challenges articulated by the lawyer respondents came alive in our analysis of the files and in our court observations. What we also observed were some concerning approaches taken by legal practitioners to trauma, disability and the complex lives of children in care. We previously described (see Chapter 2) the case of a young boy who was arrested for assaulting his carer after his efforts to reunite with his mother failed. This young boy was subsequently identified as Indigenous by the Juvenile Justice worker we spoke to after his appearance, but this was never referred to in court or noted on his court file. In this young boy's initial court appearance (we observed three in total), we saw a defence lawyer discipline this child, who was 12 at the time and was demonstrably upset. As our case notes detail:

> Case 12 Day 3
>
> Duty Lawyer: [*to the client in a harsh and strict tone*] 'If you are outside the home after 6 pm you will get locked up'. [*To the magistrate*]: 'I'm just making it clear to the young person given his age.'
>
> Boy starts crying.

This type of 'making it clear' came across more as a threat to the child. We were also struck by the lawyer's words, as they seemed to scare the child, who began to cry. The lawyer made no effort to comfort the child, after reiterating the magistrate's decision. There was no support person at court with the child. We observed little in the way of the trauma-informed approaches recommended, such as identifying trauma and adjusting the client relationship accordingly (Katz, 2019; Peña, 2019). This is of particular concern because representatives in the Children's Court are supposed to have additional training, including around how to communicate with children (NSW Legal Aid, 2019b).

Indigenous cultural competence and the professional capability of legal practitioners

Understanding the cultural difference of Indigenous children enables a lawyer to adapt their legal practice to provide a culturally holistic approach when representing Indigenous children. In that sense, there are many overlapping principles between trauma-informed lawyering and cultural competence (Katz, 2019). This section outlines what our data revealed about legal representation for care-experienced children in the Children's Court in relation to the ability of lawyers to represent Indigenous children.

Key inquiries such as the Royal Commission into Aboriginal Deaths in Custody (Johnston, 1991) and the Bowraville Inquiry (New South Wales Legislative Council Standing Committee on Law and Justice, 2014) have highlighted the importance of Indigenous cultural competency for the legal profession. More recently, there has been momentum around cultural competence in law schools to address deficits in the profession (Gainsford et al., 2020; Ranzijn et al., 2008). The NSW Legal Aid *Aboriginal Client Services Strategy 2019–2023* states that 'We will ensure our service provision is culturally competent by offering training to our own lawyers and lawyers on Legal Aid NSW panels and to Women's Domestic Violence Court Advocacy Program staff' (NSW Legal Aid, 2019b).

To some extent, our lawyer respondents acknowledged the cultural complexities of the experiences of Indigenous children in the care and criminal justice system. Some, but by no means all, provided insight into the impact of intergenerational trauma on Indigenous children and the need for professional capabilities to inform culturally informed practices that better meet the specific cultural needs of Indigenous children. For example, L11 said that 'it's not just for me about them having been in care, but in the Aboriginal community you've got Stolen Generation, you've got intergenerational trauma, you've got lateral violence in community'. A lawyer respondent we interviewed felt that Aboriginal young people had more complex needs than other young people in care:

> I think, just because of the sheer number of Aboriginal kids in care, it is definitely a matter that affects them more than it affects other kids – absolutely. And, I think if you are thinking about Aboriginal kids specifically, I think that the disadvantage that they've experienced is probably quite unique compared to other kids – the disconnection from their family. I think Aboriginal kids are much more likely to abscond back to their family, which is not supported by FACS – which often means police are involved a lot more regularly because they're reported as missing persons and they're regularly brought home and then they've got that exposure to the criminal justice system and that is not a fast step to go from that to reporting damage or assault charges. We just had – we've got a 13-year-old young person who is going through Koori Court at the moment who has a 50-page record and every single one of the offences is from the care home and he has spent a significant period of time in custody and it's only now that his offending has drastically decreased, and it is because he got moved to an intensive support service and in fact, it was a different home environment and different carers who had taken a very, very different approach, and that's why it's significantly decreased, but I raised him because the most recent offence – he just got out of custody again on Friday. The most recent offence was because he went to visit his mum. The carers hadn't arranged the visit properly and it didn't go ahead and he was really, really frustrated and basically took it out on the carer – kind of punched him on the arm and made some comments. And, I think that is more likely to happen to Aboriginal kids.
>
> (L5)

The lawyer respondents predominantly demonstrated a deficit approach to understanding Indigenous children residing in OOHC. For example, they spoke of mental health disorders, a history of family and cultural dislocation, physical and mental abuse, childhood neglect, unresolved trauma, homelessness and drug and alcohol use.

Our respondents also recognised that Indigenous children living in OOHC are known to gain more negative attention from police, to have a greater risk of imprisonment and to have more substantial criminal records than their non-Indigenous counterparts. One of the actions that was highlighted in the research as increasing the possibility of police interaction is when Indigenous children abscond from their care environment (which they often do) to seek out family connections. This cycle of 'care' removal reflects many decades of systematic removal of Indigenous children, and

Indigenous leaders have repeatedly called for an overhaul of policy and practice to focus on prevention rather than child removal. Both during and since the introduction of the policies of protection that led to the Stolen Generations, Aboriginal people have continued to resist separation from their families (HREOC, 1997).

The lawyer respondents also discussed ways to address the deficit approach, such as through more effective programming and a focus on building relationships and communication between Aboriginal communities and legal practitioners. These proposed changes can be identified as key to improving attitudes, approaches and the practices of lawyers representing Indigenous children in the criminal justice system:

> This needs to extend to more flexible programs for Aboriginal young people and a focus on building relationships.
>
> I can only speak about Aboriginal children specifically, that I feel like we don't often – feel like we need to have a different approach with Aboriginal children – both the care and within Juvenile Justice, and I think that they try and do that, like there are policies and guidelines put in that are guided by Aboriginal Elders and people in the community. But in my experience, it doesn't feel like that on the ground, especially with Juvenile Justice. They are putting kids in that same box and – I suppose flexibility is the word – not being flexible enough with them, and if you engage these kids in their environment and in their community, and if you get to know their families, you can really achieve a lot with them.
>
> Once you have that relationship with a young person, you can just achieve so much and I think that's the one thing I will say that our lawyers here who start working with our clients, if you get to understand the young person and the families of Aboriginal kids, so where did they come from? – who are their family? – and you build trust with them, they will respond a thousand times better. And the minute they don't trust someone, the minute there's that disconnection and then they just don't respond at all.
>
> (L6)

Further, a lack of resources to fund good programs was seen as a barrier to ensuring self-determination and respecting the sovereign rights of Aboriginal people and families. One respondent raised the importance of self-determination for Aboriginal children:

> The Uluru Statement, that self-determination. I mean, I just feel like we're back – I'm old enough to remember the land rights movement in the 70s, that movement towards self-determination, and I think that the welfare model has overtaken Aboriginal communities and if we can get that back out to them determining what happens within communities, and that's certainly the model that [particular communities] are

> working on with that sort of type of leadership. But there's no funding for those programs.
>
> (L11)

Our lawyer respondents explained that even though there are innovative programs that enable Indigenous communities to assert self-determined community solutions to the high number of Indigenous children in OOHC, which reduce their risk of contact with the criminal justice system, there is the constant challenge of securing sufficient funding for such programs. This raises the juxtaposition or disparity between the cost of placing Indigenous children in OOHC, the cost of delivering legal services and solutions to Indigenous children in the criminal justice system and, in the alternative, the cost of funding culturally situated prevention programs.

In relation to appropriate legal services for Indigenous children, some lawyer respondents expressed concern over what they perceived to be the ignorant and incompetent practices of other lawyers when working with Indigenous children. Areas of concern related to professional attitudes and approaches, including inappropriate cultural communication and racist terminology. One lawyer respondent provided evidence of a legal representative using racist and derogatory terminology when assisting an Indigenous child to complete a legal document:

> Legal Aid asked, 'Are you Aboriginal or Torres Strait Islander?' and the kid was – some of them can hardly read anything – education is another conversation, but the kid said, 'Well, what do I put here?' and the worker said, 'Well, are you an Abo? That's the question', and I was just like – you think they might have been trained a bit to be able to have the conversation … there must be some cultural training that you have to go through I think. But it was just shocking.
>
> (L11)

The language used by the lawyer was highly offensive and inconsistent with a responsive approach to the needs of Indigenous clients. It is hard to imagine how a child could recover from this exchange and provide full instructions to the lawyer to enable them to advocate on the child's behalf. Aboriginal activism in the 1970s led to the establishment of specialist legal services, such as the ALS. The ALS was premised on the key principles of self-determination (ALS, 2021). However, the resources available for lawyers representing children, particularly Indigenous children, are limited and funding for community services – health, legal and support – has been eroded over many years. In a recent evaluation of NSW Legal Aid's Civil Law Service for Aboriginal Communities, Williams and Ragg (2019, p. 15) observed that:

> Aboriginal and Torres Strait Islander communities have experienced countless government programs being established and/or piloted and

> not further funded, with government funding being short-term, and investments being in funding mainstream services rather than developing Aboriginal and Torres Strait Islander workforces and services.

The emphasis on 'mainstreaming' services assumes that Indigenous Australians are better served by services aimed at the whole population (Williams & Ragg, 2019). Our lawyer respondents felt that the lack of specialist services and resources has resulted in a poor experience for both Aboriginal and Torres Strait Islander children and lawyers. They spoke about it being hard to find time to undertake vital work for their clients due to the high volume of cases and systemic pressures. Moreover, the nature of the Children's Court hampered opportunities to build relationships with clients:

> Ideally, I'd love to go out and speak to kids in their house, in their home environment, with their mum, dad, uncle, auntie, around. Find out what's going on. But often it's on a list day, kid comes in, we have a chat for 10 minutes, and I try and tell him as much they can do, but I don't think that's enough.
>
> (L2)

It is extraordinary that relationship-building must occur in a room adjacent to a courtroom, and for only 10 minutes prior to the lawyer representing a child facing criminal charges. Yet that was characterised as the reality of legal practice much of the time.

In some instances, this resulted in the Indigenous status of the child not being disclosed to the court. In several of the cases we observed, there was no mention made of a child's Indigenous status, yet the file indicated that the child did identify as Indigenous. Our case file analysis revealed many inconsistencies in this regard, bringing into question how often Indigenous children are linked with appropriate support and representation. It was not clear from our file analysis whether the children's lawyers were chasing up missing or inaccurate information, or linking their client in with services or whether they even had access to the resources needed to do so.

Our court observations also revealed that the ALS was not always able to provide representation for Indigenous children appearing at court. The ALS is not present at court every day; in one of our locations, the organisation attended two to three days per week. On days when the ALS was not present, the CLS managed unscheduled cases. There were situations where an Indigenous child needed representation on non-ALS days; for example, where a child was brought into custody overnight and a bail hearing was needed the next day. However, access to specialist legal services appeared to be limited for Indigenous children.

One lawyer respondent noted the importance of access to community and that support from positive role models from community is vital for children. As detailed by Davis (2019), it is imperative for Aboriginal children to maintain connections to community and Country, and this is a legislative requirement as per the ACPP:

> 'Cause Aboriginal kids also need to learn about Aboriginal history and community, and white people can tell them about it, but it won't give as much of a connection [*laughter*]. People, like, and they get good role models and they get people – okay, I'm working, I've got a job, I'm doing this house; role models are very important and if they say, well, look, an Aboriginal person can get a job doing that, and you say, well, there's another person working down here and they're working over there, and they've got their house and family and whatever, then they go, well, there's something I can do, rather than I go back to a whole group of people where no-one has a job, or no-one doesn't drink, or no-one doesn't get in trouble. They see it as another option. Yeah. But they also see it as more diversity too, 'cause if you're from [a particular regional area], you tend to only know people from [that area].
>
> (L7)

The requirements around ensuring connection to Country and community are in legislation, yet Davis (2019) identified consistent non-compliance across the NSW sector. We know that connection to community and Country is vital to well-being, yet currently the knowledge-sharing arrangements needed to support this connection are not being supported.

Despite the recognition by the lawyer respondents we interviewed that culturally competent professional practices are essential for positive relationships with Indigenous clients, again we saw a disparity between this view and our court observations of lawyers in practice. In one case, we observed a poor interaction between a lawyer and her young Aboriginal client escalate (Day 4, Case 3; Day 5, Case 2). We saw no evidence of an acknowledgement of cultural difference or a tailored approach to communication with this client during the court proceedings. After hearing her own traumatic lived experience being recounted to the court, the young girl became increasingly distressed. She hid her face in her hands and her lawyer said, 'Are you listening?' in an authoritative and demanding tone and motioned towards the magistrate. The girl started spitting in the court and then said to her lawyer, 'Stop staring at me, I want to fucking stab you'. She was then led out of the courtroom, hitting the walls and spitting. We could hear her screaming from the cells below the courtroom for hours. The situation clearly had an emotional impact on the people sitting in that courtroom (Day 4, Case 3).

While care experience and trauma should be addressed at particular stages of the criminal justice process, timing and sensitivity are crucial. In relation to providing insight into the challenges and disadvantage that Indigenous children face in the criminal justice system, we highlight the *Bugmy Bar Book* and Canada's Gladue Report requirement. The *Bugmy Bar Book* offers cultural guidance and assistance to legal practitioners when representing

Indigenous children in the court system. It has been prepared as a resource by Indigenous peoples and legal experts, including Indigenous legal experts, and provides a basis for case preparation and the presentation of culturally informed arguments. There is a section in the *Bugmy Bar Book* on OOHC. In Canada, as a result of the Supreme Court decision in *R v. Gladue* (1999), the courts are now required to consider alternatives to prison for Aboriginal peoples and also to consider the individual circumstances of Aboriginal offenders via a Gladue Report (Hannah-Moffat et al., 2010). The reports produced are to be non-actuarial, holistic and contextual. They are more thorough than a pre-sentence report and take more than double the time to prepare (ALRC, 2017). In addition, we argue that the Gladue Report system in Canada, which, at this time, only pertains to Indigenous adults, enables the court to take into consideration culturally informed narratives developed by an Indigenous community member to situate the cultural background and lived experience of an offender. An Australian equivalent of a Gladue Report is currently being piloted in Victoria. The trial is a partnership between the Victorian Aboriginal Legal Service, the Australian Institute of Judicial Administration and academics at the University of Technology Sydney and Griffith University, and sets a requirement for the use of Aboriginal Community Justice Reports (VALS, 2022). We argue that culturally situated reports developed on behalf of the client by community can be a significant enabler of culturally appropriate outcomes for Indigenous children in the criminal justice system. These alternative approaches reveal what a trauma-informed legal system might look like, where care and trauma are identified and considered, and adjustments made to suit the client. Ultimately, the manner in which the history, context and experience of a child are raised in court should not lead to additional traumatisation or distress.

Conclusion

Our data confirm the significant role of lawyers as advocates for children in the criminal justice system. The lawyers we interviewed appeared to have a clear understanding of the trauma and the complex needs of children in care. By contrast, we saw striking examples of inappropriate practice by lawyers we observed in the Children's Court. These lawyers demonstrated little empathy, consideration or adjustments for clearly distressed young children and often seemed unaware of the cultural complexities underpinning the lives and experiences of Indigenous children. A transformation is required to enable lawyers and courts to be responsive to the diverse needs of children in care, their families and communities.

References

Aboriginal Legal Service. (2021). *Aboriginal legal service: Our history*. https://www.alsnswact.org.au/about

American Bar Association. (2014). *ABA policy on trauma-informed advocacy for children & youth*. February 10. http://www.americanbar.org/content/dam/aba/administrative/child_law/ABA%20Policy%20on%20Trauma-Informed%20Advocacy.authcheckdam.pdf

Atkinson, J., Nelson, J., & Atkinson, C. (2010). Trauma, transgenerational transfer and effects on community wellbeing. In P. Dudgeon, M. Wright, Y. Paradies, D. Garvey, & I. Walker (Eds.) *Working together: Aboriginal and Torres Strait Islander mental health and wellbeing principles and practice* (pp. 135–144). Australian Institute of Health and Welfare.

Australian Law Reform Commission. (2017). *Incarceration rates of Aboriginal and Torres Strait Islander peoples*.

Baidawi, S., & Sheehan, R. (2019). 'Crossover kids': Offending by child protection–involved youth. *Trends and Issues in Crime and Criminal Justice [Electronic Resource]*, 582, 1–23.

Baldry, E., McCausland, R., Dowse, L., & McEntyre, E. (2015). *A predictable and preventable path: Aboriginal people with mental and cognitive disabilities in the criminal justice system*. University of New South Wales.

Bugmy Bar Book Committee. (2019). Out-of-home care. *Bugmy bar book*. www.publicdefenders.nsw.gov.au/Pages/public_defenders_research/bar-book.aspx

Callander, N., Cashmore, J., Foley, S., & Kennard, D. (2020). *Care and protection: Working with children, a guide to best practice for legal representatives*. NSW Legal Aid. Working-with-Children-A-guide-to-best-practice-for-Childrens-Legal-Representatives.pdf (nsw.gov.au)

Davis, M. (2019). *Family is Culture: Review report*. Independent Review of Aboriginal Children in OOHC.

Devlin, R., Jairam, R., Asghari, M., & Eapen, V. (2022). Does assertive mental health care make a difference to children in out-of-home care? A pilot study. *Developmental Child Welfare*, *4*(1), 73–93.

Fogden, B.C., Thomas, S.D., Daffern, M., & Ogloff, J.R. (2016). Crime and victimisation in people with intellectual disability: A case linkage study. *BMC Psychiatry*, *16*(1), 170.

Gainsford, A., Gerard, A., & Bailey, K. (2020). Yindyamarra in action: indigenous cultural competence as core business within legal education and law schools. In B. Hill, J. Harris & R. Bacchus (Eds.) *Teaching aboriginal cultural competence* (pp. 61–74). Springer.

Gerard, A., McGrath, A., Colvin, E., & McFarlane, K. (2019). 'I'm not getting out of bed!': The criminalisation of young people in residential care. *Australian & New Zealand Journal of Criminology*, *52*(1), 76–93.

Gough, E. (2011). *The drift from care to crime: A Legal Aid NSW issues paper*. NSW Legal Aid Commission.

Green, J. (2020). The impacts of control, racism, and colonialism on contemporary Aboriginal–police relations. *NEW: Emerging Scholars in Australian Indigenous Studies*, *5*(1), 1–10.

Greig, H., McGrath, A., & McFarlane, K. (2019). 'Taking the wheels off': Young people with cognitive impairment in out-of-home care. *Psychiatry, Psychology and Law*, *26*(6), 920–937.

Hannah-Moffat, K., & Maurutto, P. (2010). Re-contextualizing pre-sentence reports: Risk and race. *Punishment & Society*, *12*(3), 262–286.

Howard League for Penal Reform. (2019). *Representing looked-after children at the police station: A step-by-step guide for lawyers*. https://howardleague.org/publications/representing-looked-after-children-at-the-police-station/

Human Rights and Equal Opportunity Commission. (1997). *Bringing Them Home: Report of the national inquiry into the separation of Aboriginal and Torres Strait Islander children from their families*.

James, C. (2020). Towards trauma-informed legal practice: A review. *Psychiatry, Psychology and Law*, *27*(2), 275–299.

Johnston, E. F. (1991). *Royal Commission into Aboriginal deaths in custody: National report, overview and recommendations*. Australian Government Publishing Service.

Katz, S. (2019). Trauma informed practice: The future of child welfare. *Widener Commonwealth Law Review*, *28*, 51–83.

Katz, S., & Haldar, D. (2016). The pedagogy of trauma informed lawyering. *Clinical Law Review*, *22*, 359–393.

New South Wales Legal Aid. (2019a). *Children's legal service*. https://www.legalaid.nsw.gov.au/what-we-do/criminal-law/children-and-young-people

New South Wales Legal Aid. (2019b). *Aboriginal client services strategy 2019–23*. https://www.legalaid.nsw.gov.au/for-lawyers/news/news-for-lawyers/legal-aid-nsw-launches-aboriginal-client-services-strategy-20192023

New South Wales Legislative Council Standing Committee on Law and Justice. (2014). *The family response to the Murders in Bowraville*.

Patten, E., & Kraemer, T. (2013). *Practice recommendations for trauma-informed legal services*. July. http://www.americanbar.org/content/dam/aba/administrative/child_law/5C_Patten%20Kraemer_Practice%20Recommendations%20for%20Trauma%20Informed%20Legal%20Services.authcheckdam.pdf

Peña, C. (2019). Trauma abounds: A case for trauma informed lawyering. *UCLA Women's Law Journal*, *26*, 7–16.

Ranzijn, R. O. B., McConnochie, K., Day, A., Nolan, W., & Wharton, M. (2008). Towards cultural competence: Australian Indigenous content in undergraduate psychology. *Australian Psychologist*, *43*(2), 132–139.

Ryan, J. P., & Testa, M. F. (2005). Child maltreatment and juvenile delinquency: Investigating the role of placement and placement instability. *Children and Youth Services Review*, *27*(3), 227–249.

Victorian Aboriginal Legal Service. (2022). *Aboriginal community justice reports*. Aboriginal Community Justice Reports – Victorian Aboriginal Legal Service (vals.org.au).

Williams, M., & Ragg, M. (2019). *Evaluation of legal aid NSW civil law service for aboriginal communities*. University of Technology Sydney.

6 Care-experienced children in the NSW Children's Court

Introduction

The NSW Children's Court is one of the oldest specialised juvenile courts in the world, with origins dating back to 1850 (Seymour, 1988). It is headed by a judge of the District Court who is appointed President pursuant to section 6A of the *Children's Court Act 1987* (NSW) and staffed by 15 specialist magistrates. Section 7 of the *Children's Court Act 1987* (NSW) requires Children's Magistrates to have experience and expertise in dealing with children, young people and their families. There are currently four dedicated Children's Courts in NSW, but other arrangements are in place for circuit courts or periodic Children's Court sittings of the Local Court. Where no specialist Children's Magistrates are available, typically in regional areas, the court's jurisdiction is exercised by Magistrates of the Local Court.

The Children's Court deals with care, crime, ADVO and education orders. Care and Protection matters are dealt with pursuant to the *Children and Young Persons (Care and Protection) Act 1998* (NSW). The guiding approach is known as the paramountcy principle, set out in section 9(1), which stipulates that 'in any action or decision concerning a particular child or young person, the safety, welfare and well-being of the child or young person are paramount'. Part 2 of the *Children and Young Persons (Care and Protection) Act 1998* (NSW) sets out the Aboriginal and Torres Strait Islander Principles, which refer to self-determination, participation in decision-making and the Aboriginal Child Placement Principles (ACPP). Davis found the principles are both poorly understood and poorly implemented in practice, with the evidence from the report showing agencies and individuals who provide services to Aboriginal children often fail to comply with the ACPP (Davis, 2019, pp. xxxi–ii).

For Indigenous children in NSW, there are several initiatives that challenge the colonial court structure and process. The Nowra Care Circles include Indigenous community members who provide input in matters involving Indigenous child protection. Further, Indigenous community members play a pivotal role in assisting the Children's Court of NSW to determine decisions relating to Indigenous children's care placements in the

DOI: 10.4324/9781003093367-7

Shoalhaven area. Another program is the Youth Koori Court established in 2015, which runs in conjunction with the Children's Court of NSW in Parramatta and deals with criminal and care protection cases. The Youth Koori Court provides a separate space where all stakeholders involved, including the magistrate, sit at an oval table that emulates a yarning circle. The program enables children to play a role in providing cultural contexts and to be full participants in the proceedings and planned outcomes. Both examples represent alternative court approaches for Indigenous children in specific NSW locations that are designed to improve the court experience for Indigenous children and better inform a magistrate's decision-making in the judgement and outcome process. Circle sentencing for adults has recently been found to result in fewer prison sentences and a lower likelihood of reoffending (Yeong & Moore, 2020).

The former president of the NSW Children's Court, Judge Peter Johnstone, has been critical of the inadequacy of cultural planning regarding Aboriginal children in care (Johnstone, 2016, p. 1). Further, a Queensland Children's Court study by Tilbury (2019), which included interviews with judicial officers, raised concerns about the lack of appropriate information that judges and magistrates receive concerning the specific cultural background and needs of Indigenous children. Tilbury (2019, p. 399) found that:

> [t]here are questions about the extent to which the court can rely upon or appraise family assessment reports prepared by non-Indigenous social workers, psychologists, or psychiatrists who may have limited contact, knowledge, or understanding of Aboriginal and Torres Strait Islander culture.

There have been calls for Indigenous organisations to be seen as key experts who can provide advice and be remunerated for court reports to determine the cultural needs of a child and provide an individualised strengths-based determination (Royal Commission and Board of Inquiry into the Protection and Detention of Children in the Northern Territory, 2019).

Criminal procedures in the Children's Court are dealt with under the *Children (Criminal Proceedings) Act 1987* (NSW). Section 6 sets out a number of principles that magistrates should follow when dealing with the young people who appear before them. These principles include that:

- children have a right to be heard and a right to participate in the processes that lead to decisions that affect them;
- children are responsible for their actions but require guidance and assistance because of their immaturity;
- it is desirable, wherever possible, to allow the education or employment of a child to continue;
- it is desirable, wherever possible, to allow a child to reside in his or her own home;

- penalties imposed on children should be no greater than those imposed on an adult who commits the same type of offence;
- it is desirable that children be assisted to reintegrate and maintain family and community ties;
- it is desirable that children who commit offences accept responsibility and make amends for their actions;
- appropriate consideration should be given to the impact of any crime on the victim.

Following the introduction of the *Young Offenders Act 1997* (NSW), a court appearance was seen as the final alternative for dealing with young people who commit offences, with a graded system of police cautions, warnings and other diversionary options such as youth justice conferences to be used before a matter is brought before court. Appeals from the Children's Court are heard in the NSW District Court. The exception to this is where the decision is made by the President of the Children's Court, in which case the appeal is heard in the Supreme Court.

In 2020, the NSW Children's Court finalised 5,646 criminal matters, down from 6,006 in the previous year – a drop attributed mainly to the COVID-19 pandemic (NSW Bureau of Crime Statistics and Research, 2021). Just under 77% of these young people were male (N = 4,330) and 42.5% were Indigenous (N = 2,397). Some 82.5% of these young people were convicted of an offence, with the most common offences dealt with being acts intended to cause injury (25%, N = 1,158), offences against justice procedures (e.g. breach of bail, 16%, N = 753) and theft (14%, N = 651).

Research examining the operations of Children's Courts, both in Australia and internationally, has been limited (Saunders et al., 2020). One study of 206 young people appearing before the NSW Children's Court found that young people overall thought they were treated fairly, with low levels of stigmatisation experienced, although those who did feel stigmatised were more likely to reoffend (McGrath, 2009). A follow-up study found this problem to be particularly marked for young women appearing before court (McGrath, 2014).

A recent review of the international literature identified eight qualitative studies addressing the question of what is known from Australian and international research about how children and their families understand Children's Court processes and decisions (Saunders et al., 2020). A number of key themes emerged from the authors' analyses. First, both parents and children perceived there to be significant barriers to their participation in proceedings and often lacked agency over, and even basic understanding of, what was happening in court. Second, courts lacked both knowledge and understanding of the home environment of the children appearing before them. Third, in some of the studies reviewed, support services were found to be very effective in helping both children and parents navigate the court process. This review built on an earlier national study of each jurisdiction of Australia's Children's Court by Borowski (2013), which identified significant concerns about the operation of juvenile courts in Australia, relating to children's engagement with and understanding of the court process and conflicting accounts of the courts' overall purpose and ability to balance welfare- and justice-related concerns.

In the NSW aspect of this national study, 76 respondents, including magistrates, legal practitioners and a range of government and non-governmental practitioners involved in the Children's Court, were interviewed (Fernandez et al., 2014). The respondents perceived the Court to function well, although some expressed concern about the metropolitan/regional divide and young people's engagement with the court process and ability to access the court. This last concern was particularly relevant for Indigenous and financially disadvantaged people. The overlap between care and crime was a key theme, with participants noting the social disadvantage suffered by children in the care system and the systemic disadvantage faced by Indigenous children and families, although the discussion of these factors was brief, and no concrete solutions were proposed. Our study was able to build on these findings by exploring in greater depth the overlap between care and crime as well as the intersections between social and structural disadvantage, historical trauma suffered by Indigenous people, gender and the care system.

Care-experienced children in the NSW Children's Court: background

In this book, we have reviewed evidence from both Australian and international jurisdictions showing that care-experienced children are over-represented in the criminal justice system. To summarise this evidence briefly, although explanations for the reasons for this over-representation vary, the findings from research using diverse methods and samples reveal that children who have been in contact with the care system comprise a significant proportion of the case load of juvenile and adult courts in a number of different countries (e.g. Carnie & Broderick, 2015; Malvaso et al., 2017; Ringland et al., 2015; Ryan et al., 2007; Ryan & Testa, 2005; Stewart, 2019).

In our interviews with magistrates, several respondents cited a paper by the former president of the Children's Court, Judge Mark Marien SC (2012), as providing valuable insights into the overlap between crime and care experience for children in the criminal justice system (M1, M7). We analyse this paper as it offers insights into the knowledge base used by magistrates. Marien highlights that as far back as 1992, the NSW Parliament asked the relevant departments to monitor the number of children in care in the juvenile justice system and to 'develop strategies as to how best such young people might be diverted from contact' with the juvenile justice system (2012, p. 1).

Judge Marien emphasises the criminogenic impact of time spent in juvenile detention and remand custody. Marien notes the disruptive impact of detention and that time spent in a remand facility 'is the most significant factor in increasing the likelihood of recidivism' (p. 15). Judge Marien supports calls for 'evidence-based prevention, early intervention programs and services for local communities' (p. 15). Judge Marien cites research by Judy Cashmore showing that children in care are more likely to receive punitive treatment within the juvenile justice system as a result of their care status (p. 17). Cashmore's research highlights the deficiencies in plans for young people leaving care and the inadequate support provided to these cohorts as they transition out of care (p. 18).

Options for redress examined by Judge Marien include early identification and 'coordinated agency intervention' (p. 18) that focus on 'needs' rather than 'deeds'. The examples included from Cashmore's international comparative research on juvenile models of justice and welfare highlight the importance of targeted diversion programs that are tailored to individual children's needs, with apparent success (only a conference paper is referenced to support this claim). In the final part of Judge Marien's paper, multi-systemic therapy is analysed and a pilot of a NSW intensive supervision program (ISP) is explored as offering hope. The ISP was subsequently reviewed and found to have no impact on offending frequency, although young people spent less time in custody while on the program (Poynton & Menendez, 2015). Judge Marien echoes Cashmore's concerns that a 'welfarising' approach may result in net-widening and highlights residential care as a driver of criminalisation, drawing on McFarlane's (2010) research on the link between property offences and time spent in care homes.

The *Children's Court of NSW Resource Handbook* (the Resource Handbook), maintained and regularly updated by the Judicial Commission of NSW, contains several references to Judge Marien's paper, although not the paper in full, alongside other research and commentary on the links between care experience and the criminal justice system, including one of our previous publications (McGrath et al., 2020). The Resource Handbook is intended for use by magistrates, lawyers and others who appear in the Children's Court. There is a section on 'cross-over kids', which consists of a paper by former president of the Children's Court of NSW, Judge Peter Johnstone (2016), now Chief Magistrate of NSW. In this paper, Johnstone states:

> Throughout my time as President of the Children's Court, I have observed that there is an unequivocal correlation between a history of care and protection interventions and future criminal offending.
>
> (2016, p. 13)

Johnstone focuses on similar themes to Judge Marien: identification of 'cross-over' children, discussion of some of the causes of their over-representation in the criminal justice system and options for redress and reform. He focuses on Aboriginal young people although this only comprises analysis of available statistics and a brief discussion of specialised Indigenous courts. The statistics on Aboriginal and non-Aboriginal children in care and detention demonstrate 'the over-representation of Aboriginal young people who have been removed and later appear before the criminal jurisdiction of the court' (Johnstone, 2016, p. 17). The statistical picture, which is dramatic and concerning, is offered without context or explanation. Rather, Johnstone's analysis highlights a 'number of contributory risk factors specific to Aboriginal and Torres Strait Islander children and young people' (2016, p. 19). In particular, he focuses on what he claims are the 'five well-recognised areas of disadvantage, specific to the complex manifestation of cross-over: child neglect and abuse, poor school performance/early disengagement from education, unemployment, drug and alcohol abuse and disconnection from cultural identity' (Johnstone, 2016, p. 20).

This analysis fails to consider the impacts of colonisation, rather citing the statement by the Royal Commission into Aboriginal Deaths in Custody that the 'reticulated and entrenched social, economic and cultural disadvantages experienced by Aboriginal people are root causes of Aboriginal young people "drifting" from the care and protection system to the criminal justice system' (p. 20). Johnstone also places considerable responsibility on the shoulders of young Aboriginal and Torres Strait Islander children and young people, seemingly situating 'these areas of disadvantage' in 'underlying impacts of Aboriginal cultural history', as if the legacies of colonisation are intrinsic to Aboriginal cultures rather than to imperialism. While the five areas of disadvantage are also acknowledged to be common to the non-Aboriginal population with experience of the care and criminal justice systems the claim is made that these are intensified for Aboriginal young people such that 'an impenetrable cycle of disadvantage' is perpetuated. This deficit approach contributes to a narrative of hopelessness and loss, and the normalisation of disadvantage for Aboriginal young people.

We particularly disagree with Johnstone's argument about how 'a positive characterisation of Aboriginality can act as a protective factor in ensuring that culture is used constructively, rather than destructively' (2016, p. 23). Johnstone here is critical of 'portrayals in media, social media, and within the community that define Aboriginal people as a homogenous criminogenic group of inherently antisocial people' (p. 24), and while we agree that media portrayals often comprise ignorant and discriminatory views of Aboriginal and Torres Strait Islander people, we also argue that what is set out in Johnstone's paper fails to advance recognition of the sovereign rights of Aboriginal and Torres Strait Islander peoples and communities, or understanding of the structural reasons behind the data. Johnstone states 'it is easy to see how a young Aboriginal person might see that their only option is a life of crime and disadvantage' (p. 24), as if both are a choice, or that this might even reflect the role of resistance to being subjected to criminalisation and disadvantage.

Johnstone's solutions for arresting the phenomenon of 'cross-over' are familiar and include engagement with communities, improving the number of Aboriginal staff within care and protection and justice organisations, and therapeutic justice alternatives. He is critical of the lack of cultural planning in the care and protection process and argues he has taken an activist role in relation to investigating compliance with the ACPP. The need for early intervention and pre-removal options should be 'explored to their fullest extent' (2016, p. 29) and a template for 'cultural action planning' should be included in the Care Plan. In this regard, Davis (2019) supports a more interventionist role by magistrates in ensuring care and protection decision-makers are held accountable.

Both Marien and Johnstone fail to mention the Stolen Generations or its impact, or the long history of dispossession and criminalisation of cultural difference that occurred before the introduction of the legal framework underpinning the Stolen Generations came into existence. The *Equality Benchbook* does address this historical context and is more expansive in the Indigenous perspectives presented. Overall, though, the information available in the Resource Handbook fails to provide a thorough historical context to the criminalisation of cultural difference and contemporary social realities and also lacks Indigenous perspectives. The emphasis throughout is on deficit accounts. Our chapter examining the role of lawyers discusses the *Bugmy bar book*, which is certainly relevant here.

Care-experienced children in the NSW Children's Court: findings from our study

Despite the prevalence of care-experienced children in the Children's Court, the magistrates reported only learning of the care–crime overlap through their experiences in court rather than through any initial judicial orientation training or the Resource Handbook (M7). Regardless, like the interview respondents in Sheehan and Borowski's study (2013), the magistrates we interviewed were aware of this overlap. The magistrates reported care-experienced children frequently present in the Children's Court, for reasons that are often out of their control (M6, M8). The magistrates we interviewed reported having 'too much' contact with children in residential care (M1) and that they were often asked to deal with matters originating in care, such as property offences and applications for ADVOs.

This finding was supported, in part, by our file review data, which showed that 58% of care-experienced children were involved in ADVO applications as the offender, compared to 10% of non-care-experienced children. Looking at some of these cases in more detail illustrates the difficulties of balancing the competing needs to ensure the safety of co-residents and youth workers, to identify stable and safe accommodation for children in care and to police in an equitable and fair manner. In one case at a residential home, the victim, a child in residential care, was playing music and was then threatened and assaulted by another child. The offender was subsequently bailed to live at the same home with a curfew from 8:00 pm to 7:00 am. A police compliance check conducted sometime between 8.00 and 8.20 pm found that the young person had breached this bail condition. He was subsequently apprehended and remanded in custody.

Many of the matters we observed related to ADVO orders, where the victim was either a co-resident or a care worker. The Joint Protocol outlines the obligations on police when responding to violence between residents in a residential care facility. Under s. 5 of the *Crimes (Domestic and Personal Violence) Act 2007* (NSW), the police are required to apply for an Apprehended Domestic Violence Order (ADVO) in residential care settings, as they fall within the definition of 'domestic relationship', unless the person in need of protection is 16 years or over. Under s. 5A of the 2007 legislation, a paid carer is no longer able to take out an ADVO against a child in residential care and any offences against a paid carer are not treated as domestic violence offences (see also Joint Protocol, p. 29). The Joint Protocol also sets out why the 'routine use' of ADVOs can contribute to criminalisation, is not always an effective vehicle for addressing problematic behaviour and may not be consistent with a trauma-informed approach (p. 30). Moreover, a breach of an ADVO, if it constitutes violence against a person, is defined as a significant source of aggravation and will likely result in a term of imprisonment.

As discussed in Chapter 2, there was a common understanding of the role of trauma experienced by children in care and a recognition of the impact of this on their behaviour (M5, M6, M7). The magistrate respondents believed that care-experienced children have specific and complex needs that are distinct from those of the general child population. Many magistrates perceived care-experienced children to have multiple mental health diagnoses and cognitive impairments (M6, M8). Despite the prevalence of mental health disorders in this cohort, accessing treatment was difficult and the resultant delays in treatment had a particular impact on children with care experience. As one of our lawyer respondents stated: 'As you can imagine, there's a huge waiting list. Asking these kids to wait three months for anything – their whole lives change in three months' (L13). The delay in accessing mental health services was seen as particularly difficult for care-experienced children, whose lives are more likely to be unstable and to change significantly while they wait to see a specialist.

Given the potential significance of being in care, or having care experience, one lawyer respondent told us that magistrates want to know about the lives of children appearing before them and their care status. Another observed that the first thing magistrates want to know about a child is whether or not they are in care (L13), a comment supported by several magistrate respondents (M6, M9).

There was a recognition by the magistrates of the effects of intergenerational trauma and the cycles of poverty and trauma experienced by children who appeared before them on criminal matters, in both Indigenous and non-Indigenous families, but particularly in Indigenous communities (M1, M2, M4, M6):

> The [intergenerational] thing applies across the board, more so in the Aboriginal community because of the historical trauma that they've been exposed to, but … a vast, vast majority of the kids that we have before us, the first factor you would look at commonly is where they've been parented, how they've been parented. One of the great dreams I think of all magistrates is for the wheel that just keeps producing that [intergenerational] issue somehow is disrupted.
>
> (M9)

Although the magistrate respondents recognised these familiar cycles of trauma and criminalisation, on the evidence we observed, the criminal justice system is still a long way short of adopting a trauma-informed approach to people who have suffered childhood and/or intergenerational trauma. One magistrate stated that they wanted to be notified and reminded by children's lawyers of their client's Aboriginal status and the sentencing principles that ought to be applied (M5). This magistrate respondent felt that lawyers sometimes assume that magistrates are aware of this information, but as we discussed in chapter 5, magistrates sometimes felt they needed to be reminded in a plea in mitigation to trigger consideration of the applicable sentencing principles relevant to Aboriginal and Torres Strait Islander offenders.

Several magistrates thought that they were more likely to make allowances for care-experienced children when determining bail, including any conditions of bail, and when passing sentence, and were also more tolerant of breaches of bail or court orders by these children (M2, M4, M7). We concluded from our observations of court matters and file reviews that in practice there was limited evidence of this.

The awareness of the care experience and its detrimental impact on a child's agency that came through strongly in the magistrate respondent interviews did not correspond with the discussions of care-experienced children that we observed in the courts, among either the magistrates or the lawyers. With few exceptions, the care experience and its impact were not discussed in court, and we observed a number of instances where there was information on file indicating a history of care that was not raised in court. In eight of the cases where children with care experience had been previously charged, four of the children had been charged with offences of violence, ranging from sexual assault committed against half-siblings in foster care to animal cruelty. There was also evidence of considerable trauma among these children, with one child having been abused while in OOHC, and another with a history of unsuccessful placements whose father had died by suicide. Another child had previously been found not guilty because they were suffering from mental illness.

Our Juvenile Justice respondents, like the lawyers, were more cautious in their assessment of judicial tolerance, perceiving magistrates as being initially sympathetic to care-experienced children but adopting more punitive measures if children reappeared in court for the same types of offending:

> often the kids, by the time they get to us, they generally have been charged numerous times for similar offences ... so then, yeah, the courts are trying to say, look, stop doing this or we're going to give you a more serious order.
>
> (JJ11)

The court experience for children in OOHC

Our observations of court matters and review of court files gave insight into what the experience of court was like for the children appearing. Our interview respondents also provided some vivid illustrations. In these accounts, the children suffered from structural disadvantage and dysfunction. Children often presented at court without having eaten or slept, and without any adult support. In these circumstances, getting to court was an achievement in itself:

> I just think most of these kids' lives are just different degrees of chaos. From not knowing which couch you're sleeping on, losing documents. The police will say we served your client with the brief. I'm, like, the kid is couch surfing. The kid has got an intellectual delay. He doesn't quite get it. I think they get that they're in court, but they don't understand all the nuances. Like I said, there isn't that adult to say okay, we need to be at court. You can't be late. It is important if you miss it. A lot of these kids are ringing up for themselves in the morning and going, 'Oh, I'm not coming to court; I'm sick.' Well you need to – our response, which is what we're mandated to do, is to say well you need to get a medical certificate. They're not getting to the doctor's. These kids don't have Medicare cards. It's actually quite frightening how little they have.
>
> (L13)

As to the court experience itself, we noted the pace with which matters were handled in the Children's Courts. This varied between courts and magistrates but the vast majority of matters were dealt with swiftly. Indeed, during our observations, we were struck by the fast pace of hearings. On one of our observation days, there were 100 matters on the list, and, prior to going into court, the magistrate commented this meant that an average of two minutes could be devoted to each matter so that court could finish on time. The lawyer respondents reported that client interviews were also conducted swiftly and often immediately prior to matters appearing at court (L2). Obtaining instructions by phone or audio–visual link (AVL) was difficult. One lawyer commented, 'I hate it, well, yeah, I really dislike it … having to get instructions from a kid on the phone in the morning is really bad' (L10).

Consistent with previous research (Saunders et al., 2020), our respondents expressed concern about how well children comprehended the matter. As one magistrate commented, 'all they want to know is am I getting out or am I going into custody. All the words in between, I think, go over their heads' (M3). This was perceived to be even worse when the child appeared from custody via an AVL: 'it's difficult enough for a kid to really follow what's going on in a court when they're there, so not being there is really problematic' (L10). We observed some magistrates attempting to engage the children, for instance, by asking at the end of the hearing whether they had any questions, but no child in any matter we were present at responded with anything other than a 'no'.

Sometimes, this lack of engagement turned into hostility. In one case we observed, the young person became angry, shaking his head, sighing and swearing audibly. The child then wanted to speak to the magistrate, but the lawyer advised him not to talk. The child then went to speak again before becoming frustrated and storming out of the court. The matter was held over until he had calmed down, showing a willingness on the part of magistrates to take into account the difficulties experienced by the young people appearing before them. In fact, children were often excused from attending court, particularly when held in custody. This was important as one problem identified with AVL was that the child is required to sit in the video room until their case is called, and in some cases, this might not be until well into the afternoon (L10). This is something that we thought would be more likely to impact care-experienced children as our court file data they were more likely to be in custody when appearing before the court (27.3% of care-experienced children compared to 14.3% of non-care-experienced children). Overall, the key problem we identified pertained to the actual process of appearing in court, which is alienating and bewildering for many young people. The architectural and design features of the courthouse and courtroom space, which regularly fail to accommodate Indigenous users (Anthony & Grant, 2016), compound this sense of alienation.

It is also the case that magistrates often only see a sanitised version of the child in court, given that court design places the child far from the magistrate during the hearing. In one lawyer respondent's view, this means that magistrates are not able to see the physical condition of some of the children appearing before them:

> They can't smell, see, pick up that the kid is itching and there are sores. Stuff where I go, what's going on there? We've had kids in the cells with staph – golden staph. That's really high-level neglect and medical problems. It's the first time they'll get antibiotic treatment, but we've got to wipe down the whole place and run off to the medical centres. The

> magistrate won't ever have to do that. They're not close enough to that. Like I said, everything is filtered through the lawyers, for the magistrate. It's something that I've learnt.
>
> (L13)

Yet, the physical conditions of children are at times indicative of serious abuse and health problems resulting from their living conditions. Although our magistrate respondents told us they wanted to know about the care status of the children appearing before them, these findings are also consistent with previous research demonstrating that judicial officers who deal with juvenile matters are, in most cases, unaware of the children's home backgrounds and living arrangements (Saunders et al., 2020).

Lack of support at court for care-experienced children

We frequently observed magistrates cite attendance at court of family members or other support people as a positive factor when making their sentencing remarks. The magistrates' comments included: 'It's great you have family support' and 'This shows you have good prospects'. In four sentencing matters, we saw clear evidence that the magistrate took family support into account when sentencing. In one case, where the child received a good behaviour bond with no conviction, the magistrate said: 'You have good prospects, a caring mother and father who are here in court' (Case 8, Day 1). In another sentencing matter, the magistrate was clear in relation to the impact family support had on the child's sentence:

> The seriousness of the offence means a control order. However, there is a good prospect of rehabilitation, family support, [the defendant] works with his father. I will suspend the control order and give good behaviour bonds.
>
> (Case 4, Day 1)

We also observed many defence submissions highlighted the family support experienced by the young person although this was not extended to the carers who accompanied care-experienced children. Further, on two occasions where care-experienced children had friends or intimate partners with them at court, this was not noted by either the magistrate or lawyer. For example, on Day 1, Case 10, a care-experienced child was accompanied by a female support person (not a family member) in court, yet no one made mention of this person during the hearing.

In 40 (29.9%) of the cases we observed, the young person was supported by family members in court. In an additional 16 cases (11.9%), a residential care worker was present. In the cases we observed, boys appearing in the Children's Court were more likely to be supported by family than girls – 38.6% of boys had a family member present as opposed to 19.5% of girls, representing a statistically significant difference (p = 0.009). Further, Indigenous children were more likely to have family support in court (50% of Indigenous children compared to 25.9% of non-Indigenous children – p = 0.024). We also found care-experienced children were more likely to be accompanied by a carer, and slightly less likely to be accompanied by a family member, although this latter difference was not statistically significant (22.6% for care-experienced children compared to 31.4% for non-care-experienced children).

Overall, 36% of care-experienced children were accompanied by a carer when attending court, meaning that nearly two-thirds were not. This latter figure is larger than that identified in McFarlane's (2018, p. 421) earlier file review study, in which one-third of children had no support at the police station or court. We were unable to identify the quality or effectiveness of the support provided by the carers. In this regard, the lawyer respondents expressed frustration at carers' lack of understanding of the children in their care and their behaviour management plans. As one lawyer respondent commented:

> They certainly don't have the skills and … they're often a really young worker who … will not necessarily even know anything about the client. They'll go, yeah, I'm just new, I don't really know or something like that. Often, I don't even bother talking to them other than to find out, will you take the person back or not.
>
> (L3)

> Lawyers often found that the carers who attended court did not know the young person or were not aware of any plans in place: a lot of the time you have workers that come to court that have never met the young person, which infuriates us, and so the court – this is not all magistrates – some magistrates would say I want to speak to someone that knows this young person and knows what's happening. And if we can't get that person down there, we will often make several phone calls to case workers and carers to try and get a picture of what's going on.
>
> (L6)

Davis (2019, p. 239) is critical of the absence of support provided to children in their interactions with the criminal justice system. Davis recommends that magistrates be given the power to compel a representative of FACS or of an OOHC provider to attend court to support the child. McFarlane's (2018) research revealed how attendance at court may involve case workers lobbying against children being released on bail. Following from this, we concluded that, first, the presence of family support has some influence on sentencing decisions, and second, both the nature and amount of family support differed between those with and without care experience. Those attending court to support care-experienced children consisted of grandparents, siblings, friends, OOHC workers and partners.

Research has also shown that properly designed and well-funded court support services can be very effective in assisting young people to navigate the often complex and confusing court environment. The respondents in an evaluation of a Scottish court support service reported that the support was particularly effective in helping them when held in custody: 'It made me feel a lot better because I was nervous and scared' (Deuchar & Sapouna, 2016, p. 134). They also thought that such support improved their sentence, provided them with valuable personal support and assisted them to transition from an offending lifestyle. The introduction of a similar scheme in NSW could well alleviate concerns about the disadvantages experienced by children in care, who do not have the same support other children benefit from, and in our view, this is a policy change well worth consideration.

Bail

Bail laws for juveniles in NSW have long been a source of contention (Stubbs, 2010). Bail in NSW is governed by the *Bail Act 2013* (NSW). When this Act was introduced, the test for whether bail should be granted was the 'unacceptable risk' test. This holds that bail cannot be granted if there is an unacceptable risk that the person charged will fail to reappear, commit a serious offence, endanger others or interfere with witnesses or evidence. Subsequent amendments following public controversies and high-profile events such as the Lindt Café siege have led to bail laws becoming more complex and restrictive, with a resultant rise in the number of offenders in remand custody (Hall, 2021). Klauzner and Yeong (2021) found that police refused bail for 22.7% of juveniles compared to 13.8% of adults in the period 2015–2019, meaning juveniles can spend a considerable amount of time in remand custody, particularly where no safe accommodation can be found. We found this to pose a particular danger for children in care, especially when the offending occurred in a care environment. In many cases, as we discuss below, there was literally no safe accommodation in which to place the young person, something we observed contributing to long periods in remand for what were relatively minor offences.

Section 28 of the *Bail Act* was designed to address the problem of young people being remanded in custody for extensive periods because appropriate accommodation is unavailable. Under this section, an accommodation requirement can be imposed as a bail condition for children. This means that suitable accommodation arrangements must be made before the accused person can be released on bail. Crucially, the court must ensure the matter is relisted for hearing every two days until this requirement has been satisfied. This provision aims to prevent young people spending extensive periods on remand, which is damaging to both their mental and physical health, raises the likelihood of being sentenced to imprisonment and represents a significant cost to the state – money that could be spent on diversionary and therapeutic alternatives (McGrath, 2016; Richards & Renshaw, 2013).

There was common agreement among all stakeholders in our research that bail determinations for care-experienced children are challenging. Several of the magistrates described the decision-making process underlying bail determinations (M12). Whether suitable accommodation was available emerged as a key theme. One magistrate respondent reported applying the same process regardless of whether the young person was in care or resided with their parents but found that in practice the differences were difficult to overcome:

> The typical one is, where are they going to live? Usually FACS disappears off the planet with the more difficult children. Even though the minister might have the parental responsibility. It is then a matter of Juvenile Justice trying to negotiate, trying to drag FACS into the equation to find somewhere and/or getting refuge accommodation which is highly unstable and unsatisfactory. That's the major change between a child who's got mum and/or dad or family, can have some form of stable accommodation available. Those that are in out-of-home care struggle more and more with that the older they get.
>
> (M4)

Care-experienced children face significant barriers accessing bail. Offending by care-experienced children is often related to being in care and frequently occurs in their place of residence. This makes returning children back to that same accommodation impossible in some cases, for instance, where an ADVO restricts the child from returning (M6). One Juvenile Justice respondent described this as 'cyclical' (JJ3) – the care environment produced the offending, but the child has no option but to return there. Some magistrate respondents saw several of the OOHC service providers running residential care facilities as having a strong commitment to children in residential care and noted these providers would repeatedly take children back into the same residential care facility (M1, M3, M6). However, often the child did not want to return to the same facility; indeed, one lawyer respondent told us that some children would prefer not to be bailed if it meant returning to residential care (L6). As a result, the child might abscond and breach bail and then potentially be returned to custody. Although this problem was not explicitly acknowledged by the magistrate respondents, children's concerns for their own safety in residential care have been identified as a reason why care-experienced children might not wish to return to an available placement (Colvin et al., 2018).

It was a common perception among our respondents that accessing suitable and stable housing to be bailed to is a challenge for care-experienced children. Difficulties in finding appropriate accommodation consistent with bail conditions were thought to have a number of negative impacts.

One such impact was that young people may be returned to the site of their offending:

> We see young people frequently returning to these homes where they don't want to be there, they're at risk of harm themselves, they're being assaulted by other residents, and regardless of what happens within those residences they will always take them back.
>
> (JJ15)

One magistrate respondent said that once a child has absconded from care, 'there's a difficulty with getting FACS involved again to actually look at them', making finding suitable accommodation difficult. The result of this was often that the child would be remanded in custody (M5). Our file reviews revealed some graphic examples of this. In one case, the victim and offender were co-residents in a care home. The victim, who suffered from global developmental delay and had been the victim of sexual abuse in the past, reported being indecently assaulted by the offender. Police requested that the young person be removed from the house for the victim's safety. The organisation managing the house stated that they did not have enough staff to facilitate this and so the offender remained in the house with the victim and the offences against her continued. The victim described feeling 'weak and vulnerable' after the assaults and after the most recent assault 'broken and damaged'. After some time, alternative accommodation was found for the young person accused of the indecent assault.

Some of the concerns arising in the cases discussed above were recognised by the magistrate respondents. For example, the magistrates observed that children in OOHC struggle with having a curfew as part of their bail conditions (M3, M10):

> I get many breaches of bail for breaches of curfew. So I don't see a night-time curfew as being all that useful in situations where you've got a defiant kid who's not going to obey it anyway.
>
> (M3)

Another problem identified as a challenge for care-experienced children who appear frequently in the Children's Court concerned their ability to comply with different bail conditions. Managing these conditions can be difficult for the child's solicitor, as one lawyer respondent explained:

> A lot of these kids have got – because they've got a lot of different matters, their bails sometimes don't match up. I try and go, okay, what does all your bail look like? Is there an [ADVO]? Let's make sure all the conditions look the same so you're not … unwittingly breaching something else. Because that bail says you can go back to nan's, and this one says no. So that's the other thing, these kids tend to move around a lot. They

> do hop a train. So that's the other thing that we see. It's not unusual for them to have offences in different areas.
>
> (L13)

This situation, children have different matters listed in different courts, makes complying with bail conditions more challenging and ultimately more confusing.

Section 28 of the *Bail Act 2013* (NSW) aims to address some of these problems. We heard differing views about its efficacy in this regard. According to one magistrate, section 28 is effective in that it places pressure on FACS and Juvenile Justice to respond to a child's accommodation needs (M5). A Juvenile Justice respondent said that if a section 28 is made by the court their experience was that in most cases FACS was usually unable to identify suitable accommodation quickly (JJ4). This respondent was of the view that 'kids who are actually in the care of the minister spend twice as long in custody under section 28 than those who are not in the care of the minister' (JJ4). It seemed unclear whether these legislative changes have reduced the time care-experienced children spend in custody.

Other magistrate respondents were critical of the accommodation provisions in section 28 of the *Bail Act 2013* (NSW). In the experience of one magistrate, children get increasingly agitated when accommodation cannot be found and they have to keep coming back to court or appearing through an AVL (M4). Further, in practice, section 28 has not hastened the provision of appropriate accommodation and places unnecessary strain on Juvenile Justice:

> I don't think it moves it along any quicker because I have high regard for Juvenile Justice's search powers. I have low regard for FACS assisting and since we've got no power to enforce the minister being involved, it's just using resources from Juvenile Justice unnecessarily.
>
> (M4)

Another magistrate thought the provision only highlights the schism between FACS and Juvenile Justice although also commented: 'When FACS and JJ start working together, we tend to get a much faster outcome' (M6). This cooperation, however, was not typical in the view of the majority of magistrates interviewed in our study.

Mental health

Children in care who come into contact with the criminal justice system often have mental health conditions. In NSW, judicial officers have powers in relation to 'mentally ill' defendants under sections 32 and 33 of the *Mental Health (Forensic Provisions) Act 1990* (NSW). Under the provisions of section 32 of this Act, where an offence was committed by an offender who was mentally ill or developmentally disabled, the matter can be adjourned, the offender can be bailed or the charge can be dismissed and the offender discharged unconditionally, into the care of a responsible person or into appropriate treatment facilities. Under section 33, magistrates have the power to order defendants apparently suffering from mental illness to be taken to an appropriate treatment facility for assessment and detention. The NSW scheme is explicitly diversionary and requires magistrates to determine, first, whether the defendant is eligible for diversion; second, whether such an option is appropriate and third, what a suitable outcome should be (Gotsis & Donnelly, 2008).

Our magistrate respondents saw a number of benefits arising from the use of this legislation. First, they saw the use of section 32 orders as offering an alternative to custody. One case a magistrate described involved a very serious assault that resulted in the victim's eye being irreversibly damaged. As the magistrate commented, this kind of offence on its facts certainly raised the possibility of a custodial sentence. However, the magistrate determined that 'on balance the better way forward for this was to ensure that he [the offender] had ongoing medical treatment', which the section 32 order could ensure, but which would not necessarily be available in custody (M1). The legislation, as discussed, was intended as a diversionary option, and indeed, some magistrates perceived this to be one of its main benefits. Another case was used as an example of this: 'and the mother was using [drugs] – she was actually using the court as a parenting tool and she'd bring the kid back for any breach of bail and it got annoying rather, but the mother just lacked the ability to control this kid. So his order progressed; he's currently out on section 32 orders' (M11). We thought this scenario was similar in some ways to the use of police to manage behaviour in residential homes.

The efficacy of section 32 orders was seen to rest on a number of factors: compliance, having a comprehensive plan and someone being responsible for the order. In some cases, even where there was further offending, a section 32 order was still seen as effective even if only complied with for a short period of time, given the complexities of treating mental illness:

> Look, every case depends on its own merits. But if you can see that progress is being made – if a section 32 order is made and it's immediately breached and they come back, well, then you say, okay, that's – 32 is not a vehicle here and you go down some other path. But if it's in place, say, for five or even six months has expired and there's then a gap and then there's some further offending and they come back, then there may be an explanation why this reoffending occurred because the child was not taking medication or some other explanation. So if it's another 32 and the first one was successful, well, then – and if it's a genuine case where someone has got a mental illness and they're not out there committing violent acts against the community, then 32 is an appropriate vehicle to use.
>
> (M3)

An effective and clear treatment plan was seen as crucial to section 32 orders. A number of magistrates made this observation, but the following quote best exemplifies this:

> I want to know if there's a proper treatment regime in place. After all, you're dealing with it as a matter of medicine rather than a matter of law. That's what the dichotomy is. I want to know that with a proper treatment plan in place the logistics are that they're not going to commit crime.
>
> (M1)

Our magistrate respondents also made it clear that supervision was important but often lacking: 'I make sure that someone's nominated to supervise it. But nobody has ever [reported back to me about the outcome] in my seven years in the adult court and in my time in the Children's Court (M5)'.

The lawyers also spoke about how section 32 was used in their clients' cases. One lawyer respondent said that some magistrates repeatedly offer the use of the provision to manage children's offending, but there are inconsistencies in how the provision is applied by magistrates (L9). The lawyers also felt that one of the immediate benefits of this provision was ensuring that the child would not be placed in custody. It is often the case that the children dealt with under section 32 struggle to comply with court orders, so not having to follow Juvenile Justice supervision orders, for instance, was seen as a clear advantage. Nevertheless, the lawyer respondents were unsure as to how effective section 32 was in enabling children to access treatment (L9).

Several magistrates criticised the section 32 provision. Their primary concern was that the orders were too short in length to enable effective treatment to occur. They also thought they had little power to monitor treatment plans and no ability to compel matters to come back before them. Indeed, most magistrates reported that they had rarely seen these matters return to court. They were also concerned that the police saw section 32 orders as the child 'getting away with offending', which meant that police often opposed their decision to make use of the section 32 provisions, particularly when more than one order was made. In summary, the magistrates felt that section 32 was unclear and required revision. For instance, one commented:

> It is of limited benefit to the court in that we make this order and then are never told if it's breached until the young person comes back with further offences. If we were told, say a month or two into the order, that the young person wasn't seeing the psychologist or the Mental Health Plan, et cetera, we could get involved and take further action.
>
> (M4)

This magistrate respondent felt that section 32 was particularly problematic for care-experienced children as nobody is held responsible for children getting the help they need. Another magistrate believed that perhaps a magistrate was the appropriate person to oversee any treatment plan to ensure that it is implemented:

> Sometimes it is good when somebody with more authority is there that we ask that their medication be reviewed or they go back to find out exactly what is happening.
>
> (M5)

Even though a number of reservations about section 32 orders were expressed, they were also seen as useful for matters impacted by the child's trauma and that care-experienced children often benefit from section 32 orders (M6). Such orders were seen by the magistrates as useful for enabling these children to access more specialised treatment and divert them from formal sentencing (M5).

Sometimes, the provisions of section 28 of the *Bail Act* and section 32 of the *Mental Health (Forensic Provisions) Act* were seen to conflict. For instance, in one case described by a lawyer respondent, a child was not able to obtain a treatment plan for the purposes of a section 32 application as he was in custody awaiting suitable accommodation to be found under section 28 (L9):

> I don't think any of us can probably understand his situation, it comes from so much trauma … and so I did want to do a 32 with him, the problem was initially he kept breaching his bail, I got – we got him into rehab on two separate occasions but he breached that on both times and then the last bail application when we decided we wanted to do a 32, that's the catch 22 in that they couldn't develop a treatment plan for him while he was in custody and the treatment plan's an essential part of a section 32, so you can't get it without the treatment plan, so he was pretty much stuck, he couldn't do a section 32 because of really his mental health conditions didn't allow him – made him struggle at liberty so he was really stuck there.
>
> (L9)

We saw this situation in at least one matter we observed (Case 5, Day 1). We believe that this is a problem that needs to be addressed to enable section 28 and section 32 provisions to operate in support of, rather than against, each other.

Conclusion

The findings from our study show that there is a strong awareness of the impact of care on young people appearing before the Children's Court, but that this does not necessarily translate into practice. We believe that the care status of a child should be a key factor that magistrates of the Children's Court take into account when sentencing and making bail determinations. One reason problems in the care system have a significant impact on the children appearing in court is because difficulties in identifying appropriate accommodation can lead to extensive periods in remand custody. The provisions of section 28 of the *Bail Act* are useful in this regard but need to be backed up by the agencies responsible for children in care. Mental health is also a key challenge facing children in care and it is clear from our findings that more services and greater oversight are necessary to address this.

References

Anthony, T., & Grant, E. (2016). Courthouse design principles to dignify spaces for Indigenous users: Preliminary observations. *International Journal for Court Administration, 8*(1), 43.

Borowski, A. (2013). Whither Australia's Children's Courts? Findings of the National Assessment of Australia's Children's Courts. *Australian & New Zealand Journal of Criminology, 46*(2), 268–288. https://doi.org/10.1177/0004865812470382

Carnie, J., & Broderick, R. (2015). *Prisoner Survey 2015* (Vol. 15). Scottish Prisoner Service.

Colvin, E., McFarlane, K., Gerard, A., & McGrath, A. (2018). 'We don't do measure and quotes': How agency responses criminalise and endanger the safety of children missing in care in New South Wales, Australia. *The Howard Journal of Crime and Justice*. https://doi.org/10.1111/hojo.12253

Davis, M. (2019). *Family is Culture: Review report*. Independent Review of Aboriginal Children in OOHC.

Deuchar, R., & Sapouna, M. (2016). 'It's harder to go to court yourself because you don't really know what to expect': Reducing the negative effects of court exposure on young people – Findings from an Evaluation in Scotland. *Youth Justice, 16*(2), 130–146. https://doi.org/10.1177/1473225415606815

Fernandez, E., Bolitho, J., Hansen, P.A., Hudson, M., & Kendall, S. (2014). *A study of the children's court of New South Wales*. Part of a National Assessment of Australia's Children's Courts. Sydney: University of NSW.

Gotsis, T., & Donnelly, H. (2008). *Diverting mentally disordered offenders in the NSW Local Court*. Judicial Commission of New South Wales.

Hall, M. (2021). Changes in New South Wales criminal justice since 2010. *Current Issues in Criminal Justice, 33*(2), 264–276. https://doi.org/10.1080/10345329.2020.1813388

Johnstone, P. (2016). *Children's Court Update 2016*. District Court Annual Conference 2016, Wollongong, 29 March 2016.

Judicial Commission of NSW. (2013). *Children's Court of NSW resource handbook*.

Klauzner, I., & Yeong, S. (2021). *What factors influence police and court bail decisions?* (Vol. 236). NSW Bureau of Crime Statistics and Research.

Malvaso, C. G., Delfabbro, P. H., & Day, A. (2017). The child protection and juvenile justice nexus in Australia: A longitudinal examination of the relationship between maltreatment and offending. *Child Abuse & Neglect, 64*, 32–46. http://dx.doi.org/10.1016/j.chiabu.2016.11.028

Marien, M. (2012). 'Cross-over kids': Childhood and adolescent abuse and neglect and juvenile offending. *Judicial Review, 11*(1), 97–126.

McFarlane, K. (2010). From care to custody: Young women in out-of-home care in the criminal justice system. *Current Issues in Criminal Justice, 22*, 345–353.

McFarlane, K. (2018). Care-criminalisation: The involvement of children in out-of-home care in the New South Wales criminal justice system. *Australian & New Zealand Journal of Criminology, 51*(3), 412–433. https://doi.org/10.1177/0004865817723954

McGrath, A. (2009). Offenders' perceptions of the sentencing process: A study of deterrence and stigmatisation in the NSW Children's Court. *Australian & New Zealand Journal of Criminology, 42*(1), 24–46. https://doi.org/10.1375/acri.42.1.24

McGrath, A. (2014). The subjective impact of contact with the criminal justice system: The role of gender and stigmatization. *Crime & Delinquency, 60*(6), 884–908. https://doi.org/10.1177/0011128710389589

McGrath, A. (2016). Intersections of Indigenous status, sex and age in sentencing decisions in the New South Wales Children's Court. *Australian & New Zealand Journal of Criminology, 49*(1), 90–112. https://doi.org/10.1177/0004865814551614

McGrath, A., Gerard, A., & Colvin, E. (2020). Care-experienced children and the criminal justice system. *Trends and Issues in Crime and Criminal Justice No. 600.* Canberra: Australian Institute of Criminology.

New South Wales Bureau of Crime Statistics and Research. (2021). *New South Wales Criminal Court Statistics 2020.*

Poynton, S., & Menéndez, P. (2015). The impact of the NSW Intensive Supervision Program on recidivism. *NSW Crime and Justice Bulletins, 186*, 16.

Richards, K., & Renshaw, L. (2013). *Bail and remand for young people in Australia: A national research project.* Australian Institute of Criminology.

Ringland, C., Weatherburn, D., & Poynton, S. (2015). Can child protection data improve the prediction of re-offending in young persons? *NSW Crime and Justice Bulletins, 188*, 20.

Royal Commission and Board of Inquiry into the Protection and Detention of Children in the Northern Territory. https://www.royalcommission.gov.au/sites/default/files/2019-01/rcnt-royal-commission-nt-final-report-volume-1.pdf

Ryan, J. P., Hernandez, P. M., & Herz, D. (2007). Developmental trajectories of offending for male adolescents leaving foster care. *Social Work Research, 31*(2), 83–93.

Ryan, J. P., & Testa, M. F. (2005). Child maltreatment and juvenile delinquency: Investigating the role of placement and placement instability. *Children and Youth Services Review, 27*(3), 227–249. http://dx.doi.org/10.1016/j.childyouth.2004.05.007

Saunders, B. J., Lansdell, G., & Frederick, J. (2020). Understanding Children's Court processes and decisions: Perceptions of children and their families. *Youth Justice, 20*(3), 272–292. https://doi.org/10.1177/1473225419890691

Seymour, J. A. (1988). *Dealing with young offenders.* Law Book Company.

Sheehan, R., & Borowski, A. (2013). *Australia's children's courts today and tomorrow.* Springer.

Stewart, F. (2019). *'Crossover Kids': Vulnerable children in the youth justice system. Report 1: Children who are known to child protection among sentenced and diverted children in the Victorian Children's Court.* Sentencing Advisory Council.

Stubbs, J. (2010). Re-examining bail and remand for young people in NSW. *Australian & New Zealand Journal of Criminology*, *43*(3), 485–505. https://doi.org/10.1375/acri.43.3.485

Tilbury, C. (2019). Obtaining expert evidence in child protection court proceedings. *Australian Social Work*, *72*(4), 392–403.

Yeong, S., & Moore, E. (2020). Circle sentencing, incarceration and recidivism. *NSW Crime and Justice Bulletins*, *226*, 22.

7 Gender and criminalisation

Introduction

This chapter analyses the gendered themes that emerged in our research on criminalisation, focusing on women with care experience, and Aboriginal and Torres Strait Islander women in particular. From the outset, 'colonisation was a gendered and racialized project' (Behrendt, 2019, p. 204). As Mary Spiers Williams (2021, p. 290) argues, the 'most powerful and deeply stigmatising form of deficit discourse – criminalisation – is a structural effect of colonisation that continues to affect all Indigenous peoples'. We recognise that criminalisation and deficit discourses further perpetuate harms, in sharp contrast to a strength-based approach that understands the skills, knowledge and potential of Aboriginal and Torres Strait Islander women and girls, and the import of culture (see Australian Human Rights Commission, 2020). The Australian context of colonisation and the dispossession of Aboriginal and Torres Strait Islander people necessitate that an intersectional lens is applied to the data analysis. Our analysis seeks not just to understand intersectionality but also to offer insights that transform its impact (Paik, 2017).

This chapter will engage 'legal storytelling', or narrative discourse, a process designed to enhance the visibility of marginalised voices, otherwise, excluded from analysis or obscured by quantitative data sets (Anthony, et al., 2021; Bedford, 2019; Delgado & Stefancic, 1993). Bedford (2019, p. 323) writes that in Australia, 'the importance of storytelling is particularly relevant in Aboriginal and Torres Strait Islander communities' as a result of the reliance on oral traditions to 'preserve and share' cultures and beliefs. In engaging legal storytelling as a method, we have also sought to guard against responsibilising individuals and the reification of 'categories of race, gender, and class as driving those individuals' choices' (Paik, 2017, p. 8). Thus, we have sought to situate our analysis in the broader historical, structural and cultural context.

In this chapter, we go beyond quantitative approaches to listen to narratives from key stakeholders about the factors driving the involvement of Indigenous women and girls with care experience into the criminal justice system. Three of the stakeholders we interviewed were Aboriginal and Torres Strait Islander (n = 3). In addition to these respondents,

DOI: 10.4324/9781003093367-8

we also consulted with our Advisory Board and informally with Aboriginal lawyers, carers and Elders. Through the narratives respondents provided, we piece together the factors influencing the exponential rise in the incarceration of Indigenous women. In this analysis, we operate within certain limitations arising from our research design. In our research, we spoke with key stakeholders engaged in the provision of services and the administration of the OOHC and criminal justice sectors, in addition to undertaking file reviews and court observation. However, we chose not to interview people in custody, or the care system, for three reasons. First, we decided we could not effectively surmount the institutional barriers to gaining access to people in custody, or under other forms of community supervision, or children in the care system. Second, we were also unsure of our ability to navigate and ameliorate the potential risk of harm to people participating in the research who are in the care or criminal justice systems. Third, we were keen to keep the focus on OOHC service providers and organisations within the criminal justice system as these organisations are charged with responsibility for children in care or with care experience. We sought to address this limitation in our sample by establishing an Advisory Board that included Aboriginal representation and people with lived experience of the care system. In this regard, of immense benefit to our research has been the lived experience of Wiradyuri woman Annette Gainsford (co-author of this book), who was a member of our initial Advisory Board and has experience of the care system through several roles and interactions.

We now return to a brief review of the global literature on the over-representation of women and girls with care experience in the criminal justice system, as originally outlined in Chapter 2 of this book. What follows is a contextual analysis of the criminalisation of cultural difference in Australia that has drawn Aboriginal and Torres Strait Islander people into the criminal justice system in large numbers and continues to do so. The chapter then documents the three key narratives that emerged in our research in relation to gender. The first is that gendered narratives obscure recognition that girls have experienced heightened adversity, instead portraying girls as inherently more 'difficult'. Responses are, thus, centred on the problematic behaviour of girls in care and push the adversity they experience to the periphery to be obscured from view. The second is that self-harm, which is more common for girls, intensifies criminalisation for those in care. We illustrate how self-harm by girls in care is a significant factor in accelerating their entrapment in the criminal justice system. Finally, we explore how some of the efforts of women and girls with care experience to resist their treatment within the 'care and protection' system may result in further criminalisation.

Women and girls with care experience in the criminal justice system

As Chapter 2 of this book outlined, a gendered understanding of the over-representation of women and girls with care experience in the Australian criminal justice system is lacking. Fitzpatrick et al.'s 2019 literature review on this topic identified the extant literature on the experiences of girls and women with care experience using an intersectional lens. The three themes that emerged in Fitzpatrick et al.'s literature review provide a helpful foundation for our study.

The first theme of Fitzpatrick et al.'s (2019) literature review, as explored in Chapter 2, focused on the gendered impact of ACEs. To reiterate the findings, this review found that trauma is common for girls and women with care experience and 'may elevate the risk of justice system involvement', beyond that experienced by boys and men (Fitzpatrick et al., 2019, p. 12). Girls in care were more likely to experience adversity (see Lipscombe, 2006), sexual assault and exploitation (Commissioner for Children and Young People, 2021; Dixon et al., 2005; Shrifter, 2012) and to have 'higher rates of extreme and complex trauma' (Fitzpatrick et al., 2019, p. 12). A NSW study of young women in detention found high levels of post-traumatic stress and associated psychopathologies (Dixon et al., 2005). In terms of likelihood to offend, the review found that vulnerability and adversity contribute to violent offending by girls more than boys (McAra & McVie, 2010) and that 'maltreatment' accelerates offending such that girls appear to 'catch up' with boys (Fitzpatrick et al., 2019, p. 12; see also Postlethwait et al., 2010, p. 319).

Previous research findings on young offenders show a correlation between offending and mental health concerns for girls. 'Girls involved in offending behaviour tend to have significantly greater mental health needs than boys involved in offending behaviours, being at increased risk of depression, self-harm and post-traumatic stress' (Chitsabesan & Bailey, 2006, cited in Fitzpatrick et al., 2019, p. 13). Postlethwait et al.'s (2010) study found that 'depression and delinquency in child welfare involvement is more critical to understanding girls' offending than boys' offending (cited in Fitzpatrick et al., 2019, p. 13). The review showed that the blurring of lines between welfare and justice results in more gaol time for girls (O'Neill, 2001). In Ellis's (2018) study, girls were viewed as 'vulnerable and troublesome simultaneously, regardless of the reason for their admission' (cited in Fitzpatrick, 2019, p. 18). Additionally, 'familial breakdown and domestic violence' increase the likelihood of girls being arrested as adults, with one study finding that each 'additional childhood risk factor' increased the probability of arrest by 21% (see Rhoades et al., 2016).

The intersection of race strengthens this impact, with Fitzpatrick et al (2019) noting that 'adversity may be more influential for Black girls then other ethnic groups' (Fitzpatrick et al., 2019, p. 12). Fitzpatrick et al.'s review included studies from England and Wales, the United States and Australia, which showed high rates of over-representation in the criminal justice system for particular ethno-cultural groups of girls and boys. However, ultimately, the review found a lack of research on the intersection of ethnicity, care experience and justice system involvement.

As previously acknowledged, the complexities inherent in the Australian context arising from the historical and ongoing imposition of intergenerational trauma on Aboriginal and Torres Strait Islander young people exacerbates vulnerability (HREOC, 1997). Indigenous children are more likely to experience traumatic events, or a combination of such, including illness, family violence, incarceration, financial strains, grief through death, illness or suicide of family members (Hampton & Toombs, 2013). Indigenous young people from colonised countries are more likely to experience intergenerational trauma, which has a negative impact on their physical and mental well-being (Smallwood et al., 2020). The *Royal Commission into the Detection and Protection of Children in the Northern Territory Final Report* states that for Indigenous children, cognitive disability and mental health problems are intrinsically linked to OOHC service provision and youth detention (White & Gooda, 2017).

The second theme considered by Fitzpatrick et al.'s review relates to the care experience itself. The review highlights the finding that 'sustained, consistent and nurturing relationships are key to promoting the wellbeing of children in care' (Bazalgette et al., 2015; Wood & Selwyn, 2017, cited in Fitzpatrick, 2019, p. 18). And, stable placements are important for reducing the risk of involvement with the criminal justice system (Schofield et al., 2014; Taylor, 2006). Yet, the care environment, particularly residential care, is frequently a place of criminalisation, abuse and trauma. The review also cites evidence of young people in care being the targets of predatory behaviours (Berelowitz et al., 2012; CREATE Foundation, 2018; Jay, 2014). Positive relationships, whether they be with biological parents of other carers, act as a protector against aggressive behaviours by young girls (Farruggia & Germo, 2015). For girls, a symbiotic relationship exists whereby an increase in child welfare involvement increases the likelihood of juvenile justice involvement, but this is not the case for boys (Johnson-Reid & Barth, 2000, cited in Fitzpatrick et al., 2019, p. 19).

Placement stability is critical and the review found differing results for boys and girls in this regard. Australian research has shown that placement instability increases the likelihood of conviction for girls but not for boys (Malvaso et al., 2017). Taylor (2006) identified the protective factors for girls of secure attachment and educational outcomes against youth justice involvement. In terms of educational outcomes, the review found that girls fare better than their male counterparts overall, but that girls in care fare worse than girls not in care (DfE, 2019). The review describes the link between poor educational outcomes and youth offending as 'well established' (Fitzpatrick et al., 2019, p. 14). In addition, out of area placements that involve being moved to a different local government area, exacerbate poor life outcomes (Fitzpatrick et al., 2019, p. 22). Going missing or running away from care also increases the likelihood of police reports and girls are more likely to abscond than boys as US research has shown (Baynes-Dunning & Worthington, 2013; Sarri et al., 2016, cited in Fitzpatrick, 2019, p. 23). Furthermore, girls are often blamed for their victimisation, as the Rotherham Inquiry found (Jay, 2014). The type of placement is also critical in that foster care may differ from other forms of care: a Swedish study of girls in foster care found that there was no association between justice involvement and care experience (Lindquist & Santavirta, 2014).

The third theme of Fitzpatrick et al.'s review concerns girls and women in the juvenile and adult justice systems. Women are generally sentenced to longer periods for transgressions than boys as such offending is seen as acting in opposition to gender norms (Fitzpatrick et al., 2019, p. 28). Moreover, the stigma associated with having been sentenced for an offence is a significant predictor of reoffending for young women, but not for young men (McGrath, 2014). And women's survival strategies, including running away, can often have a negative impact on sentencing (Chesney-Lind, 1999). Risk and need for women are often conflated, leading to higher sentences and net widening. For girls in OOHC, minor offending is often what brings them into the criminal justice system (Taylor, 2006). When children in care arrive in court, a lack of a support network can make a term of incarceration more likely (Fitzpatrick et al., 2019, p. 29; see also Hunter, 2022). Having an adult support worker attend court and assist with the court process is not guaranteed and not common, in contrast to the wishes of young people (CREATE Foundation, 2018, p. 52). Research has suggested that girls more than boys are affected by harsher penalties due to care status bias (Conger & Ross, 2001, cited in Fitzpatrick et al., 2019, p. 29). Although, Tam et al. (2016) found that girls were more likely than boys to be sent to a supervised group home in a Los Angeles County, but less likely to be sent to a youth gaol.

Australian research on care experience and the criminal justice system

The intersection of colonisation, the 'government of children' (Rose, 1989) and 'child saving' (Carrington & Pereira, 2009, p. 12) has fuelled the involvement of children in the care and criminal justice systems in Australia. The Australian criminal justice system is modelled on the British system, which in the 19th century became characterised by an emphasis on juvenile delinquency and a concomitant desire to address and criminalise certain types of behaviour (Platt, 1977, cited in Carrington & Pereira, 2009, p. 11). In the Australian context, a rise in practices dedicated to 'child saving' devastatingly coalesced with this trend, resulting in efforts to 'rescue delinquent children' (Carrington & Pereira, 2009, p. 12), commonly through the establishment of institutions later exposed as fostering systemic abuse. For Australia, two examples of such institutions are the Cootamundra Girls Home and the Parramatta Girls Home, discussed below.

In Australia, the colonial policies and practices of forced removal, criminalisation and dispossession have resulted in the targeting of Aboriginal and Torres Strait Islander women and children (Behrendt, 2019; Carrington & Pereira, 2009, p. 10). Writing in 1993, Kerry Carrington in her seminal book *Offending girls: sex, youth and justice* opens with the line: 'State wards comprise about a fifth of all girls processed by the Children's Courts'. As Carrington and Pereira (2009, p. 2) write in an updated edition of this collection, the 'brutal legacy of penal welfarism' has been criticised for 'net-widening, sexualising girls' delinquencies, and selectively criminalising young people from impoverished, Aboriginal and housing commission communities'. Colonisation involved dedicated strategies to 'erase the reproduction of Indigeneity through genocidal means' (Behrendt, 2019, p. 204).

The Cootamundra girls' home, located in central NSW, was established in 1912 to warehouse Aboriginal girls and young women up until the 1960s (Haskins, 2001). It provided a facility to support the Aborigines Protection Board and later the Aborigines Welfare Board in their indenturing of Aboriginal women:

> Under this 'Apprenticeship scheme' (as it was known), girls and young women were taken from their families and communities and placed in the Cootamundra Aboriginal Girls Home, in central New South Wales, prior to being sent into service in the households of middle-class white families. Their wages were artificially low and paid not to them, but directly to the Protection Board, which held trust accounts for the workers: these were rarely paid out.
>
> (Haskins, 2001, p. 13)

The policy was designed to destroy Aboriginal communities by isolating women from their Aboriginal families. As Haskins (2001, p. 19) writes:

> Girls in Cootamundra Home were actually told to look forward to the prospect of producing a fairer child, who would then produce an even fairer child, at the same time as they were taught to fear and despise Aboriginal men – basically, being exhorted to effect their own disappearance.

Haskins illustrates further using a quote from Aboriginal activist Anna Morgan, who actively opposed the policy of removal stating in 1935 that:

> At the age of fourteen our girls [are] sent to work – poor illiterate trustful little girls to be gulled by the promises of unscrupulous white men. We all know the consequences. But, of course, one of the functions of the Aborigines Protection Board is to build a white Australia.
>
> (Goodall, 1995, cited in Haskins, 2001, p. 19)

The sexual assault of girls apprenticed under this 'protection' policy was foreseeable and widespread. As Haskins (2004, p. 53) concludes, the NSW Aboriginal Protection Board colluded in systematic sexual abuse. More girls were indentured than boys, and more were sent to urban areas. Some 17%

of Aboriginal girls apprenticed in urban areas became pregnant (Haskins, 2004, p. 42).

The Parramatta Girls Home was originally established in 1887 as a way of incarcerating girls and was known by other names up until it became the Parramatta Girls Home from 1966 to 1974 (Sullivan, 2017, p. 86). It stands on the lands of the Darug people (p. 86). Corinnee Sullivan (2017) traces the history of the institution as providing of means of incarcerating Aboriginal and non-Aboriginal girls under the auspices of 'education and training'. It housed both Aboriginal and non-Aboriginal girls considered 'delinquent' and/or 'destitute' (Carrington, 1993). These labels were attributed to Aboriginal girls who were forcibly removed from their families due to the policies and practices that produced the Stolen Generations. Up to one in three Aboriginal children was removed from their families between 1910 and 1970 (Sullivan, 2017, p. 84). The systemic abuse suffered by children in these institutions has been documented in several inquiries, including the *Bringing Them Home* Report (1997), the *Forgotten Australians* (2004), the *Protecting vulnerable children report* (2005) and more recently the *Royal Commission into Institutional Responses to Child Sexual Abuse* (2017).

Accounts of Parramatta Girls Home reveal a dehumanising routine whereby girls were sent to a maximum-security facility, known as the Hay Institution For Girls, if they were not compliant (Carrington & Pereira, 2009, p. 20; see also Djuric, 2007). It is estimated that, between 160 and 200, girls were housed at the Parramatta Girls Home at any one time and approximately 30,000 girls over its lifetime (Sullivan, 2017, p. 84). Riots were common (Sullivan, 2017, p. 88). Girls were subjected to violence including sexual assault and attempted sexual assault. Cultural violence was perpetrated against Aboriginal girls as Western values were imposed and cultural connections, including visits by relatives, were prohibited in order to sever ties between Aboriginal peoples and cultures (Sullivan, 2017, p. 91). As Sullivan (2017, p. 93) writes:

> The cultural violence that Aboriginal inmates were subjected to within the Home had lifelong effects. Aboriginal inmates were denied knowledge of their families, were not formally educated and left the Home carrying the burden of guilt for being 'wrong'.

To date, there has been no redress for the treatment of the women who were incarcerated at the Parramatta Girls Home (Sullivan, 2017, p. 89). Extraordinary efforts by the 'Parragirls', a group of Aboriginal and non-Aboriginal women with lived experience of being incarcerated in the home, have shone a light on Australia's history of institutionalisation of women and children (Hibberd & Djuric, 2019). Through arts funding, Parragirls have pursued arts projects as social history mechanisms and the book *Parragirls*, charts their vision for this physical site into the future. These initiatives contribute to truth-telling and healing.

The institutionalisation of young people beyond what would be expected in a criminal matter has a long history in Australia and leaves a long legacy (Carrington, 1993). As Carrington and Pereira (2009, p. 29) write:

> Contemporary criminological research indicates that the best way to prevent juvenile reoffending is to keep young people out of custody and away from institutions which foster recidivism and secondary deviation.

Rather than being kept away from the criminal justice system, thousands of Aboriginal and Torres Strait Islander children have been forcibly placed in institutions. We know that even for those who are able to access diversionary programs, Aboriginal and Torres Strait Islander young people do not evenly share in the benefits with other young people. Aboriginal and Torres Strait Islander young people are less likely to receive a police caution than non-Indigenous people (Luke & Cunneen, 1995) and less likely to benefit from 'diversionary initiatives and restorative justice' (Blagg, 2009, p. 19).

The statistical data reveal that Aboriginal and Torres Strait Islander women are drastically over-represented in the prison population (ABS, 2021). The imprisonment rate for Aboriginal and Torres Strait Islander female prisoners is 449 persons per 100,000 of the adult female Aboriginal and Torres Strait Islander population, down from 458 persons last quarter. The imprisonment rate for all female prisoners was 32 persons per 100,000 of the adult female population for the same period (ABS, 2021). Scholarship on Indigenous young women's experiences of the criminal justice system is highly critical of the lack of disaggregated data, which makes it difficult to gain an intersectional picture of women's criminalisation (Anthony et al., 2020; Bartels, 2012a; 2012b; Tubex & Cox, 2020). Prison census data also do not record prisoners on short sentences, who are more likely to be women (Baldry, 2010).

Research by Indig et al. (2010) as part of a NSW inmate health survey conducted in 2009 found that Indigenous young offenders were more likely to have care experience, be from a non-metropolitan area, have a parent in prison, have a range of medical issues, be a parent, use drugs and have mental health problems. McGrath and Weatherburn (2012) found that 84.3% of Indigenous young offenders were likely to be reconvicted within ten years compared to 55.7% of non-Indigenous young people. Some of the tools of the criminal justice system such as risk assessment instruments have been criticised as furthering colonisation. As Leeson et al. (2015, p. 80) note, the 'uncritical adoption of risk assessment instruments may reproduce and embed systematic discrimination when considering racial, ethnic and social inequality'. The disadvantage faced by Aboriginal families has long been a factor in the policies and practices of forced removal and in the refusal of bail. It was acknowledged by a NSW magistrate interviewed as part of a study by Spiranovic et al. (2015, p. 37) that 'because Indigenous families are more disadvantaged, you're going to get kids who don't have accommodation to go to so they stay in custody because they're granted bail but there's nowhere for them to go'.

For women with care experience, the pathway from juvenile detention into the adult correctional system is not 'set in stone' but is 'highly probable' (McFarlane, 2010, p. 345), and a greater proportion of girls in detention have care experience (Kenny et al., 2008, p. 10). A 1985 Senate Standing Committee report found that a loss of connection to family and culture can increase the likelihood that an Aboriginal child in OOHC will have contact with the criminal justice system (in Davis, 2019, p. 237). According to a 2008 report evaluating the characteristics and health needs of young people in detention and subject to community orders, 39% of girls in custody had a history of OOHC compared to 28% of boys. Of young people subject to community orders, 36% of girls had a history of care compared to 21% of males (Kenny et al., 2008, p. 11). There is also a cyclical pattern whereby bail is refused for welfare reasons (McFarlane, 2010, p. 348), bail status impacts sentencing and those refused bail are more likely to receive a control order (McGrath, 2016). In McFarlane's review of 111 cases before the Parramatta Children's Court over a six-month period in 2009, 34% involved young people with care experience. Of this cohort, 26% were female and just over half were Aboriginal and Torres Strait Islander. Of the 26%, half were facing charges of property damage, whereas none of the female non-care cohort were charged with property damage offences.

A Standing Committee on Social Issues report on juvenile justice released in 1992 made recommendations that resonate today around the separation of 'care' matters from criminal matters, the need for inter-agency cooperation, the importance of having appropriately trained and qualified staff working with young people, the importance of diversion and the need for culturally appropriate programs and Aboriginal and Torres Strait Islander staff. The committee's findings in relation to girls in the criminal justice system are familiar: 'Girls who are state wards are forty times more likely to be detained in custody than other girls. Boys who are state wards are seventeen times more likely to be detained in custody than non state wards' (1992, p. xxxi). Further, Kerry Carrington testified before the committee at the time, stating that:

> Rates of female delinquency in NSW are not surprisingly correlated with the indicators of social disadvantage … in my statistical analysis of female delinquency in Local Government Areas of NSW, the single most over-represented group were girls from Aboriginal communities … The fact that Aboriginal youth are the single most over-represented cohort in the ward population … it is my firm belief that some, if not many, of the Aboriginal youth in detention centres today, would not be there had they not been forcibly, and often unnecessarily removed from their families and communities as children by child welfare authorities.

After the separation of the care and protection jurisdiction from the criminal jurisdiction of the Children's Court, the age of clients for DOCS dropped dramatically (Carrington & Pereira, 2009, p. 34).

Recent public advocacy by a group of Aboriginal grandmothers in NSW known as Grandmothers Against Removal led to a significant and far-reaching inquiry. In 2016, the NSW Government commissioned Professor Megan Davis to deliver an independent report into Aboriginal and Torres Strait Islander children and young people in OOHC. The review was tasked with identifying the reasons behind the high and increasing rates of Aboriginal children in OOHC in NSW and strategies to reduce this trend. Among its 125 recommendations, the review found the ACPP to be 'poorly implemented and misunderstood' (Davis, 2020, p. XIV). The report's ultimate conclusion was that 'it is time for the NSW Government to formally acknowledge to Aboriginal communities, as well as the broader Australian community, that as an ostensible "parent", it can and does cause harm to children for whom it has parental responsibility' (Davis, 2020, p. XXXV).

The fervour with which the Australian care and protection and criminal justice systems have sought to ensnare children, particularly Aboriginal children, has cast a long shadow that persists today (Behrendt, 2019). These are practices of institutional racism in that they regularly occur on the back of ostensibly 'facially neutral' laws and policies that operate in an uneven or unfair way to the detriment of Aboriginal people (Blagg et al., 2005, p. 12). The next section will analyse our data to facilitate a gendered analysis focusing on Aboriginal and Torres Strait Islander girls and women.

Gendered understandings of care experience among criminal justice stakeholders

Talking to our respondents about gender revealed different understandings of how girls and boys with care experience interact with the criminal justice system. There was little insight shown into the characteristics of either girls or boys who become involved in the criminal justice system, as explicated by the literature reviewed above. Several of our police and NGO respondents felt that there were no gendered differences between the involvement of boys and girls with care experience in the criminal justice system (OP1, OP2, NGO4, NGO3). Among the lawyers, perceptions differed as to whether girls were more likely to get bail (L4&L5) or less likely to get bail (L3). One magistrate commented that boys more often tune out of the court process (M14).

Our respondents differed in their perceptions of offending by boys and girls with care experience. There was a common perception that more boys in care were involved with the criminal justice system, but only by a small proportion (M10, M14, JJ6, JJ5). Several respondents remarked that either that gap was narrowing or that offending by girls with care experience was on the increase (NGO1, M12). A number of respondents, including magistrates and juvenile justice officers, observed that violent offending by girls with care experience was increasing (JJ5, JJ6, M12). However, boys were seen as being more likely to engage in physical offending (L4&L5) or serious offending. In contrast, girls with care experience were understood to commit minor offending, and not break-and-enter offences (M11):

> We get a fair proportion of young girls. They don't tend to be involved in the break-and-enter type offences. A lot of them are drug affected. A lot of shoplifting type petty theft offences and a lot of violent matters where they get involved in assaults. In terms of numbers, I don't know that I could give you any useful guide there. Most of the girls who do come tend to be younger than the boys; they're usually very young... They commit offences themselves and in groups and with boys, related to drugs sometimes, it's alcohol infused ... And I think it's normal behaviour for these girls to react that way. So if they're confronted with something that they disagree with they're more inclined to lash out rather than think about it. And I find that the girls, I think, more than the boys tend to overreact when the police get involved. There's a lot of swearing at the police and the police react to the swearing and so one thing leads to another and they find themselves jailed with resisting and assaulting police.
>
> (M11)

As Sprott and Doob (2009, p. 25) note, any increase for women is likely to be dramatic as their numbers are low in comparison to men's offending. Speaking about the North American context, Sprott and Doob (2009, pp. 42–43) observe that girls are 'less likely to be in court than boys, and ... they are more likely to have been involved in the least serious forms of offending'. Magistrates, police officers, OOHC service providers and lawyers were all unable to articulate the gendered characteristics of children in care and how this intersects with their exposure to, or experience with, the criminal justice system.

Censoring vulnerability: the perceived difficulties of working with girls and women with care experience

Our interviews with the respondents revealed gendered understandings of the complexities faced by girls with care experience. A juvenile justice respondent felt that it was more difficult to build rapport with girls (JJ6). Several of our respondents (OP5, NGO1) stated that girls with care experience were harder to deal with than boys with care experience as girls were more manipulative or 'attention seekers' (OP5), whereas boys 'just got on with it' (NGO1). A police officer respondent commented:

> To be honest, I've mainly dealt with the females. Off the top of my head, I'm only thinking about the females. The males can be aggressive, but I

> just find the females are more of the troublemakers; they're more of the ones we get called for. They're more of the attention seekers, I would say.
>
> (P6)

The adversity that lies behind these behaviours was recast as a gendered propensity to make trouble and seek attention. The assumption here is that the attention-seeking behaviour of girls is a nuisance that requires a police response and uses valuable police resources.

Juvenile justice workers commented on the extensive and complex needs of girls in care, highlighting mental health problems, exposure to trauma and/or being easily triggered. One JJ respondent was critical of the way in which the complex needs of young people were being managed by youth workers in OOHC, most of whom do not possess specific or adequate skills for dealing with heightened vulnerability:

> [Y]ou get a lot of casuals in the residential youth work setting, so people that are studying or coming through that are really just developing skillsets and kind of using them as a stepping stone into bigger and better things. So kids end up with – they might have one or two permanent youth workers, and then they get people that haven't got a strong English background at the same age as them, 18, and the youth worker might be 18 or 19, and they're 17, and this 18 year-old is trying to enforce boundaries and put things in place on them. So the dynamics are really kind of sometimes complex and difficult for the young people, and just that inconsistency doesn't allow for those relationships to always get built up.
>
> (JJ7)

Secure attachment and placement stability, so critical as protective factors against involvement in the criminal justice system, are hard to ensure in this environment. Rather, calling for police intervention becomes the norm. This structural deficit in the care system results in children having increased exposure to the criminal justice system.

Girls were seen as more manipulative and better able than boys to navigate the criminal justice system to avoid harsh consequences. One NGO respondent, an OOHC provider, felt that girls would 'bat their eyelids' to get out of trouble (NGO1), despite being 'more vicious' in their offending:

> A lot of females will play the innocent role. I'll bat my eyelids, I'm sorry. I'll cry and I'll get away with it. Where the boys were generally, I'm tough, I'm macho. I'm not going to admit to anything. And I'll just do whatever punishment I'm given. That's a stereotype, I know, but that's pretty much the way a lot of it goes, because quite often, especially in relation to violence, quite often females can be far more vicious than

> males in their offences, or the facts around their offending. Females can be a lot more manipulative, and can be quite more vicious in that, and even to each other when they're in – again, I haven't done any research in it, but I think you'll find that there's a lot more – well, I knew from working in the prisons that female inmates are a lot more harder to work with and deal with than men, because of those underlying behaviours, and manipulating. And again, like I said, it probably comes back from being a child, and seeing what happens in your own family, sort of thing.
>
> (NGO1)

This respondent, thus, described a continuation of the behaviour of young women in OOHC into their time spent in prison. Women with care experience were described as vicious, manipulative and harder to work with than men. This was attributed by the above respondent to a traumatic family environment and upbringing, yet the impact of this adversity was ignored. Instead, the offending is addressed and made visible, and results in the punishment of this child. Therefore, across our interviews, the impact of trauma or maltreatment for girls with care experience was effectively pushed to the periphery.

'Once they are in trouble, we fall on them with an axe': on girls becoming parents while in OOHC and the criminal justice system

The sexualised habits of young girls were the focus of comments by the respondents throughout the interviews. One respondent felt that girls were sexualised early and were promiscuous as a result (L13). Some NGO respondents felt that they needed to protect themselves from false claims of sexual assaults made by girls in residential care (NGO10). One said that they were conscious of the risk of working alone with young girls in care (NGO10), adding to the perception of girls in care as being manipulative and prone to making false claims. Staines (2016) similarly highlights this trend amongst carers who fear allegations from girls in their care. More recent research by Fitzpatrick (2022, p. 24) noted the 'damaging cultures that develop amongst staff in some care and criminal justice settings, whereby girls may be dehumanised, and their vulnerability and experiences of trauma rendered invisible, particularly when they are viewed as sexually knowledgeable'. Fitzpatrick argues for more support to practitioners alongside raising aspirations and tackling negative stereotypes for girls and women.

Our respondents also observed that action is not taken to address the victimisation of girls who have been sexually assaulted while in OOHC (L13). One respondent said that many children in care engaged with porn and were sexualised as a result (L13). Residential care was said to characterise girls as sluts and boys as alpha males, depending on how sexualised they were (JJ1), clearly denigrating girls in care and leaving questions unanswered about the care and protection provided to them while in OOHC. The damaging gender roles cultivated in the residential care environment impacted girls and boys. In other studies, these characteristics have been identified as factors contributing to misogyny and rape culture (Death et al., 2021; Salter, 2016). One respondent said that girls in care were mums at age 14 and 15 and several had two kids by 17:

> It's very complicated. It is really complicated. When you imagine that – it's a complicated situation with people who have deficits, who are compromised, who have no sophistication. Absolutely none. They're not worldly in any way. They're quite street smart, but they're not mature. Sometimes I get really cranky with the Department when they say, you know, say a 16 year old has had a baby – oh, she hasn't done this and she hasn't gone to – I've said it lots of times. A switch doesn't get flipped from her being a child to an adult just because she's popped out a baby. She's still a child. Where's the care application for that mother? Why hasn't someone been charged? She was pregnant at 15. That's the other thing we see. Maybe because it's just such an enormous task to bring those people to justice. Especially when you have the victim being non-compliant. My view is it doesn't matter – take the DNA. There's nothing to argue after that. I think that the system lets the kids down. And then once they're in trouble, that's when we fall on them with an axe.
>
> (L13)

The above respondent felt that the system is letting children down as it expects children who have had a child themselves to be mature and assume adult responsibilities. This respondent also commented that the fact that a child has had their own child is unlikely to be followed up by law enforcement and charges of sexual offences against this child sought. This was also the finding of the Commission for Children and Young People (2021) in a recent Victorian study, which found that children in residential care were exposed to sexual and criminal exploitation that received inadequate responses by police, OOHC service providers and child protection agencies.

One of the gendered narratives to emerge that exacerbates criminalisation, and which has been previously documented (McFarlane, 2010), was the sense that magistrates would try to protect girls from potential assault by refusing them bail. One lawyer respondent felt that if girls with care experience come before a magistrate they would be less likely to get bail if there was a risk of sexual assault or danger for that young girl were she to be released:

> I guess, if women – sometimes I think with women that possibly if there's any suggestion that they're at any kind of risk of sexual assault

> or danger in that area, that they may be less likely to get bail because the courts – the magistrates will take a more protectionist approach maybe.
>
> (L3)

This approach is thus resulting in children being detained in custody for being 'at risk'. This shows that earlier criticisms, outlined by McFarlane (2010), of bail being used to perpetuate a cyclical pattern of criminalisation are continuing.

Mental health, care experience and criminalisation

Self-harm was seen by some of our respondents as being more common for girls with care experience who become involved in the criminal justice system (M11). One juvenile justice officer characterised girls in care as being prone to self-harm and boys in care as being prone to 'bravado' (JJ2). It was a common perception that girls are more likely to self-harm than boys (JJ5, OP5, NGO12, SP1):

> The only thing that the girls do seem to represent more in – is in self-harm. My experience here is that we can get very few males that will do superficial cutting of the wrists or whatever it might be, or harm themselves with a sharp implement, won't hurt themselves. The girls seem to do that more regularly, self-harm, the boys just go off and use physical violence against the workers or they'll go out and do whatever they do. But we don't have – I couldn't tell you of any males here that I've had here that have self – done self-harm. They will talk about killing themselves, but they don't do that. So the girls seem to do that.
>
> (SP1)

Our study provided evidence of how self-harm can lead to criminalisation for young women, who were understood as more likely to self-harm in the first place as a result of traumatic childhood experiences (SP1, OP4). Service providers responded to girls who self-harmed by calling the police to address the self-harming behaviour. Yet, increased police contact often resulted in subsequent criminalisation. The following story shared by an NGO respondent reveals how this occurs:

> The boys are more likely to be involved with the police, but having said that, girls with mental health issues will always be involved with police, because the self-harming and suicidal girls are going to be refusing treatment, they'll be the ones that the police and ambulance are called for, or the ambulance called for, they refuse to attend the hospital with the ambulance, and then the police are called to restrain them, there's all that, sort of, stuff that happens with the girls actually.
>
> (NGO2)

The marked difference between girls' and boys' experiences of OOHC here is clear. Girls are more likely to self-harm and police are more likely to be called as a result of their self-harming. This can lead to resist arrest and subsequent charges.

The vulnerability of kids in care to criminalisation was confirmed by the senior police respondents interviewed in our study. This was illustrated by one respondent (P1), who discussed the experiences of a young woman called Linda (a pseudonym) and the processes that contribute to criminalisation. Critically, in this case it was clear that the impact would be felt over a lifetime:

> We have a young lady here that's about to turn 18 [Linda], and she's a self-harmer and we've been through the assault phases with her and tried to get AVOs and changes of workers and all these sort of things, but what that does is increase the profile of the young person, so that later in life, when police talk to them on the side of the road, and they say I'm talking to, in this case [Linda], the first thing that comes up, for the rest of her life, will be all the warnings that applied to her as a young person – in all the contacts with police by numerical number. And what that does is that if the police don't know about it, they will be forgiven for drawing an adverse conclusion from a very good start, and that is sadly, I think, what sometimes happens.

For Linda, police involvement in relation to assault, AVOs and self-harm increased the chances that she would be visible to police and would have more contact with the police over time. In this regard, one police respondent explained the consequences of being reported to police for self-harm:

> [This] is a young girl yet to turn 18, and she already has a hundred events. But by comparison to some of our – worst is not a word I'd use – but I'll say worst kids, we have some in the high two hundreds and some in the three hundreds … But what you'd see is when you pull up these events, like, it does say she's been charged four times, she's got legal process; she's got all these warnings … she's got all this – and that stays with her all her life, in as far as contact with police.
>
> Anyone who's got one hundred events, that's really unusual for anybody. And here are – so these are the warnings that come up – self harm – unarmed resist, threatened resist, in the police resist, will lose it, false allegations, habitual liar … that warning can't come off unless the officer who put it on takes it off. If that officer resigns or dies, that's it, that's there. And every time police have contact with her that warning comes up. And extensive self-harm, so straight away, if she's acting strangely, the police will think, oh, she's mad, we need to schedule to take her into custody for her in care, when – and that's been done many, many times with very poor results. So, you see, here are what these one hundred things are – apprehended violence orders, more apprehended

> domestic violence, domestic violence, mental health, assaults, domestic violence, mental health, mental health, mental health and mental health, you see, this is what's been recorded for a young person in care. There's a missing persons – and this is what a lot of their profiles will look like.
>
> (SP1)

The same police respondent was of the view that this scenario is not uncommon for children in care. This kind of record narrows the options available to police when dealing with children, or indeed adults, with such a record.

> This would be representative of the kids that are really in trouble in out-of-home care. They will have a history there of all of those sort of things. And that number has a big influence on police. Straightaway, if it comes up, you know, [Linda], three events, straightaway, as far as we're concerned she's clean, no problems, she won't lie to us, no warnings, take her on face value. And you pull this poor young girl up with all that there, which I'd have to say most of it is legitimate, sadly, perceptions are gone to straightaway. And [Linda] is a big and aggressive young girl. She's over 110 kilos, and she can be very aggressive and obnoxious. And, so, if this is in the back of your mind, and you form an opinion and then you see and meet [Linda] then the opinion is cemented, therefore the options that the police are likely to consider are very narrow. And that is just how it is, and that's what we're trying – trying desperately to work with FACS and our partners, to get away from.

The same senior police respondent then compared his own record to this young person's to illustrate the point:

> I'll just, in fairness to [Linda], I'll bring myself up and I'll show you the difference – and I'm [older]. And, you know, I'm not going to show you – there will be nothing too secretive about that. But, you see, here I am … no warnings [laughs], which you wouldn't expect from a policeman, I know, but five events, right. So if, when I do my walk after work – at work, I usually do it in my flannelette shirt and my stubbies, and look like some sort of yobbo walking along the road, a local cop pulls me over and I say, mate, I'm just walking along the road here, he says, what have you got that stick for, I said for the dogs that aren't on a chain or magpies, they're in nesting season. And if he wants to check me up he'd have a look at that and he'd probably say it nicely. If he – [Linda] was walking along the same road with a big stick and he pulled her up and her profile came up – give me that stick, and why aren't I charging you with carrying an implement? See, this is the difference.

The abundance of detail on the police record of this young person stayed with them for a considerable period and shaped their interactions with the police force. It was also reflective of a drain on police resources. In this regard, research from SA and NSW confirms the influence of prior criminal record. In Gale et al.'s study from 1990, prior record was the main determining factor for sentencing, with unemployment and non-nuclear family structures more likely to lead to a custodial sentence (Gale et al., 1990 cited in Luke & Cunneen, 1995, p. 27).

A further illustration provided by a more junior police officer based in a regional location further reveals how vulnerability intersects with criminalisation for those with care experience. In the incident described below, the police were called out by an OOHC service provider on account of the behaviour of a young person:

> I have gone to a motel room where this young lady was not allowed to be at home, in the group home, so they've put her in a motel room. Yeah. She's been mucking up. She's threatened to climb out the window. So I've gone there and said, like, 'What's the go? Why do you want to climb out the window?'. 'I don't really want to climb out the window, but he's annoying me', being the carer. Now I'm talking to the carer and I hate to sound racial, but I'm talking to the carer and I'm going, unfortunately, for you, buddy, I'll take my report and I'll be very professional – however, if I can't understand you, and I'm a professional and I'm getting frustrated with you, you can imagine a young person who is already frustrated with the world, who is frustrated with adults, who is frustrated with the cops or just naughty in general, why she would muck up on you, because even I am frustrated with you. So I've told this young lady, 'You need to just be very, very mindful of him. He's here doing you – a job for you, looking after you, respect him, otherwise he'll call us back.' She responds to that and we don't get another call that night. The next night is a different story. But I walk away going, it's no wonder they're frustrated – these kids are frustrated and acting out, it's because the carers are frustrating. I am frustrated. I'm the professional. These kids are no doubt going to be frustrated. There's no boundaries, there's no rules, they're allowed to do whatever they like. Another example would be where they've – she's walking down the street at 3 o'clock in the morning and there's four coppers there trying to nicely take her back into custody, because she's obviously got some issues. And the carers, you know, we've said, well, come on carer, you can come and give us a hand, you know this young lady better than what we do; how about you use some of your rapport with her to get her to do what we need her to do. Now come on such and such, you know I can't touch you, you know I can't put a hand on you, but can you come a bit closer to me? I'm thinking, don't remind her that you are not allowed to put a hand on her and you're not allowed to have some type of control on her, because when she comes close to me and starts carrying on, I'm allowed to grab her, and I'm happy to grab her, because that's what I will do. And we ended up taking her to the ground, because she carried on.

> But the carer, instead of trying to help us, was saying, you know I can't touch you, come on, you know, I'm not going to touch you, you know I'm not allowed to do that. She needs no reminding. It's like, man, shut up, because you're not helping. You're not helping at all.
>
> All you're doing is reminding her that she has rights. And, of course, she's got rights and of course she's got a job to do, but right now that is not appropriate. We are trying to actually corral her so she doesn't get hurt, for her own safety, and here you are reminding her that she can just walk away and keep going and no-one's going to lay a hand on her. That's crap. I'm going to lay a hand on her. I'm going to have to secure her, if it's in her best interests and the safety of everybody else … Frustrating. Day in and day out.
>
> (P2)

The above narrative paints a clear and devastating picture of how self-harm, or threats to self-harm, leads to criminalisation and danger for children in care. The inability of the staff member to manage the complex needs of the child, the characterisation of this behaviour as a drain and waste of police resources and the inevitability of a police response that takes the person into custody, with considerable force, are all painfully demonstrated.

Our research was undertaken at the same time as the coronial inquiry into the tragic death of a 15-year-old girl known as MK. MK had a history of sexual assault and died of an overdose in a youth refuge in Pennant Hills, NSW. The psychologist at her coronial inquiry stated that there was not enough funding to support traumatised children. MK had been in care since she was 12 months old and was allegedly raped by two male carers at a youth refuge in Sydney. She was due to give evidence at the rape trial in the weeks after her death (Boney, 2016). The coronial inquest into MK's death revealed how unsafe her care placements had been. Even after she was removed from the placement where she was allegedly sexually assaulted by carers, she was placed in a residential care home. At that home, a man described as her 'boyfriend', despite the age difference between them constituting a criminal offence under the *Crimes Act 1900* (NSW), was able to enter her room and engage in drug taking with her, during which she overdosed (Lee, 2016). The inquiry into the death of Tiahleigh Palmer also demonstrated the vulnerability of girls in foster placements (Bentley, 2021). Our research demonstrates that girls in care, residential care, in particular, are still at risk of sexual abuse in care placements. As noted in Chapter 3, the juvenile justice respondents discussed a case where a girl was sexually assaulted by another child in care and experienced retaliation from other children for reporting. In another case, Case 63 of our file reviews, the victim was a co-resident of the offender in a group home. She and the defendant had previously been in a sexual relationship, but after it ended, he assaulted her. She had low intellectual functioning as a result of a traumatic brain injury and was, therefore, particularly vulnerable being left in the same home environment as her alleged offender. These cases indicate how unsafe the care environment can be for girls and young women and the structural factors exacerbating their vulnerability.

Self-placing as resistance

The respondents in our study stated that absconding was common (L13 JJ8). In some cases, children, particularly Aboriginal and Torres Strait Islander children, have historically absconded to return to their families from whom they had been forcibly removed (McFarlane, 2021). As our previous research has highlighted, absconding is a form of resistance by young people and can also make children more vulnerable to sexual and criminal exploitation (Colvin et al., 2018). One respondent provided a vivid account of how this absconding as resistance occurs, by using the example of Michelle (a pseudonym) who was before both the care and criminal jurisdictions of the Children's Court. This young person was the child subject in care proceedings, and she also faced criminal proceedings for AVOs and breaches of that AVO:

> So [Michelle] was removed from her mum – I'm not sure if she was removed, to be honest, or if it was an informal care arrangement. But she's been living with her grandparents for most of her life. That placement has broken down and [Michelle] is a teenager. [Michelle] has decided to vote with her feet and go back and live with mum. That relationship is toxic and volatile. AVOs and breaches ensue. Because she left the grandparents – and there were real concerns about the grandparents – there was a care proceeding brought to basically have her placed in the care of the Minister, not her grandparents. Her grandparents have got some real issues. And that's the thing – she's not living with her mum, but she was no better living with her grandparents. Maybe even worse. But because she's been with her grandparents – and she's quite damaged by that placement. She has significant mental health issues. She is a self-harmer. She runs away. I think she's currently missing. So a lot of our kids will go missing.
>
> (L13)

This storytelling highlights the fraught nature of the overlap between care and criminal proceedings and the predicament faced by young people who are forced into certain living arrangements, against their wishes and ultimately to the detriment of their well-being. It illustrates the strength and resilience of this young person, in taking herself out of a dangerous environment that was sanctioned by the state but ended up perpetuating her exposure to violence. It also demonstrates how this led to her criminalisation and that was the behaviour that was prioritised in terms of a response.

Conclusion

The Stolen Generations Organisations (SGOs) (Aboriginal Affairs, 2018, p. 2) write that:

> The Bringing Them Home report was a watershed moment in our nation's history. But 20 years later it's not just about bringing Aboriginal people home; it's also about keeping them home. We are deeply distressed by the rate Aboriginal children today continue to be removed from their families. As survivors of the Stolen Generations, our voice and perspective on child protection issues are important, and we could play a unique role in supporting the restoration of families.

This statement from the Stolen Generations Organisations attests to the continued resistance and advocacy of Aboriginal and Torres Strait Islander people. The right to self-determination is not currently applied in the Aboriginal child protection system in NSW despite the fact that it has been 20 years since the publication of the *Bringing Them Home* Report which advocated the recognition of a strong form of self-determination in Aboriginal OOHC. However, the Queensland *Human Rights Act 2019* (QLD), under Section 28 Cultural Rights, states that Aboriginal and Torres Strait Islander peoples have the right to 'enjoy, maintain, control, protect and develop their kinship ties'. The right to self-determination is seen as enabling community advocacy and a culturally informed justice system can play a pivotal role in addressing the 'intergenerational impacts of child protection interventions' (Radke & Douglas, 2020).

Our research on the intersections of gender and criminalisation among those with care experience, focusing on Aboriginal and Torres Strait Islander women, revealed that acute and complex needs are obscured in favour of prosecution and a police response. Vulnerability increases the likelihood of exposure to the criminal justice system and acts not as a trigger for transformative care but as a catalyst for criminalisation. The impacts of exposure to the criminal justice system are long-lasting and follow a child into their adulthood. Young people resist these unsafe environments but in doing so often become the target of law enforcement. Given the specific needs of young women and their likelihood of possessing certain vulnerabilities, more needs to be done to address the propensity of the criminal justice system to criminalise young women and girls.

References

Aboriginal Affairs. (2018). *Unfinished business, progress report to parliament*. NSW Government. http://cootagirls.mediajam.com.au/wp-content/uploads/2021/03/unfinished business_report_2018.pdf

Anthony, T., Sentance, G., & Bartels, L. (2020). Transcending colonial legacies: From criminal justice to Indigenous women's healing. In L. George, A. N. Norris, A. Deckert, & J. Tauri (Eds.) *Neo-colonial injustice and the mass imprisonment of indigenous women* (pp. 103–132). Palgrave Macmillan.

Anthony, T., Sentance, G., & Behrendt, L. (2021). 'We're not being treated like mothers': Listening to the stories of First Nations mothers in prison. *Laws*, *10*(3), 74.

Australian Bureau of Statistics. (2021). *Corrective services*. https://www.abs.gov.au/statistics/people/crime-and-justice/corrective-services-australia/sep-quarter-2021

Australian Human Rights Commission. (2020). *Wiyi Yani U Thangani (Women's Voices): securing our rights, securing our future—report.*

Baldry, E. (2010). Women in transition: From prison to... *Current Issues in Criminal Justice*, *22*(2), 253–267.

Bartels, L. (2012a). Painting the picture of Indigenous women in custody in Australia. *Queensland University of Technology Law and Justice Journal*, *12*(2), 1–17.

Bartels, L. (2012b). Twenty years on: Indigenous deaths in custody and lessons from the frontline. In I. Bartkowiak-Thron & N. L. Asquith (Eds.) *Policing vulnerability* (pp. 181–197). The Federation Press.

Bartels, L., Spiranovic, C., Clare, J., Bartels, L., Clare, M., & Clare, B. (2015). Aboriginal young people in the Children's Court of Western Australia: Findings from the National Assessment of Australian Children's Courts. *University of Western Australia Law Review*, *38*(2), 86–116.

Bedford, N. (2019). Storytelling in our legal system: Healing for the stolen generations. *Australian Feminist Law Journal*, *45*(2), 321–331.

Behrendt, L. (2019). Stories and words, advocacy and social justice: Finding voice for Aboriginal women in Australia. *Australian Feminist Law Journal*, *45*(2), 191–205.

Bentley, K. (2021). *Inquest into the death of Tiahleigh Alyssa-Rose Palmer.* Coroners Court of QLD. https://www.courts.qld.gov.au/__data/assets/pdf_file/0008/687131/cif-palmer-ta-20210618.pdf

Berelowitz, S., Firmin, C., Edwards, G., & Gulyurtlu, S. (2012). *'I thought I was the only one. The only one in the world': The Office of the Children's Commissioner's Inquiry into Child Sexual Exploitation in Gangs and Groups – Interim Report.* Office of the Children's Commissioner.

Blagg, H. (2009). *Youth justice in Western Australia.* Report prepared for the Commissioner for Children and Young People WA.

Blagg, H., Morgan, N., Cunneen, C., & Ferrante, A. (2005) *Systemic racism as a factor in the over-representation of Aboriginal people in the Victorian criminal justice system.* https://tr.uow.edu.au/uow/file/64419d5f-d183-49c2-90d9-d81c8dc44f17/1/2005-blagg-1-210.pdf

Boney, B. (2016). Faster response needed to help teenager who died of overdose in state care, inquest hears. *ABC News.* https://www.abc.net.au/news/2016-09-12/teen-who-overdosed-in-sydney-needed-faster-response/7835890

Carrington, K. (1993). *Offending girls: Sex, youth and justice.* Allen and Unwin.

Carrington, K., & Pereira, M. (2009). *Offending youth: Sex, crime and justice.* Federation Press.

Chesney-Lind, M. (1999). Challenging girls' invisibility in juvenile court. *The Annals of the American Academy of Political and Social Science*, *564*(1), 185–202.

Colvin, E., McFarlane, K., Gerard, A., & Mcgrath, A. (2018). 'We don't do measure and quotes': How agency responses criminalise and endanger the safety of children missing in care in New South Wales, Australia. *The Howard Journal of Crime and Justice*, *57*, 231–249. https://doi.org/10.1111/hojo.12253

Commission for Children and Young People. (2021). *Out of sight: Systemic inquiry into children and young people who are absent or missing from residential care.*

CREATE Foundation. (2018). *Youth justice.* https://create.org.au/wp-content/uploads/2021/07/CREATEs-Youth-Justice-Report-Young-Persons-Version-2018.pdf

Crimes Act 1900 (NSW). https://legislation.nsw.gov.au/view/html/inforce/current/act-1900-040

Davis, M. (2019). *Family is Culture*: *Review report.* Independent Review of Aboriginal Children in OOHC.

Death, J., Moore, T., McArthur, M., Roche, S., & Tilbury, C. (2021). Young people's perceptions of sexual assault in residential care: 'It does happen a lot'. *Journal of Child Sexual Abuse*, *30*(1), 4–20.

Delgado, R., & Stefancic, J. (1993). Critical race theory: An annotated bibliography. *Virginia Law Review*, *79*, 461.

Department for Education. (2019). *Outcomes for children looked after by local authorities in England, 31 March 2018.* https://assets.publishing.service.gov.uk/government/uploads/system/uploads/attachment_data/file/794535/Main_Text_Outcomes_for_CLA_by_LAs_2018.pdf

Dixon, A., Howie, P., & Starling, J. (2005). Trauma exposure, posttraumatic stress, and psychiatric comorbidity in female juvenile offenders. *Journal of the American Academy of Child & Adolescent Psychiatry*, *44*(8), 798–806.

Djuric, B. (2007). *14 years of hell.* Women about Hay.

Ellis, K.H. (2018). Contested vulnerability: A case study of girls in secure care. *Children and Youth Services Review*, *88*, 156–163.

Farruggia, S. P., & Germo, G. R. (2015). Problem behavior among older youth in foster care: Examining gender. *Children and Youth Services Review*, *48*, 20–30.

Fitzpatrick, C. (2017). What do we know about girls in the care and criminal justice systems? *Safer Communities*, *16*(3), 134–143.

Fitzpatrick, C. (2022). Challenging perceptions of care-experienced girls and women. *Prison Service Journal*, *258*, 19.

Fitzpatrick, C., Hunter, K., Staines, J., & Shaw, J. (2019). *Exploring the pathways between care and custody for girls and women: A literature review.* https://eprints.lancs.ac.uk/id/eprint/142892/1/CareCustodyLiteratureReview.pdf

Hampton, R., & Toombs, M. (2013). *Indigenous Australians and health: The wombat in the room.* Oxford University Press.

Haskins, V. (2001). On the doorstep: Aboriginal domestic service as a 'contact zone'. *Australian Feminist Studies*, *16*(34), 13–25.

Haskins, V. (2004). 'A better chance'? Sexual abuse and the apprenticeship of Aboriginal girls under the NSW Aborigines Protection Board. *Aboriginal History*, *28*, 33–58.

Hibberd, L., & Djuric, B. (2019). *Parragirls.* New South Publishing.

Human Rights Act 2019 (QLD). https://www.legislation.qld.gov.au/view/html/asmade/act-2019-005.

Human Rights and Equal Opportunity Commission. (1997). *Bringing Them Home: National inquiry into the separation of Aboriginal and Torres Strait Islander children from their Families.* Report of the National Inquiry into the Separation of Aboriginal and Torres Strait Islander Children from their Families.

Hunter, K. (2022). 'Out of place': The criminalisation of black and minority ethnic looked after children in England and Wales. *Prison Service Journal*, *258*, 13–18.

Indig, D., McEntyre, E., Page, J., & Ross, B. (2010). *2009 NSW inmate health survey: Aboriginal health report*. NSW Justice Health.

Jay, A. (2014). *Independent inquiry into child sexual exploitation in Rotherham 1997–2013*. Rotherham Metropolitan Borough Council.

Kenny, D.T., Nelson, P.K., Schreiner, I., Lennings, C.J., & Butler, T. (2008). *Young offenders on community orders: Health, welfare and criminogenic needs*. Sydney University Press.

Lee, D. (2016) *Inquest into the Death of M*. NSW Coroners Court. https://coroners.nsw.gov.au/documents/findings/2016/m-finding.pdf

Leeson, S., Rynne, J., & Smith, C. (2015). Incarcerating Aboriginal and Torres Strait Islander women in Australia: Finding a balance in defining the 'just prison'. *Australian Indigenous Law Review*, *19*(2), 76–96.

Lindquist, M. J., & Santavirta, T. (2014). Does placing children in foster care increase their adult criminality? *Labour Economics*, *31*, 72–83.

Lipscombe, J. (2006). *Care or control? Foster care for young people on remand*. BAAF.

Luke, G., & Cunneen, C. (1995). *Aboriginal over-representation and discretionary decisions in the NSW juvenile justice system*. Juvenile Justice Advisory Council of NSW.

Malvaso, C.G., Delfabbro, P.H., & Day, A. (2017). Child maltreatment and criminal convictions in youth: The role of gender, ethnicity and placement experiences in an Australian population. *Children and Youth Services Review*, *73*, 57–65.

McAra, L., & McVie, S. (2010). Youth crime and justice: Key messages from the Edinburgh Study of Youth Transitions and Crime. *Criminology & Criminal Justice*, *10*(2), 179–209.

McFarlane, K. (2010). From care to custody: Young women in out-of-home care in the criminal justice system. *Current Issues in Criminal Justice*, *22*(2), 345–353.

McFarlane, K. (2021). *Children and youth reported missing from out-of-home care in Australia*. Australian Federal Police.

McGrath, A. (2014). The subjective impact of contact with the criminal justice system: The role of gender and stigmatization. *Crime and Delinquency*, *60*(6), 884–908.

McGrath, A. (2016). Intersections of Indigenous status, sex and age in sentencing decisions in the New South Wales Children's Court. *Australian and New Zealand Journal of Criminology*, *49*(1), 90–112.

McGrath, A., & Weatherburn, D. (2012). The effect of custodial penalties on juvenile reoffending. *Australian and New Zealand Journal of Criminology*, *45*(1), 26–44. https://doi.org/10.1177/0004865811432585

New South Wales Upper House Standing Committee on Social Issues. (1992). *Juvenile Justice in NSW*. New South Wales Government Printer.

O'Neill, T. (2001). *Children in secure accommodation: A gendered exploration of locked institutional care for children in trouble*. Jessica Kingsley.

Paik, L. (2017). Critical perspectives on intersectionality and criminology: Introduction. *Theoretical Criminology*, *21*(1), 4–10.

Postlethwait, A.W., Barth, R.P., & Guo, S. (2010). Gender variation in delinquent behavior changes of child welfare-involved youth. *Children and Youth Services Review*, *32*(3), 318–324.

Radke, A., & Douglas, H., (2020). Indigenous Australians, specialist courts, and the intergenerational impacts of child removal in the criminal justice system. *The International Journal of Children's Rights*, *28*(2), 378–400.

Rhoades, K. A., Leve, L. D., Eddy, J. M., & Chamberlain, P. (2016). Predicting the transition from juvenile delinquency to adult criminality: Gender-specific influences in two high-risk samples. *Criminal Behaviour & Mental Health*, *26*(5), 336–351.

Rose, N. (1989). *Governing the soul*. Routledge.

Royal Commission into Institutional Responses to Child Sexual Abuse. (2017). *Final report*.

Salter, M. (2016). Real men do hit women: The violence at the heart of masculinity. *Meanjin*, *75*, 97–104.

Schofield, G., Ward, E., Biggart, L., Scaife, V., Dodsworth, J., Larsson, B., Haynes, A., & Stone, N. (2014). *Looked after children and offending: Reducing risk and promoting resilience*. BAAF.

Senate Community Affairs References Committee. (2004). *Forgotten Australians*. https://apo.org.au/node/190271

Senate Community Affairs References Committee. (2005). *Protecting vulnerable children: A national challenge*. https://apo.org.au/node/1787

Shrifter, C. N. (2012). *Child welfare and delinquency: Examining differences in first-time referrals of crossover youth within the juvenile justice system*. Portland State University.

Smallwood, R., Woods, C., Power, T., & Usher, K. (2020). Understanding the impact of historical trauma due to colonization on the health and well-being of indigenous young peoples: A systematic scoping review. *Journal of Transcultural Nursing*, *32*(1), 59–68.

Sprott, J. B., & Doob, A. N. (2009). *Justice for girls?* University of Chicago Press.

Staines, J. (2016). *Risk, adverse influence and criminalisation: Understanding the over-representation of looked after children in the youth justice system*. Prison Reform Trust.

Sullivan, C. (2017). Aboriginal inmate experiences of Parramatta girls home. *Australian Aboriginal Studies*, *2*, 84–97.

Tam, C.C., Abrams, L.S., Freisthler, B., & Ryan, J.P. (2016) Juvenile justice sentencing: Do gender and child welfare involvement matter? *Children and Youth Services Review*, *64*, 60–65.

Taylor, C. (2006). *Young people in care and criminal behaviour*. Jessica Kingsley.

Tubex, H., & Cox, D. (2020). Aboriginal and Torres Strait Islander women in Australian prisons. In *Neo-colonial injustice and the mass imprisonment of indigenous women* (pp. 133–154). Palgrave Macmillan.

White, M., & Gooda, M. (2017). *Royal Commission into the protection and detention of children in the Northern Territory*. NT Final Report. Commonwealth of Australia.

Williams, M. S. (2021). Judgement: Bugmy v R [2013] HCA 3. In *Indigenous legal judgments: Bringing Indigenous voices into judicial decision-making* (pp. 77–91). Routledge.

8 Reducing criminalisation

Innovations from England and Wales

Introduction

The globalisation of criminal justice reform is usually about the proliferation of punitive approaches. However, in our NSW pilot study, several of our respondents referred to initiatives underway in parts of England and Wales that were resulting in a decrease in the criminalisation of children in residential care. These initiatives were being mirrored in some parts of NSW in an attempt to similarly decrease the criminalisation of this cohort. As a result, we built into our study an international snapshot and undertook qualitative research with key informants from relevant criminal justice and social welfare agencies in England and Wales, including care leavers.

We acknowledge that there is a direct link between the legacy of British colonialism and the criminalisation of Aboriginal and Torres Strait Islander children in OOHC. This theme has been explored extensively in other chapters and is recognised as a point of difference between the Australian and international research on the involvement of children in care in the criminal justice system. The international snapshot presented here provides an interesting comparison between the coloniser and the colonised. There are limitations to our analysis of England and Wales, however. International comparisons with countries that share a legacy of colonisation, such as Aotearoa New Zealand and Canada, would offer insights related to the shared experience of criminalisation and the over-representation of Indigenous peoples in the criminal justice system and in OOHC (see Stanley, 2017).

There are historical similarities in the development of the United Kingdom and Australian juvenile justice and welfare systems. While colonisation and the over-representation of Indigenous peoples comprise a major distinction, both systems feature the warehousing of often impoverished children for delinquency and neglect, as well as for offending, in reformatories and industrial schools. Similar to the Australian context, several UK inquiries have also exposed abusive practices in children's homes (Jay, 2014; Shaw & Greenhow, 2021; Utting, 1997; Warner, 1992). These inquiries resulted in fewer children living in residential care settings, which are now predominantly provided by private enterprises (Narey, 2016, p. 9). Research has also

DOI: 10.4324/9781003093367-9

shown how criminalisation and decriminalisation practices in England and Wales have a differential impact on children, such that 'black and minority ethnic' (BAME) children are over-represented in the care population and in the criminal justice system (Hunter, 2022).

In situating this case study, this chapter first canvasses the wave of recent reviews, reports, policy formulation and scholarship that has characterised the landscape of care experience and the involvement of care-experienced children in the criminal justice system over the past five years. Second, it analyses the key informant interviews undertaken according to three themes: shifting cultures, policing and inter-agency cooperation and custodial settings. We met with key informants (n = 10) from organisations in England and Wales involved in developing, researching and implementing policies and practices to shift the culture and establish a shared understanding of how to reduce the over-representation of people with care experience in the criminal justice system. These agencies were engaged with both children and adults with care experience, so practices aimed at both cohorts were captured. Finally, the chapter explores what insights this case study might offer that relate to the NSW context. In drawing on these decriminalisation practices in the United Kingdom, we do not promote the blind adoption of reforms from international jurisdictions. We also acknowledge the work of critical scholars who have highlighted the dramatic increase in the child detention population between 1989 and 2009, which rose 795% (Cunneen et al., 2018). Cunneen et al. (2018, p. 425) argue that:

> youth justice policy reforms might be taken to signal *change* (the size and shape of the penal landscape) but they have ultimately failed to displace *continuities* in the form of systemic human rights violations.
>
> [original emphasis]

What we observed in our case study is not definitive evidence of success or a panacea. Rather, we aim to enrich the findings of our NSW case study and promote further reflection by analysing how decriminalisation pathways might be imagined.

The criminalisation of people with care experience in the United Kingdom

Our research took place at a time of considerable momentum in the United Kingdom around policy review and closer interrogation of the links between care experience and involvement in the criminal justice system. In a systematic review of youth justice policy between 1991 and 2016, Cunneen et al. (2018, p. 406) conclude that England and Wales had 'evolved into one of the most retributive and punitive youth justice sites in the western world'. However, towards the end of this time scale, the numbers of children in custody had begun to decline. Austerity measures, targets to reduce 'first time entrants' (FTEs), diversionary schemes promoted from the centre and not the periphery and a political softening 'albeit tentative and beset with ambiguity' are provided as explanations for this reduction (see Bateman, 2012, p. 43; Cunneen et al., 2018). Care experience and its intersection with the criminal justice system had also started to receive more attention.

In late 2015, the UK Prime Minster and the Secretary of State for Education commissioned an independent review of residential care (Narey, 2016). At around the same time, two national charities – Prison Reform Trust and the Howard League – had begun exploring the links between care experience and criminalisation by conducting research and reviews. The Howard League launched a campaign to reduce the over-representation of children in care in the criminal justice system. National law enforcement agencies were also developing new strategies focused on young people, specifically aimed at reducing their contact with police and other parts of the criminal justice system.

Additionally, there were also reviews underway into the adult and youth justice systems more broadly, alongside policy formulation in this area by national law enforcement agencies. Charlie Taylor, at the time the Chief Executive of the National College of Teaching and Leadership, was commissioned by the Ministry of Justice to review the youth justice system (2016). The Honourable David Lammy MP, a former Minister of State, barrister and Chair of the All Party Parliamentary Group on Race and Community since 2010, conducted an independent review of the treatment of and outcomes for BAME people in the criminal justice system (2017). However, the terminology of 'Black, Asian and Minority Ethnic' is widely seen as inappropriate (see Khunti et al., 2020). Its use by UK public sector agencies is soon likely to be discontinued since the Prime Minister's Commission on Race and Ethnic Disparities (2021) has recommended it be replaced by a focus on developing specific understandings of ethnic groups. Thus, where this term is used in this chapter, it reflects the terminology used in the official government reports cited.

Finally, momentum among UK academics was also building. Notwithstanding the existing research programs of several academics who had been analysing the intersection of care and criminalisation for some time, new and continued research programs brought additional insights to these long-standing issues (see, for example, Day, 2017; Fitzpatrick, 2009; Fitzpatrick & Williams, 2017; Hayden, 2010; Shaw, 2014, 2016; Shaw & Greenhow, 2021; Staines, 2016; Taylor, 2006), including those generated by intersectional approaches (Fitzpatrick et al., 2019).

A clear benefit of this momentum and its ability to achieve results has been an improvement in the available data used to record and monitor children and adults with care experience engaged with the social service and criminal justice systems, including data capturing earlier contact between police and residential homes. This is now possible because since 2018 children's homes have been required to report data on police contact in the pre-inspection questionnaire administered by the Office for Standards in Education, Children's Services and Skills (Ofsted) that such homes must complete (Shaw & Greenhow, 2021, p. 11).

To put this international snapshot into context, it is helpful to understand some of the characteristics of OOHC in the United Kingdom. First, approaches to child social services differ according to jurisdiction. Our study focused on England and Wales. Second, the only available statistics were from England and showed that there were 70,440 children in care, referred to as 'looked-after children' in the United Kingdom, at the beginning of March 2016 (Department of Education [DfE], 2016). This rate of children in OOHC is similar to that of Australia overall, but the disaggregated Australian picture reveals that Indigenous Australian children are in OOHC at 11 times the rate of non-Indigenous children (AIHW, 2021). Returning to the statistics from England, the number of children in OOHC in 2016 represented an increase of 5% on the number of looked-after children in 2012. Much of this increase is a result of the dramatic rise in the number of unaccompanied asylum seeker children entering OOHC (DfE, 2016). Most looked-after children are male (56%), white (75%) and over ten years old (62%; DfE, 2016). Black and minority ethnic children are disproportionately represented (Hunter, 2022). Most children (75%) in OOHC are placed in foster care, while 11% are placed in a secure unit, children's home or hostel (DfE, 2016, p. 8). Statistics from 2015 show that 'residential care' in the United Kingdom is made up of children's homes (64%), secure units (2%), hostels (13%) and residential schools (8%) (Narey, 2016, p. 4). Third, the majority of group homes are run by the private sector (67%), and a significant proportion are run by local authorities (28%; p. 9). Eleven companies operate almost a quarter of all children's homes in the United Kingdom (p. 9). There are fewer staff at privately run children's homes, where staff are paid £9.39 per hour, almost £4 less than their counterparts at children's homes run by local authorities. Since January 2015, residential care staff have been required to possess as a minimum a level 3 diploma (p. 56). An assessment of this qualification is particular to occupation and organisation/industry, but in broad terms, it is the equivalent of a diploma in the Australian Qualifications Framework. Residential care is more costly than foster care. The National Audit Office estimated that 'in 2017–18, local authorities spent £1.61 billion on the 79,000 looked-after children in foster care, £20,400 per child. In contrast, they spent £1.25 billion on the 26,750 looked-after children placed in residential care (a category that includes secure units and children's homes), which amounts to £46,600 per child' (NAO, 2018, p. 23).

Statistics from 2019 show that almost half of the children sentenced in the United Kingdom have a history of care (Youth Justice Board [YJB], 2020, p. 4). According to the Youth Justice Board report, 'a sentenced child is one who received a Referral Order, Reparation Order, Youth Rehabilitation Order or custodial sentence between 1st April 2018 to 31st March 2019' (YJB, 2020, p. 4). More than half the children in prison have been in care, and more than half of this cohort are from 'Black, Asian and Minority Ethnic backgrounds (BAME)' (Greater London Authority, 2021, p. 5). While overall numbers of children in custody dropped by 74% between 2007 and 2017 (Ministry of Justice, 2018), the number of 'BAME' children has increased as a proportion of all children in custody (Hunter, 2022). An analysis of data by the Youth Justice Board found that 'Black, Asian and Mixed ethnic children' were more likely to be sentenced to custody by significant margins (YJB, 2021, p. 9). A gender breakdown of these statistics was not available. Hunter's (2022) research with youth justice professionals gave some context for this statistic, observing that looked after children were perceived as not having supportive backgrounds and that this led to harsher sanctions as a way of intervening. Moreover, looked after children were understood as not having the necessary support structures in place to ensure a diversionary approach would succeed.

An independent review led by David Lammy investigated improvements for reducing the number of so-called BAME offenders in the criminal justice system (Lammy, 2017). The Lammy Review criticised a youth justice system as slow to respond to the increase in the proportion of numbers of BAME offenders coming into contact with the criminal justice system. Among its 35 recommendations, the Lammy Review called for better data and monitoring, race-blind decisions and greater transparency around Crown Court sentencing remarks as well as more diversity in judicial and other justice system appointments. Many of the recommendations were structural in nature and aimed at improving education and understanding of how the system operates to sustain the over-representation of specific ethnic minorities in the youth justice system.

The *Review of the Youth Justice System in England and Wales* by Charlie Taylor (2016) celebrated the declining numbers of young people coming into contact with the youth justice system but focused on the high numbers of 'black, Muslim and white working class boys; many [of whom] are in care, and mental and other health problems, and learning difficulties, are common' (Taylor, 2016, p. 2). It made 36 recommendations to address what it saw as a multi-system failure and prioritised a more devolved justice system and a greater focus on education. Some of the recommendations sought increased training of staff in children's homes around the resolution of minor incidents and supported the development of protocols with the police. Taylor's review also recommended that children always be accompanied by their carer or social worker in court (Taylor, 2016, p. 52).

Many of the above reviews, as well as academic scholarship, have highlighted the lack of a gendered analysis of care experience and criminalisation, particularly one that applies an intersectional lens (Fitzpatrick et al., 2019; Prison Reform Trust [PRT], 2016). In this regard, a gendered focus on the pathway to custody in the United Kingdom for women and girls with care experience was provided in a recent literature review by Fitzpatrick et al. (2019). As we examine in more detail in Chapter 7, in

2019, Fitzpatrick et al. published a literature review on *Exploring the pathways between care and custody for girls and women* as part of a larger UK Nuffield Foundation project aimed at disrupting the trajectory from care to criminalisation. This review captured the English-language literature from the past 20 years on the experiences of girls and women with care experience, evaluated using an intersectional lens. In considering women as well as girls, it extended the focus to women involved in the adult criminal justice system. The review explores the overlap of care experience and criminal justice system involvement, the care experience itself and girls and women in the criminal justice system. It remains the case that disaggregated data on the involvement of particular cohorts in the criminal justice system are lacking.

An independent review of residential care, led by the Chief Executive of social services voluntary agency Barnardo's, Sir Martin Narey (Narey, 2016), focused primarily on children's homes, which at the time accounted for 64% of placements in residential care, or 5,300 children, and accrued administration costs totalling £750 million per year. In 2015, 15% of children in children's homes had been convicted or been subject to a warning or reprimand, a much higher rate than the 5% of looked-after children not residing in children's homes (Narey, 2016, p. 6). The Narey report also found that the vast majority of children's homes were run well and that some children chose to live in residential care over foster care, contrary to popular stereotypes that residential care is a last resort.

Narey made 34 recommendations related to staffing profiles and numbers, access to education and reviewing placement and foster care. Of the recommendations pertaining to the criminalisation of children with care experience, replication of protocols and uptake of restorative justice were two strategies endorsed. Narey also recommended clearing up any legal uncertainties around the use by staff of restraint and containment on children in care, and the ability of police to use their discretion to not record crime in children's homes. Narey recommended against requiring those who work in children's homes to have graduate qualifications. Instead, he argued that the 'best staff, irrespective of their qualifications, develop a vital ability to make and maintain good relationships with troubled and challenging children' (Narey, 2016, p. 55). Narey argued that ensuring that staff possess this ability was dependent on sound recruitment strategies, including hiring staff with a diploma.

A second independent review was commissioned in 2015 by the Prison Reform Trust to investigate the involvement of children with care experience in the criminal justice system in England and Wales (PRT, 2016). *In Care, Out of Trouble* took over 200 submissions and involved a review panel consisting of children and young people's consultation groups. The report was delivered in 2016 and made 10 recommendations that aimed to reduce the involvement of children with care experience in the criminal justice system. Many of the recommendations focused on the need for early intervention and support, national leadership in police and other agencies and greater cooperation among agencies. The recommendations were related to those in care and leaving care and those in custody.

A third report by the Howard League was also delivered in 2016 (Howard League, 2016). The report, entitled *Criminal care*, contained pointed criticism of children's homes and what it termed the 'excessively high rates' of criminalisation. The Howard League undertook to focus on addressing the criminalisation of children in residential care in a campaign launched in 2016. It began with a scoping paper and has since also published six briefing papers, including the *Representing looked-after children at the police station* (2019) guide for lawyers and *Best practice in policing* (2017). While the previous focus of the Howard League had been on the minor offending of young people that brought them into the criminal justice system, its latest report, published in 2020, examines intersections of residential care and child crime exploitation (Howard League, 2020). From this perspective, children in residential care are viewed as vulnerable to exploitation by criminal gangs and other networks that capitalise on the low levels of oversight within such facilities where already vulnerable children reside. The Howard League argues that its advocacy has culminated in a reduction in the criminalisation of children in residential care, from 15% in 2013–2014 to 5% in 2019–2020 (Neilson & Sands, 2021).

The Narey Report is critical of the Howard League for making what it called 'simplistic' and 'unfair' arguments and using 'dramatic license' about the routine criminalisation of children in care. It argues that criminalisation for minor incidents is not 'remotely typical' (Narey, 2016, p. 34). In discussing unnecessary criminalisation, Narey further remarks that:

> However severe the problem of unnecessary criminalisation has been, I am confident that this has substantially been addressed by homes, by the police and by the Crown Prosecution Service.
>
> (p. 38)

The unnecessary criminalisation of those with care experience in the United Kingdom is consistent with that occurring in the NSW context (Cashmore, 2011; Gerard et al., 2019; McFarlane, 2017; McFarlane et al., 2019; Wong et al., 2009). Yet, pockets of practice in the United Kingdom are seeing a shift away from a punitive approach, and less contact with the criminal justice system among children (DfE, 2018, pp. 5–6), although criminalisation for certain cohorts of children have intensified (Hunter, 2022). The next section of this chapter looks briefly at the respondent views on the over-representation of care-experienced children in the criminal justice system in the United Kingdom, before moving to an analysis of the initiatives undertaken to arrest this trend in three sites – the residential care environment, policing and custodial settings. The final part of the chapter offers insights for the NSW context.

Key informant views on care experience and criminalisation in the United Kingdom

There was universal agreement among the ten UK key informants we interviewed that care-experienced children are over-represented in the criminal justice system in England and Wales. It was also consistently acknowledged that traumatic childhood experiences were compounded by the limitations and poor performance of the care system itself. As one respondent observed, there was 'concern that children in care are perhaps held to higher account maybe for their behaviour than children who live in private homes' (UK1). The key informants argued that the care-experienced population faced certain aspects of the criminal justice system in a different, and more disadvantageous way than other children. As a police respondent observed:

> [T]he strongest advocate for a child is their parent, and so where their parent is missing because they are in the care system, you remove that advocate, so actually they tend to be the young people who are more likely to spend longer in police custody because there isn't a parent there saying, 'What are you doing? What's going on with my child? Why are you doing this?' And it changes the conversation because nobody seems to care about this child, so actually the police officers dealing with it don't care either and so it replicates that whole forgotten, abandoned child, the behaviour is replicated by all those dealing with them, which is terrible and a real indictment [on] our system … a young person in the care system is more likely to come in quicker I think because of that.
>
> (UK4)

Without an advocate, children were thus worse off in the criminal justice system. The respondents estimated that care-experienced children were between 6 (UK2) and 12 (UK10) times more likely to be in the criminal justice system than other children. Care experience was also seen to severely compound the already considerable challenges facing children in the criminal justice system in the United Kingdom.

Part of the impetus for change in how institutions respond to kids in care has been a recognition, as described by the key stakeholders, that incidents involving care-experienced children quickly escalate. As a respondent from one local authority explained, past practice involved relying heavily on the criminal justice system to manage challenging behaviour:

> [W]e, as carers, as corporate parents, were calling on the criminal justice system to manage the behaviour too much, too often … where we were in the UK as a whole … 10 years ago was, we were scooping up almost any child who kind of had any minor misdemeanour with the criminal justice system and getting a criminal record which stays with them for life.
>
> (UK6)

As we examine below, the prevalence of unnecessary criminalisation has been tempered by initiatives intended to change agency practice to reduce the habitual reliance on the police to manage children's behaviour. The respondents provided examples of successful or promising initiatives designed to reduce the involvement of those with care experience in the criminal justice system.

Shifting cultures: 'getting ahead of the behaviour' in care environments

Our key informants spoke about the significant work undertaken in specific counties in the United Kingdom around shifting the culture within the residential care sector. This involved a new emphasis on inter-agency collaboration to identify new ways of becoming 'more mindful of the experiences that children will have been through', which might help agencies 'respond more appropriately' (UK6). In Surrey County, for example, initiatives undertaken to 'reinforce' a holistic approach have meant that the number of young people entering the criminal justice system for the first time decreased by 92% in the ten years between 2007–2008 and 2017–2018 (DfE, 2018, p. 6). In the past decade, across the United Kingdom, the number of first-time entrants in the youth justice system has reduced by 85% (p. 5).

As one of our key informants noted, the strategies developed were based on a rejection of the assumption that 'looked-after children' are necessarily more likely to commit crime. In place of this assumption, the aim was described by the respondents as understanding offending as 'an indicator of responsibility to protect, to see offending as a flag that we need to raise our game and see it as an indication of vulnerability' (UK6). The approach also embraced a commitment to recognising that the types of offences that were drawing children in care into the criminal justice system were arising as a result of the care environment itself, rather than occurring in the wider community (UK6). A key focus in shifting the culture was to build the skills of residential care staff. Carers were trained in 'social pedagogy' (UK10) theory and practice, which represents an intersection of the social work and education disciplines. The goal was outlined by one key informant as follows:

> We need to create an environment for children where they are living which is going to be conducive to their wellbeing and is going to acknowledge the stuff they bring with them.
>
> (UK6)

Shaw and Greenhow (2021, p. 70; see also Narey, 2016) provide an overview of the social pedagogy approach, which was shown in official evaluations to not have had a measurable impact overall when trialled in England.

One respondent stated that, typically, children brought into care have experienced trauma and, therefore, that certain behaviours should be anticipated to arise in the care environment. This means that staff have a 'duty to get ahead of that behaviour and be as good as we can possibly be' (UK6). This respondent also articulated that the type of care environment that adopts such an approach would not, or should not, have to rely on law enforcement to respond to a child's challenging behaviour. As this respondent outlined, calling the police sets off a chain of events that results in criminalisation:

> It was blue lights, it was drag the kid off, it was – and the train leaves the station in terms of the criminal justice process and it's like, well, you called the police so therefore this is what's going to happen and we're going to take control now. So it was about stopping the train leaving the station and recognising there might be cases where kids had to go and talk to the police. Where we might call the police to help us because there's a riot in the home but that doesn't mean we'd actually want them to prosecute every child in the home.
>
> (UK6)

The need for a partnership between residential care providers and the police to ensure that children are not placed on the train that arrives at criminalisation was identified as critical. An analysis of respondent perceptions of how this shift in policing has occurred is provided in the next section of this chapter. Trust in multiagency relationships is difficult to achieve, particularly in hierarchical organisations such as the police force (see Shaw & Greenhow, 2020, p. 98). Shaw and Greenhow's evaluation of a multi-agency safeguarding team working to support children in care found that whilst there were benefits, the challenges outnumbered these advantages. The obstacles needed addressing before the multiagency team could fulfil its function. As they conclude, 'the idealised version of multi-agency working so often advocated by government reports and inquiries in response to safeguarding failures ...appears to be very different from the reality of such practice' (Shaw & Greenhow, 2021, p. 104).

The key informants spoke about how the changes to the care environment needed to be more than 'words on paper' (UK6). Instead, the shift needed to be 'more about our hearts and minds and a culture thing around people doing the right things' (UK6). Changing the culture in a children's home was said to involve modelling that behaviour from the outset. The key informants involved in these initiatives told us that what they did not do was blame staff for their poor behaviour or criticise their work:

> What we didn't do is go in and with a big stick and say, you're doing your job badly and we're here to tell you how to do it differently. And because that's what they were doing to the kids. So what we did instead was to go in and model what it is we wanted them to do. So we went in and we gave them a damned good listening to. And we were interested

> in their ideas around how things could be better, how they could support one another as a group to be a more consistent parent. We encourage them to reflect on, you know, what are the things that they do well? What are the – what does contribute to the times when things are relatively calm and peaceful in their environments? What's their understanding about what makes that possible? … I think by modelling, by helping them to see that they were affirmed and valued and by empowering them they were more able to see the value in them empowering the children and sharing responsibility, you know, helping them to – rather than be the people responsible for control and the social order in these environments and then a whole load of sanctions that they can call upon to achieve it, trading that with a kind of, you know, how can you help the children in their home to feel that this is their home and responsibility for wellbeing and safety and health and happiness is the child's – is everybody's responsibility within that environment. So let's trust the kids, you know?
>
> (UK6)

As this respondent highlights, there are good reasons for children to have a say in their own safety, health and wellbeing. As this respondent outlined, in order to shift the culture, managers modelled the behaviour that they wanted staff to show the children residing in these homes. The staff then developed skills that they could deploy to manage situations better and de-escalate conflict. In doing so, they sought to shift the narrative from one based on control and social order to one focused on shared responsibility with children to achieve a safer care environment.

Over the last decade, the number of children in the youth justice system has declined dramatically. The child prison population has fallen by over 70% (Hunter, 2022). The number of care experienced children in the United Kingdom who have been criminalised has also reduced. Between March 2015 and March 2020, the number of children convicted or subject to a youth caution has fallen from 15% to 5% (Howard League, 2020). However, the disproportionate representation of looked after children and 'black and minority ethnic' children have increased (Hunter, 2022). As the police key informant told us during the 2017 interview:

> Surrey County have managed for the last two years to not bring somebody new from the care system into the criminal justice system who wasn't already there at all, so they've managed to get to zero of anybody entering the criminal justice system from the care system for the first time, so that's a really good result.
>
> (UK4)

In Surrey County, the number of young people entering the criminal justice system for the first time reduced by 92% in the ten years between 2007–2008 and 2017–2018 (DfE, 2018, p. 6). The use of physical restraints has also been reported to have significantly decreased (UK10).

While the impact in this particular UK county has, thus, been considerable, our respondents said that this was the result of the immense work undertaken in this location and was, therefore, not indicative of practice or statistics across the country. Perhaps, it is, therefore, more appropriate to talk about pockets of change in the United Kingdom rather than a wider shift. However, in the past decade, across the United Kingdom, the number of first-time entrants in the youth justice system has reduced by 85% (DfE, 2018, p. 5).

In counties that have seen a reduction, monitoring and reflective practice have been introduced to evaluate the individual cases of children in residential care who are still being criminalised despite the changes in the sector. As one of our key informants observed:

> Well, the other thing we've done, I think, is … monitored, really quite forensically, you know, who are the children who we still continue to criminalise and lots of inquests about individual cases. We've just had this latest set of numbers for this year, overall, the looked-after children population has gone up, but so with this year we've got 16 young people who have been formally dealt with by the criminal justice system. And we will now go through each one of those cases and review and think, you know, what could we have done differently to avoid that outcome? And we'll do that with partners and there's a whole infrastructure of forums and – that bring people together to do that work. So it's like the – this stuff doesn't happen by itself. You need more than ambition, you need to put the work in.
>
> (UK6)

This comment indicates a firm commitment to a multi-agency approach to reviewing incidents in cases where care-experienced children are criminalised and to collaboratively developing new strategies or practices as required. While NSW and the United Kingdom share similar realities in terms of the unnecessary criminalisation of those with care experience, the initiatives undertaken to address this issue are different and are implemented in different ways. For the United Kingdom, the focus on reducing criminalisation through active monitoring and reviewing is apparent. In the next section, we return to the role of the police, who have formed partnerships to, in effect, prevent 'the train from leaving the station' (UK7).

Policies aimed at 'stopping the train leaving the station': policing and inter-agency cooperation

We start this section with an exploration of what the key informants characterised as a shift in the policing of looked-after children in the United

Kingdom, comprising a national policy framework, investment in cultural change and relationship building at the local level to stop children being arrested and brought into custody. We note that in only talking to key informants we have not been able to capture the perceptions of frontline staff as we did in our NSW study. It is likely that staff at senior levels are more informed on strategies and best practice and this knowledge is likely to be inconsistent within and across an organisation.

Our UK case study respondents spoke of the *South East Protocol to Reduce Offending and Criminalisation of Children in Care*, a multi-agency protocol involving several local authorities and a number of corresponding police services. The protocol sets out certain key principles as well as specific principles governing police involvement, children placed outside their local authority and responses to incidents occurring outside the care placement. The protocol is aimed at reducing the prosecution of care-experienced children using restorative justice approaches. The requirements on all involved are described as follows:

> It will be an expectation of all local authorities that staff and carers of children in care will strive to manage challenging behaviour at the placement address by way of internal resolution without involvement of the police wherever possible. Where this is not appropriate such as where there is concern about immediate safety, and where police become involved, the police should consider use of discretionary powers to apply an informal resolution response (such as community resolution). In circumstances where such a response is inadequate in the face of the seriousness of the offence then police should routinely consider potential for diversion from criminalisation/prosecution.
>
> (Protocol, p. 3)

As one key informant described, this protocol represents a commitment to doing 'something better than just sticking them [children] on the escalator and hurtling them off towards court rooms and prisons' (UK6). Instead, the protocol was designed to make people 'stop and think about informal alternatives to formal criminal justice' (UK6).

The UK Police has also developed a national strategy that heralds a new approach to managing children, in particular, care-experienced children. The National Strategy for the Policing of Children and Young People was endorsed by the National Police Chiefs Council in April 2015. It focuses on four key areas, one of which is 'looked-after children' (children in care). The other key areas are stop and search; detention, custody and criminalisation of children and young people and the relationship between young people and the police. The strategy recognises the over-representation of care-experienced children in the youth justice system and the impact of the trauma that many from this cohort have endured. Additionally, it affirms the need to minimise the risk to the significant proportion of care-experienced children who regularly go missing and to avoid the unnecessary criminalisation of care-experienced children. Again, in this strategy, the emphasis is on working with partners to 'make every effort to avoid the unnecessary criminalisation of children in care, making sure that the criminal justice system is not used for resolving issues that would ordinarily fit under the umbrella of parenting' (National Police Chief's Council, 2015, p. 11).

According to the police key informant, this framework has formed the basis of a child-centred policing strategy for the United Kingdom (UK4). Its focus on looked-after children speaks directly to many of the concerns police have been raising for some time. As our police key informant respondent explained:

> So [the national strategy] set us off on this journey of focusing on looked-after children and within our own force … we then started to look at what we knew about children's homes and children in the care system because officers on the ground would be constantly moaning about children's homes, children in care and the amount of calls, them always going missing, but we had no evidence, no data to support that actually this was an issue because our system was not focusing on recording it in such a way that you could pull that out quite easily.
>
> (UK7)

When the data were collected, the results were staggering. Among the almost 50 children's residential homes in a particular county, over 3,500 calls had been made to police in a one-year period (UK7). Of this huge number of calls, only 10% were related to criminal offending, while the rest pertained to a missing child or welfare issues (UK7).

Exposure of the police workload in this area coincided with the Lord Laming Review (PRT, 2016) into the unnecessary criminalisation of children in care, and at the same time, the lived experience of children placed in juvenile detention for what would not be considered offending in the home environment increased in visibility in the public domain through advocacy and campaigning. This was characterised by the police key informant as the perfect storm in which to bring about change. The need for central coordination of such change became a focus of the UK Police (UK4). The police recognised that without a national protocol, the uptake and impact of changes would be uneven across the United Kingdom. A national protocol was signed in November 2018 although, as Shaw and Greenhow (2021) highlight, it has no statutory status. A further protocol for London was signed in 2021 that incorporates the principles set out in the national framework, reportedly adjusted to the pan-London context (Greater London Authority, 2021, p. 10).

The child-centred focus of the UK Police national strategy was targeted at shifting police perceptions of, and responses to, looked-after children.

Our police respondent spoke about how understanding the vulnerability of the children they come across can influence police responses:

> Our child-centred policing strategy is all about how actually the young people that the police come across are vulnerable by the very nature of the fact that the police have come across them. And if you start thinking about the fact that this young person is a vulnerable young person and they are a child, then actually as a police officer you treat them differently than if you just looked at the stroppy, difficult, abusive, threatening language … because that's their defence mechanism … So understanding the impact of trauma on a young person and how it contributes to their behaviour and how as a police officer you can defuse that and help them and support them, if you start to put that lens into your conversation it's a very different conversation and it's just that shift in attitude that we're trying to get officers to take on board and think differently about young people than just see them as a pain.
>
> (UK4)

In this regard, the strategy includes training for police members on the vulnerability of care-experienced children. Our police key informant was also eager to highlight that, while training is important, a shift in attitude is required. This shift requires police to ask, 'why is this person here in this position and what can I do about it?' (UK4).

A critical way of shifting police attitudes was said by our key informant to be learning from the lived experience of those with care experience. The UK police sought to draw out the lived experience of children in care and to hear directly from people with care experience at conferences, seminars and in training, to great effect, according to the following key informant:

> So what we've done to address that is get the voice of the young people out there … we've … run several conferences where we've had young people talking about their experience of the care system and how they were treated by the police and how they've been arrested for basically some very minor type offences and when they describe the whole situation from their perspective it sounds ridiculous that the police have turned up. One young woman was – had a spat with her carer because the carer put tomatoes in her shepherd's pie, she doesn't like tomato, she wouldn't let her cook it herself, they ended up having a row and she got really cross and angry and threw a plate across the room and so the carer called the police and basically said she was being threatened by this young woman with a knife, so the police turn up with their tasers, she almost got – was tasered, yet this young woman was sitting on a table with her head in her arms sobbing because she had tomato in her shepherd's pie. Now, when you tell that story, that young woman tells that story to an audience of police officers I don't think there was a dry

> eye in the room actually and those police officers then resolved to go and do something about it because actually you're not just saying this isn't just one young person, there are countless other stories of young people talking about their experience and so we put these young people in front of a police audience and they told their stories and they said that was really, really powerful to the point one officer just stood up and said, 'Would you give us another chance? We've got this so badly wrong, we need to get – we need to do this better. Will you give us another chance to get this right?' And that's when you – because this is about – it's about a shift in attitude not in practice really, it's about the officers thinking differently about the young people they're dealing with.
>
> (UK4)

While this key informant was seeking a shift in the attitudes of police, they were also mindful that the nature of the police organisation means that this message might best be communicated utilising the hierarchical structure of the organisation. As the UK police respondent went on to outline:

> Policing works with a carrot and stick approach I think for lots of things in that police officers are very good at basically doing as they're told so you need to find the carrot and stick to make them do what you want them to do and encourage them to do it, but if they don't do it make them do it, so it's things like that you're making it really clear that actually we don't want to be arresting young people. I get told very grumpily by some officers, 'Well, apparently we're not meant to arrest kids anymore.' Well, that's fine, you've got the message, it might not be getting back in the right way, but you have got the message so actually what that officer is now doing is thinking, well, I can't arrest this young person so I'll have to deal with them differently. They're grumpy about it but they're getting to the point we want them to get to.
>
> (UK4)

With the introduction of the new strategy, this respondent perceived that police have received the message that custody is not the right place for children and that the arrest of children is inappropriate. This shift has seen the police engaging restorative interventions designed to divert children from the criminal justice system (UK4). Further research is required to determine how restorative justice operates in the context of the care environment.

For care-experienced children who 'go missing', different counties in the United Kingdom have trialled various initiatives. One initiative involved collaboration between non-government agencies and the police around talking to children about their situation. Whereas police might only do a welfare check that involves asking children if they are ok, an agency experienced in the delivery of social welfare would talk to the child more openly and provide them with some support (UK4). In another county, specialist police officers were focusing on missing children and working within agency forums to address any identified issues. In one instance, this led to police temporarily removing all children from a residential care home for their protection as the level of services being provided to those children was so poor (UK5). In the view of one non-policing key informant, 'this is what good policing should look like' (UK5).

In relation to offending by care-experienced children that took place in the community, a consistent policing response was sought. Our key informants in the United Kingdom spoke about the need to 'build in a pause' to repress the 'urge' of criminal justice agencies to continually default to criminalisation:

> We then also have to have a strategy for when they offend in the community, which is particularly important when we come in with our police partners to say, okay, you've picked a kid up in the community who's offended, what responsibility – who have we got as professionals to ensure that the right responses are followed? And I think we talked about, earlier, about the pause and it was just – tactically it's a really important thing because the urge for criminal justice agencies is to make a decision, to react. And that informed decision-making is, I think, just such an important aspect.
>
> (UK6)

This approach meant that even if the offending took place outside the residential care home, the same processes and practices would be considered to ensure that criminalisation was not the default response.

The range of measures adopted in the United Kingdom that are aimed at reducing involvement in the criminal justice system for those with care experience have introduced opportunities to divert a matter before a child is placed before a judge or magistrate (UK6). This was said by our respondent to be supported by most magistrates, who were frustrated that children keep appearing before them on minor charges, which, in their view, reflected poor corporate parenting (UK6). This echoed the concerns of the magistrates interviewed in our NSW study. In this regard, a key informant explained that the narrative 'that unless we round them up and put them in front of a court then we're not going to get them the help they need' (UK6) is being consciously rejected. In this respondent's view, therapeutic approaches needed to be adopted outside the criminal justice system before the child gets to court. One key informant told us that a child could only be remanded in custody for a 'very serious risk to the public' or 'very prolific offending' and that welfare needs or homelessness could not be used as a reason to remand a child (UK6).

The use of restorative justice approaches has led to a significant decline in the number of children appearing in the courts. One of our key informants stated that the youth restorative intervention, a multi-agency partnership, seeks to address both the offence and the young person responsible for it.

This intervention was characterised as not a 'light touch' and suitable for serious offending, and it has become the default practice, according to one respondent:

> It's what we do, so long as we've got an admission ... We had four courts, we've now got one quiet court. So, you know, we've really moved away from the use of formal cautioning and lots of that sort of stuff. And much more relational – we're much more inclined now, to listen, to try and understand and to empower people to take responsibility.
>
> (UK6)

This respondent also stated that they were more inclined to use diversion repeatedly for care-experienced children than to escalate the matter, even though the child might frequently have matters in the criminal justice system (UK6). As noted above, restorative justice – which emphasises a relational rather than punitive approach – has reportedly become the default practice in some parts of the United Kingdom. Recent research has highlighted how whilst the numbers of children coming into the youth justice system has reduced, 'it has had the perverse effect of increasing the disproportionate representation of two particularly vulnerable groups; Black and Minority Ethnic (BME) children and looked after children' (Hunter, 2022, p. 13). Further research is required to evaluate how this approach withstands the criticisms often levelled at it in the Australian context, including, that it is no more effective at reducing reoffending (Smith & Weatherburn, 2012), or that Indigenous children 'are less likely to receive the benefit of these diversionary options compared to their non-Indigenous counterparts' (Cunneen et al., 2021, p. 176).

Care experience and custodial settings

Several UK key informants spoke about the positive impact of leaders and 'champions' in terms of identifying, promoting and responding to the needs of people with care experience at all stages of engagement with the criminal justice system. The Ministry of Justice launched a Care Leavers Champion initiative in 2013, and a respondent we interviewed was adamant that, through its focus on care leavers, this initiative was pitched at the right level (UK4). This initiative formed part of the UK Government's 2013 *Care leaver strategy: A cross departmental strategy for young people leaving care* (DfE, 2013), which was designed to ensure that care leavers receive the same level of care and support that other young people receive from their parents. Care leavers were identified as receiving little support, whereas young people aged 15–18 were seen to have access to more resources (UK4). One respondent stated that the Care Leavers Champion initiative drove advocacy around recognising the complex and unique needs of care leavers within the criminal justice system and implementing strategies to identify and support this cohort. Before turning to discuss some of the related initiatives, it is noteworthy that a key informant characterised these initiatives as the exception rather than a reflection of the national setting (UK6). Notwithstanding this, prisoner numbers overall have fallen in the United Kingdom over the last decade (UK6), and the changes discussed below were seen by many respondents to have been a contributing factor to this reduction.

One key informant from the UK case study spoke about the Care Leavers Champion initiative as driving effective change (UK4). The strategy outlines the work being undertaken 'to reflect the needs of care leavers' (DfE, 2013, p. 5) and the work to be pursued in the key government departments relating to education, health, employment, financial support, housing, ongoing support and the justice system. Under the strategy, the Care Leavers Champion is tasked with advocacy for care leavers within government and for ensuring that agency staff are provided with guidance (p. 18).

Increased guidance around and understanding of the impact of care on young people's involvement in the criminal justice system equips criminal justice professionals with the skills to understand both the criminalisation and vulnerability of young people. The following quote from a senior manager within the criminal justice system highlights the impact of a deeper understanding of care experience:

> When I was [in a senior position] and we had juveniles, we had that 15- to 18-year-old cohort, I used to look at their previous convictions sometimes and think, blimey, for a 15 or 16 year old you've done an awful lot. Gosh, look at all this criminal damage and look at all this threatening and abusive behaviour, in terms of convictions. Well, looking back on that now I think to myself, well, what was the criminal damage? Was that kicking a door in a care home, was that threatening and abusive – the sort of thing I get off my son occasionally? What are we talking here? It's made me think about that. So I think, after all, having a better understanding of what that criminalisation does in terms of – even things like previous convictions would be really helpful because looking back I really do wonder how many of those young men who had terrible criminal records as far as I could see didn't actually have terrible criminal records in a sense I would understand normally, that their criminal damage and their threatening behaviour was actually pretty minor, but because they were in a care home, the police were called.
>
> (UK7)

This respondent, thus, reflects on how they would now interpret a child's criminal record differently, understood in the context of that child's care experience. Instead of assuming that the presence of a significant criminal record means that the person has committed many criminal acts, one would instead consider how this offending occurred in the context of a care environment and consider the issues around recourse to law enforcement for so-called offending in this context.

According to one respondent, the focus within custody was on better identification of those with care experience and of the resources to which they were entitled (UK7). The care leaver respondent from the United Kingdom that we interviewed stated that there was a lack of awareness among care leavers of what entitlements and support services they could access, highlighting the need for greater coordination among agencies (UK8, UK9). As these respondents informed us, most [care leavers] don't know what they can access and are, therefore, not receiving their entitlements. An obstacle to receiving appropriate entitlements this were the IT systems used within the justice system, which, historically, had no facility to record whether someone had been in care. So, these IT systems were rebuilt to accommodate and record care experience. Identification of those with care experience on its own, however, was not enough. It had to be accompanied by an understanding of why this information was important and what services or entitlements were available to care leavers. The stigma associated with care can make people reluctant to identify (Michell, 2015). As others have recently pointed out, it needs to be asked in appropriate ways that create safe environments to foster disclosure (see Gooch et al., 2022). Gooch et al. (2022, p. 9) conclude that whilst there is evidence of good practice as regards recording care experience, this is not standard practice.

The limitations in the provision of support to care-experienced children were felt by our respondents to impact on their chances of successfully re-entering society upon release from custody. This was regarded as fundamentally important 'because [there's] a very high reoffending rate of young people coming out of custody. It's nearly 70% of any year, so it's really high' (UK1). The poor accommodation options available to children leaving custody were thought to contribute to the high rates of reoffending among care-experienced children as these children were being placed in unsuitable accommodation while in a vulnerable state. As one respondent with responsibility for reviewing children's custodial arrangements observed:

> [I]t's almost unheard of for children to go out [of custody] without accommodation in England [but] it is something that definitely disproportionately impacts on looked-after children, and we have seen people going out to bed and breakfasts, we've seen them going out to hostel-type accommodation as well.
>
> (UK6)

A lack of coordination and communication between prison agencies and the local authorities tasked with providing support was resulting in the misalignment of entitlements for care leavers in custody. One of our key informants working in custodial services stated that:

> In some cases, local authorities actually are trying to give [support and entitlements]; they're visiting and they're engaging with the young

> person. But because we didn't know that, we haven't been engaging with the local authorities, so, ironically, you've got this situation where you've got local authorities who are actually engaged in the care, they're writing a plan for this young person, and we're busy in prison writing a plan for this young person both for inside and for outside, and the two are running in parallel and not actually meeting. So we've done some work on that as well. There's obviously masses of issues around support and I feel like we're really kind of doing tip-of-the-iceberg stuff with that around what support do care leavers need and what are the issues for them.
>
> (UK7)

As this respondent suggested, while such collaboration is a good first step, a swathe of other support initiatives is required to meet the needs of care leavers. Ensuring that all local authorities and youth correctional services were aware of the entitlements available for care-experienced children was an important goal, but the respondents felt that more needs to be done (UK7).

The establishment of care leaver support groups run by people with care experience was reported to be an important initiative introduced within several UK prisons (UK7). One of our key informants said that these 'worked really well' and had grown over time in both men's and women's prisons:

> I know one of the female prisons has just started one and in fact is looking at having a separate support group for older women than the younger women just because they'd identified different issues. So the idea is that we found it really useful to have [a facilitator with care experience] there for the support group because it was about having somebody who understood the care experience and could engage with them, and it was very much about not just getting together to complain about having been in care, but let's deal with the issue. So I think that's really good and I think that's really positive, and in fact at [one facility], they've now got champions out on the wing... We're now having care leaver reps out on wings in one of the prisons.
>
> (UK7)

This respondent went on to say that an important consequence of having care leaver representatives on wings in the prison was that they could help mitigate the stigma of having been in care. The impact of this stigma was referred to by our care leaver respondents from the United Kingdom as a significant and challenging issue. The development of support groups and the presence and visibility of care champions, although in their nascent stages of development, were seen as reducing the stigma associated with being in care and providing much-needed support networks for care leavers.

One final initiative discussed by this respondent related to staff training and development within prison and probation services that equips staff with the skills to recognise care leavers and the issues that this cohort faces so that adequate support can be provided:

> We have focused on communication and awareness, which sounds like the same as the first one [identifying and recording care status], but actually what we realised was that identifying care leavers is one thing, actually part of that process is that our staff don't know – most of our managers don't know why we're having this conversation, why we're talking about care leavers. So without that we can't actually have the conversation with prisoners, because even if we get out to prisoners and say to them or people in the community 'Tell us that you're a care leaver', you know, and they say, 'Why?' and our staff just look at them blankly, and, kind of, shrug their shoulders and say, 'I don't know; I've just been told to do it', so because of that there's a massive communication and raising awareness piece of work that we've been trying to do.
>
> (UK4)

Not only were frontline prison staff unaware of the relevance and significance of recognising care leaver status, but, as this respondent observed, managers were also ill equipped to understand why this information is collected and how it is relevant to service delivery. Staff training was, therefore, focused on providing a context to explain why knowing about a person's care leaver status is critical (see also Gooch et al., 2022).

The key informants in our UK case study expressed the view that custody numbers had fallen across the United Kingdom in recent years. The decline among girls was described as particularly significant (UK2). The changes that have occurred within both policing and the care environment have, thus, had a flow-on effect by reducing the numbers of people in custodial facilities.

Insights from England and Wales relevant to the NSW context

Overall, there has been a significant reduction in the number of looked-after children coming into contact with the criminal justice system in England and Wales, and a significant decrease in the child prison population. As a proportion however, looked after children and 'black and minority ethnic' children have experienced an increase in their disproportionate representation (Hunter, 2022). Stakeholders in the NSW criminal justice system ought to reflect on the policies and practices, and their interactions in England and Wales, to evaluate how they may address criminalisation now and into the future.

By way of preliminary analysis, we highlight that youth justice is a complex process with many parts. There is no one attributable reason for the decline seen in England and Wales. Austerity measures have accompanied the reduction in the prison population (Cunneen et al., 2018). England

and Wales were starting from an extraordinarily high child prison population base and had some of the most punitive measures in the Western world according to scholars (Cunneen et al., 2018). In 2008, England and Wales had the second highest rate of child incarceration in Western Europe (Bateman, 2012). It then tumbled, and Bateman's (2012) analysis sets out several of the reasons why this may have occurred, likening it to a similar dramatic decline during Thatcher's beginnings in the late 1970s up until the mid-1990s when the numbers began to again rise. Bateman's analysis of the reasons behind the dramatic fall this century include the depoliticisation of youth crime; minor demographic changes in the youth population; an increase in diversionary approaches; a focus by the Youth Justice Board on avoiding custody; the change in 2007 to make youth justice a joint responsibility of the Ministry of Justice and the Department for Children, Schools and Families; new performance indicators for local authorities; targets to reduce first time entrants and a shift in tone by governments that spurned harsher sentences for children. Bateman (2012, p. 46) argues these gains are 'vulnerable to reversal'. Yet fortunately, the downward trend has continued. Cunneen et al. (2018, p. 410) privilege fiscal imperatives as the principal driver in the reduction of the youth justice population and highlight that it does not represent 'a deliberative expression of human rights compliance'. In grappling with these viewpoints, we identify what we see as key mechanisms that offer insights to NSW.

The first mechanism driving change with the criminal justice system in England and Wales is data collection and data monitoring. While some of the disaggregated data collection has yet to be harmonised across public sector and non-government agencies, this development represents a considerable improvement on the situation in NSW. The obscuring of a complete picture on the involvement of specific cohorts of young people with care experience in the criminal justice system in NSW is preventing accountability and the formulation and evaluation of evidence-based policy. The sector appears opaque and resistant, defensive to authentic and meaningful monitoring and accountability. The priority instead is on the familiar groove of detection, arrest and progression through the criminal justice system behind closed doors. In the England and Wales context, performance frameworks for local authorities have made the numbers visible and the agencies accountable.

Second, a centrally coordinated diversionary approach that has used the hierarchical nature of the police force to 'stop the train leaving the station' has been effective in the United Kingdom. Matters are stopped before they get to court. Many of the magistrates in our study lamented that it was difficult to intervene once matters were at the Children's Court. In the key informant interviews conducted in England and Wales, we heard about the way that policing organisations were applying the national strategy on children, looked-after children in particular, to ensure diversion and adopt stringent non-arrest strategies. Looking at the NSW context, it is hard to imagine that police would intervene to remove children from a residential care home where the standard of care was very low. In the UK setting, this action demonstrates a commitment to higher standards for children in care and for the agencies responsible for delivering that care. Diversion reduces the custody population (Bateman, 2012). Reducing the age of criminal responsibility would support this shift. Moreover, making youth justice a joint responsibility may see more effective and integrated responses that can influence the process of youth justice, rather than achieving narrow and isolated reforms.

Both the England and Wales case study, and the NSW study, show real barriers in the provision of support to children who come into contact with the criminal justice system. The result of this is that children in care are often appearing in court unaccompanied. This is not conducive to a best practice outcome for the child, albeit that there is evidence in NSW of carers trying to get the children in their care put into custody. Those responsible for supporting children should provide that support in the criminal justice system. Without it, harsher sentences result (Hunter, 2022).

Stakeholders in OOHC and the criminal justice system in NSW should be more alert to the recruitment and exploitation of children in residential care for organised crime. The United Kingdom is far more advanced in its thinking around vulnerable children and the risk of exploitation and recruitment into organised crime (see Shaw & Greenhow, 2021). This is likely to be an emerging area of research, policy and practice in NSW, particularly in light of Victoria's recent report on exploitation by the Commission for Children and Young People (2021).

Conclusion

Several trends are observable in the UK case study. First, while the number of young people coming into contact with the criminal justice system has dropped, this is not true of the proportion of certain populations coming into contact with this system, namely, unaccompanied asylum seekers. The availability of disaggregated data is still poor, and as a result, a complete picture remains lacking. Second, while there has been a flurry of reports and inquiries on the youth justice system and looked-after children, it is unclear which recommendations have been implemented. This aligns with the NSW context in that there is consistently very little engagement with sector-wide reports, such as the recent *Family is Culture* report by Professor Megan Davis (2019). Third, Australia can certainly learn from the effectiveness of local-level cooperation in the United Kingdom, which has produced a number of protocols, but the commitment to these protocols needs to be at all levels and meaningful. Monitoring is a key part of such initiatives, and as successive reports have identified, this is not happening effectively in the NSW context (Davis, 2019; McFarlane et al., 2019). We conclude this chapter with a quote from Shaw and Greenhow (2021, p. 119) on the imperatives and conditions necessary for effective multi-agency cooperation in the United Kingdom, which in our view strongly resonates with the NSW context:

> Multi-agency work needs to be adequately resourced, its practitioners educated, and consideration given to how individuals with often different perspectives and legislatively mandated priorities can successfully work together to safeguard children. Indeed, the importance of building trusting and productive relationships is vital, both within the context of the immediate team and increasingly with professionals from further afield. It seems that despite the good intentions of the practitioners in this research, there is still a long way to go in terms of achieving universally good practice and positive, child-centred outcomes.

References

Australian Institute of Health and Welfare. (2021, May 18). *Rate of children in out-of-home care remains stable.* https://www.aihw.gov.au/news-media/media-releases/2021-1/may/rate-of-children-in-out-of-home-care-remains-stabl

Bateman, T. (2012). Who pulled the plug? Towards an explanation of the fall in child imprisonment in England and Wales. *Youth Justice*, *12*(1), 36–52.

Cashmore, J. (2011). The link between child maltreatment and adolescent offending: Systems neglect of adolescents. *Family Matters*, *89*, 31–41.

Commission for Children and Young People. (2021). *Out of sight: Systemic inquiry into children and young people who are absent or missing from residential care.*

Commission on Race and Ethnic Disparities. (2021, March 2021). *The report.* https://assets.publishing.service.gov.uk/government/uploads/system/uploads/attachment_data/file/974507/20210331_-_CRED_Report_-_FINAL_-_Web_Accessible.pdf

Cunneen, C., Goldson, B., & Russell, S. (2018). Human rights and youth justice reform in England and Wales: A systemic analysis. *Criminology & Criminal Justice*, *18*(4), 405–430.

Cunneen, C., Russell, S., & Schwartz, M. (2021). Principles in diversion of Aboriginal and Torres Strait Islander young people from the criminal jurisdiction. *Current Issues in Criminal Justice*, *33*(2), 170–190.

Davis, M. (2019). *Family is Culture: Review report.* Independent Review of Aboriginal Children in OOHC.

Day, A. (2017). Hearing the voice of looked after children: Challenging current assumptions and knowledge about pathways into offending. *Safer Communities*, *16*(3), 122–133.

Department for Education. (2013, October). *Care leaver strategy: A cross-departmental strategy for young people leaving care.* https://assets.publishing.service.gov.uk/government/uploads/system/uploads/attachment_data/file/266484/Care_Leaver_Strategy.pdf

Department for Education. (2016, September 29). *Children looked after in England (including adoption) year ending 31 March 2016.* https://assets.publishing.service.gov.uk/government/uploads/system/uploads/attachment_data/file/556331/SFR41_2016_Text.pdf

Department for Education. (2018, November). *The national protocol on reducing unnecessary criminalisation of looked-after children and care leavers.* https://assets.

publishing.service.gov.uk/government/uploads/system/uploads/attachment_data/file/765082/The_national_protocol_on_reducing_unnecessary_criminalisation_of_looked-after_children_and_care_.pdf

Fitzpatrick, C. (2009). Looked after children and the criminal justice system. In K. Broadhurst, C. Grover, & J. Jamieson (Eds.) *Critical perspectives on safeguarding children* (pp. 211–228). John Wiley & Sons.

Fitzpatrick, C., Hunter, K., Staines, J., & Shaw, J. (2019). *Exploring the pathways between care and custody for girls and women: A literature review.* https://eprints.lancs.ac.uk/id/eprint/142892/1/CareCustodyLiteratureReview.pdf

Fitzpatrick, C., & Williams, P. (2017). The neglected needs of care leavers in the criminal justice system: Practitioners' perspectives and the persistence of problem (corporate) parenting. *Criminology & Criminal Justice, 17*(2), 175–191.

Gerard, A., McGrath, A., Colvin, E., & McFarlane, K. (2019). 'I'm not getting out of bed!': The criminalisation of young people in residential care. *Australian & New Zealand Journal of Criminology, 52*(1), 76–93.

Gooch, K., Masson, I., Waddington, E., & Owens, A. (2022). *After care, after thought?: The invisibility of care experienced men and women in prison. Prison Service Journal, 258*, 4–12.

Greater London Authority. (2021, March). *Reducing criminalisation of looked-after children and care leavers: A protocol for London.* https://www.london.gov.uk/sites/default/files/reducing_criminalisation_of_looked_after_children_and_care_leavers-_a_protocol_for_london.pdf

Hayden, C. (2010). Offending behaviour in care: Is children's residential care a 'criminogenic' environment? *Child and Family Social Work, 154*, 461–472.

Howard League for Penal Reform. (2016). *Criminal care: Children's homes and criminalising children.* https://howardleague.org/wp-content/uploads/2016/02/Criminal-Care.pdf

Howard League for Penal Reform. (2017). *Ending the criminalisation of children in residential care: Briefing two – Best practice in policing.* https://howardleague.org/wp-content/uploads/2017/12/Ending-the-criminalisation-of-children-in-residential-care-Briefingtwo.pdf

Howard League for Penal Reform. (2019). *Representing looked-after children at the police station: A step-by-step guide for lawyers.* https://howardleague.org/publications/representing-looked-after-children-at-the-police-station/

Howard League for Penal Reform. (2020). *Victims not criminals: Protection children living in residential care from criminal exploitation.* https://howardleague.org/publications/victims-not-criminals-protecting-children-living-in-residential-care-from-criminal-exploitation/

Hunter, K. (2022). 'Out of place': The criminalisation of black and minority ethnic looked after children in England and Wales. *Prison Service Journal, 258*, 13–18.

Jay, A. (2014). *Independent inquiry into child sexual exploitation in Rotherham 1997–2013.* Rotherham Metropolitan Borough Council.

Khunti, K., Routen, A., Pareek, M., Treweek, S., & Platt, L. (2020). The language of ethnicity. *BMJ, 371*, 1–2.

Lammy, D. (2017). *An independent review into the treatment of, and outcomes for, black, Asian and minority ethnic individuals in the criminal justice system.* https://www.gov.uk/government/publications/lammy-review-final-report

McFarlane, K. (2017). Care-criminalisation: The involvement of children in out-of-home care in the New South Wales criminal justice system. *Australian and New Zealand Journal of Criminology, 51*(3), 412–433.

McFarlane, K., Colvin, E., McGrath, A., & Gerard, A. (2019). Just another policy document? Can a protocol end the criminalisation of kids in care? *Alternative Law Journal*, *44*(1), 37–42.

Michell, D. (2015). Foster care, stigma and the sturdy, unkillable children of the very poor. *Continuum: Journal of Media & Cultural Studies*, *29*, 663–676.

Ministry of Justice. (2018, January 25). *Youth justice statistics 2016/2017, England and Wales*. https://assets.publishing.service.gov.uk/government/uploads/system/uploads/attachment_data/file/676072/youth_justice_statistics_2016-17.pdf

Narey, M. (2016). *Residential care in England: Report of Sir Martin Narey's independent review of children's residential care*. Department for Education.

National Audit Office. (2018). *Pressures on children's social care*. https://www.nao.org.uk/wp-content/uploads/2019/01/Pressures-on-Childrens-Social-Care.pdf

National Police Chief's Council. (2015, April). *National strategy for the policing of children and young people*. https://www.npcc.police.uk/documents/edhr/2015/CYP%20Strategy%202015%202017%20August%202015.pdf

Neilson, A., & Sands, C. (2021). *Criminal care? Closing reflections*. https://howardleague.org/blog/closing-reflections/

Prison Reform Trust. (2016). *In care, out of trouble: An independent review chaired by Lord Laming*.

Shaw, J. (2014). *Residential children's homes and the youth justice system: Identity, power and perceptions*. Palgrave Macmillan.

Shaw, J. (2016). Policy, practice and perceptions: Exploring the criminalisation of children's home residents in England. *Youth Justice*, *16*(2), 147–161.

Shaw, J., & Greenhow, S. (2021). *The criminalisation and exploitation of children in care: Multi agency perspectives*. Routledge.

Smith, N., & Weatherburn, D. (2012). Youth justice conferences versus children's court: A comparison of re-offending. *Crime and Justice Bulletin*, *160*, 1–24.

Staines, J. (2016). *Risk, adverse influence and criminalisation: Understanding the over-representation of looked after children in the youth justice system*. Prison Reform Trust.

Stanley, E. (2017). From care to custody: Trajectories of children in post-war New Zealand. *Youth Justice*, *17*(1), 57–72. https://doi.org/10.1177/1473225416669145

Taylor, C. (2006). *Young people in care and criminal behaviour*. Jessica Kingsley.

Taylor, C. (2016). *Review of the youth justice system in England and Wales*. Ministry of Justice.

Utting, W. (1997). *People like us: The report of the safeguards for children living away from home*. Department of Health.

Warner, N. (1992). *Choosing with care*. HMSO.

Wong, K., Bailey, B., & Kenny, D. T. (2009). *Bail me out: New South Wales young offenders and bail*. Youth Justice Coalition.

Youth Justice Board. (2020). *Assessing the needs of sentenced children in the Youth Justice System 2018/2019 England and Wales*. https://assets.publishing.service.gov.uk/government/uploads/system/uploads/attachment_data/file/887644/assessing-needs-of-sentenced-children-youth-justice-system.pdf

Youth Justice Board. (2021). *Ethnic disproportionality in remand and sentencing in the youth justice system: Analysis of administrative data*. https://assets.publishing.service.gov.uk/government/uploads/system/uploads/attachment_data/file/952483/Ethnic_disproportionality_in_remand_and_sentencing_in_the_youth_justice_system.pdf

Conclusion

'Hope tropes' and routine criminalisation

Introduction

Our research documents and analyses contemporary fault lines in the interactions between the child protection and youth justice systems in NSW. As we document throughout this book, these fault lines have historical continuities that began with the colonisation of Australia and the resultant criminalisation of cultural difference. These tensions are also a product of imperialism, which brought with it assumptions that Australia inherited about children, 'child saving' and dangerousness or managing risk, that caused ongoing harm to Indigenous and non-Indigenous children. While there is a new legal architecture arising from in the ACPP, which represents the formal dismantling of the Stolen Generations and the recognition of self-determination, in practice, we heard from practitioners that these legislative requirements are peripheral; and a recent systematic review of contemporary practice in NSW found that '[i]t is very clear that the ACPP is not implemented' (Davis, 2019, pp. 25, xvi). When these and our findings are analysed alongside the recommendations of other seminal reports that have also been poorly implemented or not implemented at all – the *Royal Commission into Aboriginal Deaths in Custody* (Johnston, 1991) and the *Bringing Them Home* Report (HREOC, 1997), the ALRC's *Pathways to Justice* Report (2017; see Cubillo, 2021) – a pattern of hope 'tropes' emerges. Our empirical work has led us to the theoretical concept of 'hope tropes' to capture the interplay of good policy and parlous implementation, as we outline in this chapter.

In our study, we saw many ways in which good policy kept hope alive but also served to distract from the ongoing systematic criminalisation of children with care experience, particularly those with experience of residential care. Three discrete examples from our research illustrate this best. The first is the Joint Protocol, which aims to get multiple agencies on board to prevent children in care becoming involved in the criminal justice system and provides a mechanism for reducing criminalisation. The Joint Protocol, in place since 2016, was referred to mainly in our conversations with senior managers but was unknown to many of the OOHC service providers, police,

DOI: 10.4324/9781003093367-10

lawyers and magistrates that we interviewed. This reminds us of what Scraton (2007) calls gatekeeping, where senior leaders shape official discourse to suit institutional needs and agendas. As for the Protocol, we saw no evidence of its implementation and there is no publicly available information on its monitoring or evaluation despite the Protocol being in its second iteration (2016 and 2019). The newest version, like the first, commits to a process of review and evaluation of the Joint Protocol. The second example is the therapeutic care framework (TCF), which was reportedly in effect according to our respondents, yet barely any noticeable impact or application surfaced in our fieldwork. Some of our respondents defensively referred to the TCF as though it was a panacea, and both universally and holistically implemented. The TCF was used to explain away their agencies' accountability for historical and contemporary harms committed against children and young people by the interaction of the child protection and youth justice systems. Finally, international law and NSW legislation spell out the commitment to ensuring that the removal of children from their families, and the placement of children and young people in juvenile detention, is a 'last resort'. However, Davis's (2019) report is clear that this commitment is not being honoured in child protection, a view supported by the former President of the Children's Court, the Honourable Judge Peter Johnstone. Moreover, as we saw in our research, children and young people are being remanded in custody for extended periods because of a lack of suitable accommodation, even in situations where bail has been granted. We even saw instances of bail being refused for welfare reasons, for example, through the use of section 28 of the *Bail Act 2013* (NSW).

We do not claim to have new solutions to the problems we identified in this research, but we add our support to the many recommendations that have been neglected by government agencies and non-government service providers over many years. As university academics, we are working to implement the Universities Australia whole-of-sector strategy to make universities more culturally safe for Aboriginal and Torres Strait Islander staff and students and build Indigenous cultural competence (Behrendt, 2012; Gainsford, 2018, 2021; Universities Australia, 2011a, 2011b, 2017). These initiatives strive to meet the recommendations of the Royal Commission into Aboriginal Deaths in Custody on how the higher education sector can take action and lead change in transforming its services.

We call upon the government to implement the recommendations of the *Family is Culture* report (Davis, 2019). This report was the first review to focus entirely on Aboriginal and Torres Strait Islander children in OOHC and the first to be led by an Aboriginal Chairperson, Professor Megan Davis. The independent review was secured through community campaigning and advocacy and its recommendations concluded that the government department charged with ensuring adequate care for Indigenous children in OOHC, the Department of Family and Communities, had 'lost focus on achieving the fundamental goal of the ACPP: keeping children and young people connected to family, community, culture and country and, recognising community as a strength for children' (Davis, 2019, p. xiv). Compliance with the ACPP is a legislative requirement and non-compliance is having a 'devastating impact' on Aboriginal families and communities in NSW, as Davis (2019, p. 248) illustrates.

The government's decision to delay consideration of legislative reforms recommended by Professor Megan Davis (as part of the *Family is Culture* Review) is harmful to Aboriginal children, families and communities. It also represents a loss to the staff who stand to benefit from these recommendations through improved working conditions. The *Family is Culture* report provided 125 recommendations to address systemic failures impacting children and young people, particularly Aboriginal and Torres Strait Islander young people. Implementing these recommendations would reduce the number of Aboriginal children in care, but the report has been ignored by the government. The recommendations have been pushed aside until 2024 when a review of the *Children and Young Persons (Care and Protection) Act 1998* (NSW) is due to take place. Megan Davis has been critical of the lack of detail on other recommendations reportedly stuck in the 'scoping' and 'planning' phases (Davis, 2021).

We refer to the interplay of good policy and parlous or no implementation as 'hope tropes'. Hope tropes enable key stakeholders to talk about the ways in which problems that are widely identified across the sector are being addressed and places on the horizon a pathway out of trouble that sounds reasonable and evidence based. However, the associated policies are not resourced; recommendations are ignored; protocols are not adequately implemented, monitored or evaluated and, as a result, routine criminalisation continues largely unabated.

In our formulation, 'hope tropes' are made up of five elements. The first is an identified problem, tension or issue. The second is investment in an inquiry, review or report aimed at addressing the problem and providing recommendations or solutions. The third is an articulated framework for addressing the problem that is publicly available on a website and visible in formal reporting requirements. This framework also needs to be understood by senior managers. The fourth is a lack of resources or training to genuinely shift values, attitudes and practices, which results in a lack of, or partial, implementation of the framework. Finally, hope tropes are characterised by a vague or non-existent system of monitoring and review to track progress against recommendations. Hope rhetoric provides a buffer that allows systematic criminalisation to continue. It does not buffer decision-makers and stakeholders against criticism, as this is critical to the cycle of routine criminalisation. Instead, hope tropes buffer key decision-makers and stakeholders against accountability for harms and transformative change and provide a defence against criticism.

These tropes ensure that the only people with real skin in the game, children and young people involved with the criminal justice system and their families/communities from which they are removed, continue to be unable to influence the cycle of routine criminalisation. This is despite the significant visibility of documentary evidence attesting to lived experiences of criminalisation. Eventually, as identified by Davis (2019), children, families and communities will stop participating in the activities designed to capture their feedback. In this regard, as outlined in the *Family is Culture* report, communities warned that the report would be ignored; yet they participated in the review anyway, indicating that expectations of change perhaps shift over time, but participation may not stop entirely.

The hope rhetoric we observed is reliant on the concept of 'ritualism' applied by Davis in the *Family is Culture* report to characterise the Department of Families and Communities in NSW. In this, Davis cites Merton's identification of five modes of bureaucratic normative order: conformity, innovation, ritualism, retreatism and rebellion. Ritualism is 'acceptance of institutionalised means for securing regulatory goals while losing all focus on achieving the goals or outcomes themselves' (Merton in Davis, 2019, p. 25). Davis uses this theory to characterise the way in which case workers focus on familiar tasks of risk assessment and, in doing so, lose their focus on the goal of reuniting children with their families. She found that 'the outward appearance of compliance … shields a culture of non-compliance' (Davis, 2019, p. xiv). Hope tropes similarly support the appearance of a commitment to reform, policy development and cooperation across the child protection and youth justice sectors.

Hope tropes enable people from different parts of the child protection and youth justice sectors to come together and denounce the catastrophic statistics on Indigenous children in OOHC, 'cross-over kids' and the involvement of people with care experience in the criminal justice system. This rhetoric of hope also needs individual activists to lament the systemic problems and profess their commitment to being champions of the reforms or frameworks designed to address the underlying problems. These individuals benefit from the ability to set themselves apart from the system, which allows them to continue their work in this area, despite the prevalence of routine criminalisation.

Transforming routine criminalisation

Routine criminalisation courses through the child protection and youth justice systems. Arresting this pattern requires a transformation in values, attitudes and practices. It requires working at multiple levels, from the top down, from the bottom up and laterally, to shift what has been 'ritual' practice and well-worn grooves in the operations of OOHC service providers, law enforcement, criminal justice professionals, the legal profession and judging, for so long. We argue that attention to four factors could shift policy and legislation away from 'hope tropes' towards genuine transformative change: monitoring and accountability mechanisms; trauma-informed and strength-based approaches and the tools and resources needed to address complexity. Each of these elements is now explored in turn.

Monitoring and accountability

In our study, we saw many examples of how a lack of monitoring and accountability meant that problems were inadequately understood or scoped, and progress against recommendations, policy development and legislative reform was not measured. Ultimately, this led to a lack of accountability for individuals and organisations, apart from the young person who was more often than not held accountable for their behaviour and/or transgressions.

With the appropriate protocols in place regarding data sovereignty, the collection of and access to data that can provide a complete picture of the intersection of child protection and youth justice is the necessary first step to moving beyond hope rhetoric towards transformation. In this area, it is useful to learn from the UK's experience of data collection, specifically the way in which some counties collect and access data on:

- call-outs from residential care facilities to police;
- the charges arising from each residential care facility;
- the application of any Protocol; and
- how diversion is utilised, and if not, why not?

This is not an exhaustive list, but it does set out some of the critical aspects of processes within the OOHC and justice systems that need to be tracked and monitored.

In Australia, data sovereignty needs to be a central consideration in any efforts to better account for and monitor the contemporary realities in the child protection and youth justice systems in NSW. The *Family is Culture* report recommended a roundtable with Aboriginal stakeholders to discuss what data sovereignty means and how data should be collected and used. Davis's report also recommended the establishment of an Aboriginal Quality Assurance Unit to foster the promotion, tracking and implementation of reforms set out in the report. Transparency and accountability will drive transformative change, and improvements for Aboriginal children will improve the approach taken for all children in OOHC – 'If you get it right for Aboriginal and Torres Strait Islander people, you can get it right for everyone' (see Williams & Ragg, 2019).

A trauma-informed criminal justice system

As we have argued in this book, an approach to care that focuses on the traumatic histories of the children being cared for rather than on their current behaviour is widely viewed as offering the best outcomes for both children and carers. In NSW, this trauma-informed approach is at the heart of the TCF, although, as we discussed in Chapter 2, implementation of this framework is patchy. Indeed, this could be seen as an instance of the hope tropes discussed above and, thus, a way of diverting attention from current practices that may not be meeting best practice standards. Nevertheless, it is clear that there remains considerable support for the principles of this framework throughout the care system in NSW.

Adoption of a trauma-informed approach by the criminal justice system may at first seem a counter-intuitive proposition, given the emphasis on 'individualised justice' (*Bugmy vs Queen* (2013) 249 CLR 571) in a system that aims to identify and punish law-breaking behaviour as well as rehabilitate offenders. However, in our view, a trauma-informed approach to criminal justice is consistent with a long history of common law, which holds that the background characteristics of offenders must be taken into account in sentencing decisions. This approach is also recommended by the ALRC in its *Pathways to Justice* report (2018, p. 28), who support the introduction of 'Indigenous Experience Reports' prepared by Indigenous people in order to culturally situate Indigenous people who come before the court for sentencing, although the criminal justice system is about more than just sentencing. The criminal justice system must be concerned with the histories of the children appearing before the courts, especially when those histories involve trauma, and these histories of trauma should be at the forefront of all decisions that affect these young people. This requires transforming the criminal justice system in a way that puts a trauma-informed approach at its centre and decentres behaviour, which will allow a focus on the needs of Aboriginal and Torres Strait Islander peoples. In doing so, the criminal justice system ought to recognise that these needs 'are an effect of the ongoing adversities of colonisation', rather than constitutive of 'Aboriginal identity' (Spiers Williams, 2021, p. 278), and can thereby pivot to a strengths-based approach.

The earliest point of contact with the criminal justice system for those with care experience is usually with police. When speaking to police who had been called to care homes on a regular basis, we found that many had little interest in the lives of care-experienced young people and perceived their role to be confined to identifying whether a criminal offence had been committed, and then arresting and charging the young person if this were the case. Even those who were understanding of the chaos of residential care settings would at best delay a response that amounted to criminalisation, rather than avoid it. We also saw clear examples of re-traumatisation through contact with police, for instance, where evidently distressed children were handcuffed and forced into police vans, and taken to hospital as involuntary patients (see Chapter 2).

Changing attitudes and practices such as these requires a shift in police culture to keep police out of children's lives, which will minimise the involvement in the criminal justice system that often results from police interaction (see Cunneen, 2001). Certainly, police should be educated about the principles of trauma-informed care as part of their basic training, but support for these principles needs to come from all levels of the police force and requires action on implementation. We were heartened by the quite different attitudes to the care-experienced population expressed by more senior officers of the police force. We also see the introduction of the Joint Protocol as a welcome step, although at the time of writing there was no evidence of any evaluation of the Protocol. But changing attitudes among police who come into contact with care-experienced children is of the highest importance. Moreover, our research from the UK revealed that a change in police procedures and strategies around monitoring and preventing new entrants to the youth justice system has led to a reduction in young people entering the system, although this has been less effective for certain groups of children, including BAME and 'looked after' children. Applying the UK experience to Australia suggests that more action is required to ensure that children with care experience, including Indigenous children, receive the same responses as their non-care (and non-Indigenous) counterparts.

We have written elsewhere of the often-fraught relationship between police and the care system, in particular, where residential care workers are perceived to use police to manage disciplinary infractions in the home (Gerard et al., 2019). It is clear that if the principles of trauma-informed care were properly observed, police would be called to care homes only in the case of serious criminal offending. When police are called to homes, information about the child's background should be provided to police, and these interactions ought to be dealt with by specialist officers. Where there is evidence of offending, a trauma-informed system would see diversionary options adopted, with criminal charges being the last resort. This is, of course, already a guiding principle of youth justice in NSW; however, it is especially important to observe for children with traumatic histories. There should also be a clear assumption in favour of bail, and bail determinations should as a matter of course note the child's care status. Further, this should be managed in a trauma-informed way, that is, gently, respectfully and with adequate regard for the child's privacy.

Magistrate bail determinations need to take into account both the care status and the background of the child. Experiences of trauma should be brought to the attention of the magistrate and this should be a key determinant of bail outcomes. As we have shown, one cause of children experiencing extended periods on remand is where appropriate accommodation cannot be located. Traumatised children should only be placed in detention as a last resort, so solving the problem of accommodation is a key challenge. In this regard, the contracting out of residential care is not always in the best interest of the child. Crisis accommodation provided by the Department of Community and Justice should be available to ensure that children are not remanded in custody purely because of a lack of appropriate accommodation.

When sentencing, care status should be brought to the magistrate's attention and histories of trauma should be explicitly dealt with in all presentencing reports, or specifically in 'Indigenous Experience Reports' akin to Canada's Gladue Reports (ALRC, 2018). Magistrates should refer to these histories in sentencing and show how they have been taken into account in passing sentence. These are not radical suggestions and indeed are consistent with current practice. Transformative change is needed in how the state deals with care-experienced children. In our court observations, we saw clear examples of alienated and traumatised children and a pace that did not allow for effective consideration of the histories of these children and the circumstances that brought them to court. A non-adversarial approach would avoid these problems and provide a forum that enables the criminal justice system to implement the principles of trauma-informed care. In our view, such a change would benefit all involved.

Harmful impacts of rapid responses to complexity in the Children's Court

As researchers, we found the fast pace of the Children's Court remarkable given the complexities of the lives and experiences of the children who appeared before it. Our respondents informed us that children, the subject of the Court's gaze, regularly found the court experience incomprehensible, and this was also evident to us as observers. The requirements on all parties are to address complexity quickly, which, from what we observed, often meant that any complexity was simply not addressed. This rapid system appears unable to effectively deal with complex needs. We support calls for magistrates to have access to better information so that they can adopt a trauma-informed approach to dealing with the children who appear before them. In many of the cases we observed where the child was required to have their history discussed in court, they became distressed. The increased use of reports that privilege Indigenous stakeholders, including Indigenous community-controlled organisations and their employees, would go some way towards enabling complexities to be acknowledged and addressed, and therefore, the decisions made would be based on a higher quality of information. These reports would ensure that the needs of each child were carefully set out and considered. In these circumstances, a child's needs would not be left to a short interview on the morning of the court appearance, sometimes via AVL, where relationships stand little chance of being developed and instructions are difficult to obtain. These mechanisms, however, do not in themselves ensure self-determination (see Blackstock et al., 2020). Blackstock et al. write that 'the remaining challenges are to affirm self-determination in Indigenous child raising, ensuring substantively equal funding to enable Indigenous experts and community members to address the multi-generational impacts of colonialism and to educate and engage non-Indigenous peoples in the effort' (p. 9). On this, we note that in response to the latest (2022–2023) Australian Government federal budget, the Chief Executive of the National Aboriginal Community Controlled Health Organisation described it as 'short-changing' Indigenous Australians (Allam, 2022).

Finally, we know that one of the benefits of the NSW Intensive Supervision Program was that children spent less time in detention when they were on the program. We can infer from this that more attention to a child's decarceration equates to less time in custody. This means that additional oversight and surveillance do reduce the amount of time children are kept in custody. To address complexity quickly, magistrates need to start from a strong basis of understanding. Judicial education needs to extend beyond the yearly conferences and bench books, which are not capturing all magistrates, according to our findings.

Advocacy and challenging systemic discrimination require the centring of Indigenous stories (Behrendt, 2019). Anthony et al. (2021) argue that '[s]tories challenge assumptions, biases and stereotypes that pivot on deficit'. They also provide counter-narratives and have the 'power to heal communities, nurture and build relationships, and advocate for the needs, priorities an aspirations of First Nations women, families and communities' (p. 74). Currently, the pace of the Children's Court reflects an inability to listen to stories and understand and hear a counter-narrative of 'strength, resilience and resistance' (p.74).

Indigenous strengths-based approaches to influence change

Indigenous people's cultures and traditions are diverse and unique, and, as we have highlighted in this study, Indigenous children in the child protection and youth justice systems require individual cultural consideration and support. Indigenous children have both individual and collective rights to receive care that connects them with their culture, including their Country and kinship ties. These connections are seen as integral to strengthening an Indigenous child's identity and play a pivotal role in their social, emotional and cultural well-being. The Royal Commission into the Detention and Protection of Children in the Northern Territory (White & Gooda, 2017) recommended that organisational reform to recognise Indigenous children's strengths, rather than positioning Indigenous culture as a deficit, is essential across the criminal justice system (see also Blackstock et al., 2020; Spiers Williams, 2021). A recent extensive study by the Australian Human Rights Commission (2020, p. 53), which sought out the voices of Aboriginal and Torres Strait Islander women and girls, found that a deficit model is 'based on lingering patriarchal assumptions and racist ideology which continues to perpetuate intergenerational trauma and disadvantage and entrenches intersectional discrimination'. This study found that a significant shift is required to move towards a strengths-based approach that is respectful and recognises the skills, knowledge, leadership and potential of Aboriginal and Torres Strait Islander women and girls.

A strengths-based approach enables children to recognise and develop their own individual, cultural and aspirational strengths, which then contribute to their pathway to success. However, to build the strengths-based approaches as recommended in the Royal Commission report requires significant sectoral reform and partnership building with Indigenous communities and organisations to support the agency of Indigenous children. The ability of Indigenous communities to advocate for their children provides autonomy to assert Indigenous sovereign rights and supports these communities to deliver localised solutions that place cultural needs at the centre of a child's well-being. Enabling an Indigenous child to connect to culture and success needs to be normalised, not neglected.

To deliver culturally informed services requires organisations to build collaborative partnerships with key Indigenous stakeholders. This form of engagement requires organisational staff and practitioners to understand communication and relational approaches when working with and for Indigenous peoples and communities. Mandating change in professional attitudes and approaches to ensure that practitioners work more effectively with Indigenous children and communities involves these practitioners recognising how past and current policies continue to impact Indigenous peoples. One issue that was highlighted throughout the research was the need for culturally competent practitioners who can appreciate and interpret cultural difference in relation to Indigenous children in the care and criminal justice systems. Another suggested sectoral reform involved increasing the employment of Indigenous people and recognising their cultural knowledge and lived experience as professional expertise. Despite repeated calls, the cultural and community voice is often disregarded by professionals in both the care and justice sectors and the system more broadly. While Davis's (2019) report and recommendations relate to Indigenous children and families, her recommendations, if implemented, would have widespread benefit for all children in care. These recommendations would strengthen the whole care system, from which all children, and their families, stand to benefit. Therefore, building better collaborative partnerships with Indigenous communities can create new pathways of working together to advocate for Indigenous children's rights and the need for systemic change.

Emerging trends to note: Unaccompanied minors and child exploitation

Our case study from England and Wales provides insight into what may lie ahead for NSW, and we have chosen to focus on two issues that emerged from this case study that are of particular relevance to our analysis of the Australian context. The first is the increase in the number of unaccompanied minors in OOHC. Unaccompanied minors are children who cross international borders without an adult or carer, who usually go on to seek refugee protection. This population is increasing among the OOHC cohort in the

United Kingdom and warrants consideration in the Australian context. The second issue is the criminal exploitation and recruitment into organised crime of children in OOHC. This was highlighted as an issue in the Rotherham Inquiry (Jay, 2014) and was the focus of Shaw and Greenhow's (2021) latest book, and has important implications for Australia.

Unaccompanied minors

A strong trend evident in the UK statistics is the rise in the number of unaccompanied minors in OOHC. In England and Wales, the number of children entering OOHC would have been reducing if it were not for the increase in the number of unaccompanied minors entering care. In the NSW context, the number of unaccompanied minors in OOHC remains unclear and it is likely that unaccompanied minors are being administered through the Department of Immigration, with the Minister for Immigration as their legal guardian. Historically, unaccompanied minors were kept in detention in Australia.

Of particular concern in relation to the trend of unaccompanied minors entering OOHC in Australia is the potential trajectory of criminalisation that could result in deportation. As a result of Australian reforms introduced in 2014, non-citizens can now be deported if they fail a character test (Gerard, 2019; Gerard & Weber, 2019). We already know of cases where children who have offended in residential care have been deported (see *QDVJ and Minister for Immigration, Citizenship, Migrant Services and Multicultural Affairs (Migration)* [2021] AATA 1841 (1 June 2021)). Given what our research and other studies have revealed about the pervasiveness of systemic failings that contribute to the involvement of children in OOHC in the criminal justice system, this is a worrying trend. In effect, the government is placing vulnerable children in an environment like residential care that is known to be criminogenic, and when they offend they are either sent to detention or deported. This constitutes a manifestly unfair chain of events.

Sexual and criminal exploitation of children in OOHC

Children in OOHC are susceptible to exploitation, including recruitment for organised crime. Sexual and criminal exploitation featured in our NSW case study. A recent report by the Commission for Children and Young People (2021) in Victoria found that children in residential care were particularly exposed to risk and that girls and young women were more likely than boys to be absent and subject to sexual exploitation. Shaw and Greenhow's (2021) research in the UK setting revealed systemic deficiencies that created risks for children in OOHC that are particularly heightened for children in residential care. These risks included those arising from 'the lack of permanent, secure and protective relationships available to children in care and the apparent dichotomy of profit-making and safeguarding' (Shaw &

Greenhow, 2021, p. 80). Residential care increases the risks faced by children given the prevalence of children who go missing and the makeup of the residential care population, many of whom have experienced multiple unstable placements.

In their interviews with practitioners working in Multi-Agency Safeguarding Hubs (MASH) – a co-location of professionals from different services supporting children in OOHC – Shaw and Greenhow found that knowledge among practitioners of the risks of exploitation for children in care was lacking and that more needed to be done to build understanding of the risks and to safeguard children. While NSW does not have the marketisation of OOHC to the same extent as the United Kingdom, there are other similarities between the two jurisdictions that give rise to the same concerns. First, there are considerable numbers of children in OOHC that leave care and 'go missing'. Second, there are significant gaps in the provision of secure placements for children in OOHC. Third, given the geographic distances between some residential care homes in NSW, being moved out of area is likely to enhance vulnerability. The UK sector has a greater understanding of the links between criminalisation and exploitation that was not yet visible among the criminal justice and OOHC stakeholders that we interviewed. Perhaps, one of the key findings of Shaw and Greenhow's research that is particularly relevant for the NSW context is that effective multi-agency relationships, often lamented in our research as a real gap, are 'only as good as the knowledge brought by individual professionals' (Shaw & Greenhow, 2021, p. 112). Children are already vulnerable to exploitation as a result of their histories of trauma, and the OOHC system should ameliorate and not exacerbate that vulnerability.

Conclusion

Our research has found that routine criminalisation is largely unhindered by 'hope tropes'. Good policy alone is not able to reduce the over-representation of children in OOHC in the criminal justice system or alter the current statistical picture that sees Aboriginal and Torres Strait Islander children disproportionately placed in care and criminalised. This book has sought to understand the historical context and contemporary social realities of criminalisation using an intersectional lens that enables structural determinants to be considered together – Indigeneity, gender and disability. In studying the processes of criminalisation, we have sought to decentre criminology's obsession with 'crime' to understand the continuing impact of colonisation (Aliverti et al., 2021). In this regard, 'Colonialism embedded western ontology as the baseline upon which First Nations child-rearing and children's rights would be defined and judged' (Blackstock et al., 2020, p. 2). Criminology has long ignored the impacts of colonisation, and under its gaze, the criminalisation of Indigenous peoples in Australia has intensified (Porter, 2019), as has the pace of child removal (Behrendt, 2019). Our findings promote a conceptual framing that aims to puncture the assumption, prevalent among particular groups of respondents in our research, that good policy legitimately hides atrocious practice. Implementation, monitoring and accountability are required to proliferate strengths-based approaches that privilege self-determination and in the process build relationships and community partnerships and transform the sector for the benefit of all children, families, communities and workers.

References

Aliverti, A., Carvalho, H., Chamberlen, A., & Sozzo, M. (2021). Decolonizing the criminal question. *Punishment & Society*, *23*(3), 297–316.

Allam, L. (2022, 30 March). Federal budget continues 'unconscionable' failure to close the gap in Indigenous health. *The Guardian*. https://www.theguardian.com/australia-news/2022/mar/30/federal-budget-continues-unconscionable-failure-to-close-the-gap-in-indigenous-health

Anthony, T., Sentence, G., & Behrendt, L. (2021). 'We're not being treated like mothers': Listening to the stories of First Nations mothers in prison. *Laws*, *10*(3), 74.

Australian Human Rights Commission. (2020). *Wiyi Yani U Thangani (Women's Voices): Securing our rights, securing our future report*. Aboriginal and Torres Strait Islander Commissioner.

Australian Law Reform Commission. (2018). *Pathways to justice report*. https://www.alrc.gov.au/publication/pathways-to-justice-inquiry-into-the-incarceration-rate-of-aboriginal-and-torres-strait-islander-peoples-alrc-report-133/

Bail Act. (2013) NSW. https://legislation.nsw.gov.au/view/html/inforce/current/act-2013-026.

Behrendt, L. (2012). *Review of higher education access and outcomes for Aboriginal and Torres Strait Islander People Final Report*. Australian Government.

Behrendt, L. (2019). Stories and words, advocacy and social justice: Finding voice for Aboriginal women in Australia. *Australian Feminist Law Journal*, *45*(2), 191–205.

Blackstock, C., Bamblett, M., & Black, C. (2020). Indigenous ontology, international law and the application of the Convention to the over-representation of Indigenous children in out of home care in Canada and Australia. *Child Abuse & Neglect*, *110*, 104587.

Bugmy vs Queen. (2013) 249 CLR 571.

Children and Young Persons (Care and Protection) Act 1998 (NSW). https://legislation.nsw.gov.au/view/html/inforce/current/act-1998-157.

Commission for Children and Young People. (2021). *Out of sight: Systemic inquiry into children and young people who are absent or missing from residential care*.

Cubillo, E. (2021). 30th anniversary of the RCIADIC and the 'white noise' of the justice system is loud and clear. *Alternative Law Journal*, *46*(3), 185–192.

Cunneen, C. (2001). *Conflict, politics and crime: Aboriginal communities and the police*. Routledge.

Davis, M. (2019). *Family is Culture: Review report*. Independent Review of Aboriginal Children in OOHC.

Davis, M. (2021, November 8). Still they take the children away while our report gathers dust. *Sydney Morning Herald*. https://www.smh.com.au/national/nsw/still-they-take-the-children-away-while-20211107-p596oy.html

Gainsford, A. (2018). Connection to Country: Place-based learning initiatives embedded in the Charles Sturt University Bachelor of Law. *Legal Education Review*, *28*(2), 1–14.

Gainsford, A. (2021). *Embedding Indigenous knowledges in the design of higher education curriculum: An international study in law education*. Charles Sturt University.

Gerard, A. (2019). Crimmigration and the Australian legal lexicon: Reflecting on border control, theory and the lived experience. In P. Billings (Ed.) *Crimmigration in Australia: Law, politics, and society* (pp. 89–115). Springer.

Gerard, A., & Weber, L. (2019). 'Humanitarian borderwork': Identifying tensions between humanitarianism and securitization for government contracted NGOs working with adult and unaccompanied minor asylum seekers in Australia. *Theoretical Criminology: An International Journal*, *23*(2), 266–285.

Human Rights and Equal Opportunity Commission. (1997). *Bringing Them Home: Report of the national inquiry into the separation of Aboriginal and Torres Strait Islander children from their families*.

Jay, A. (2014). *Independent inquiry into child sexual exploitation in Rotherham 1997–2013*. Rotherham Metropolitan Borough Council.

Johnston, E. F. (1991). *Royal Commission into Aboriginal deaths in custody: National report, overview and recommendations*. Australian Government Publishing Service.

Porter, A. (2019). Aboriginal sovereignty, 'crime'and criminology. *Current Issues in Criminal Justice*, *31*(1), 122–142.

QDVJ and Minister for Immigration, Citizenship, Migrant Services and Multicultural Affairs (Migration). (2021). AATA 1841 (1 June 2021).

Scraton, P. (2007). *Power, conflict and criminalisation*. Routledge.

Shaw, J., & Greenhow, S. (2021). *The criminalisation and exploitation of children in care: Multi-agency perspectives*. Routledge.

Spiers Williams, M. (2021). Judgement: Bugmy v R [2013] HCA 3. In N. Watson & H. Douglas (Eds.) *Indigenous legal judgments: Bringing Indigenous voices into judicial decision-making* (pp. 77–91). Routledge.

Universities Australia. (2011a). *National best practice framework for Indigenous cultural competency in Australian universities*.

Universities Australia. (2011b). *Guiding principles for developing Indigenous cultural competency in Australian universities*.

Universities Australia. (2017). *Universities Australia Indigenous Strategy 2017–2020*.

White, M., & Gooda, M, (2017). *Royal commission into the protection and detention of children in the northern territory: Final Report*. Australian Government.

Williams, M. & Ragg, M. (2019). *Evaluation of legal aid NSW civil law service for aboriginal communities*. UTS.

Index

Note: **Bold** page numbers refer to tables and *Italic* page numbers refer to figures.

For Product Safety Concerns and Information please contact our EU representative GPSR@taylorandfrancis.com
Taylor & Francis Verlag GmbH, Kaufingerstraße 24, 80331 München, Germany

www.ingramcontent.com/pod-product-compliance
Lightning Source LLC
LaVergne TN
LVHW021126300926
849160LV00010B/877